CATERPILLAR CHRONICLE

THE HISTORY OF THE WORLD'S GREATEST EARTHMOVERS

Eric C. Orlemann

MBI Publishing Company

First published in 2000 by MBI Publishing Company, 729 Prospect Avenue,
PO Box 1, Osceola, WI 54020-0001 USA

MBI Publishing Company books are also available at discounts in bulk quantity
for industrial or sales-promotional use. For details write to Special Sales Manager
at Motorbooks International Wholesalers and Distributors, 729 Prospect Avenue,
PO Box 1, Osceola, WI 54020-0001 USA

Library of Congress Cataloging-in-Publication Data Available

ISBN 0-7603-0667-2

On the front cover: The Caterpillar 5130 series of hydraulic excavators,
introduced in October 1992, is one of the industry's leading mining machines
in its size class. The 5130 ME Mass Excavator shown in 1996 is equipped with
a 13-cubic-yard bucket and has a maximum digging depth of 27 feet 6 inches.
Eric C. Orlemann

On the frontispiece: Even though the Caterpillar D2 was the smallest diesel
tractor built by the company, 45,615 model series types were produced between
1938 and 1957. This 1939 vintage D2 (Serial No. 3J3433 SP) belongs to Tom
Novak of Ohio. *ECO*

On the title page: To own a perfect 1936 Caterpillar RD-8 is a rare thing, but
to have it parked next to its predecessor, a 1934 Diesel Seventy-Five, is rarer
still. These tractors are part of the Max Tyler Collection of Montana. *ECO*

On the back cover: *Top:* Behold the world's largest mechanical-drive hauler—
the 797. As of the year 2000, there isn't another one larger. This giant is
powered by a 3,224-flywheel-horsepower, 24-cylinder Cat 3524B diesel engine
and has a 360-ton capacity. The engine alone is about as large as the Chevrolet
S-10 Blazer parked next to the hauler. *Caterpillar*
Bottom: When it comes to classic gas-engined tractors, the model Sixty is at the
top of almost everyone's list. Starting out as the Best 60 in 1919, it would
become a Caterpillar model in 1925. This pristine 1929 Sixty (Serial No.
5089A) belongs to Doug Veerkamp of California. *ECO*

Editor: Paul Johnson
Design: Rebecca Allen and Tom Heffron

Printed in China

CONTENTS

ACKNOWLEDGMENTS

A book of this nature, concerning some of the greatest Caterpillar equipment ever built, would have been impossible without the cooperation of Caterpillar, Inc. of Peoria, Illinois. I would like to personally thank the following individuals, both currently employed and retired, of Caterpillar for without whose help and guidance, this project would not have been possible. They are: Jeff Hawkinson, Sharon L. Holling, Sandie Watson, Lea McCall, Mary Turpin, Carl Volz, Ron Nusbaum, Angela H. Myers, Benjamin S. Cordani, Catherine Wells, William F. Pullman, Lorri Porter, Shirley Streib, Pete J. Holman, John Ingle, Doug Bailey, Bill Burris, Sam Kershaw, Tom Passarelli, Eldon D. Oestmann, James A. McMillan, Bob Price, David C. Janzen, Robert J. Grob, Paul Corcoran, Elmer Crabb, Ed Staley, Bob Purcell, James E. Gee, Larry Clancy, and John F. Cooper.

I would also like to thank Stephan Ihnken, Paul N. Hurlbut, and Naldo B. Coelho of the Caterpillar Image Center, who watched over much of the image work concerning historic and rare equipment from the Caterpillar Corporate Archives.

For the help in obtaining new images of historic Best, Holt, and Caterpillar machinery, I thank the following individuals for granting me access to photograph their tractors, both at rest and at work, and to the individuals that assisted in the set-up of these treasures. They are: Dave Smith of Oregon; Marv Fery of Oregon; Keith Clark and John Ives of Washington; Ron Miller of Michigan; Larry Maasdam of Iowa; George E. Logue of Pennsylvania; Doug Veerkamp of California; Ed Akin of California; Wayne Swart of California; Bob Russell of California; Dick Railing of California; Allen F. Anderson of Oregon; Laurence Darrach of California; Paul Kirsch of Oregon; Don Dougherty of California; Bill Santos of California; Tom Novak of Ohio; and Max Tyler, Paul Tyler, and Mike Tyler of Montana.

For the people that helped me find the machines, and make the process of setting up photo sessions and verifying historical information a lot easier, I would like to thank Josy Applegate and Allen Konkel of Altorfer, Inc.; Eileen Grafton of Peterson Tractor Co.; Don "Bart" Bartholomew, General Tractor; Thomas Berry and the Historical Construction Equipment Association; the Antique Caterpillar Machinery Owners Club; Dick Ryan of Oregon; Tom Osborne of Wyoming; and Nance Dania of Ohio.

Last but not least, I would like to acknowledge fellow authors Randy Leffingwell of California; Keith Haddock of Alberta, Canada; Lorry Dunning and the Joseph A. Heidrick, Sr., Foundation, Davis, California; and photographer Urs Peyer of Switzerland, for their unselfish help in making this project all that it could be. I thank you all.

Eric C. Orlemann
Decatur, Illinois 2000

INTRODUCTION

On April 15, 2000, Caterpillar, as a corporate entity, the world's largest manufacturer of earthmoving equipment, celebrated its 75th anniversary. The "Caterpillar" trademark also turned 90 in the same year. But Caterpillar's rich heritage actually extends back to 1870 when one of its founders, Daniel Best, put his first transportable grain cleaner to work in California. From then on, innovation after innovation propelled Best and Caterpillar's other founding member, Benjamin Holt, into agricultural and eventually earthmoving history.

It seems that the tracked crawler tractor has been with us forever. This vehicle is another one of our fabulous mechanical creations from the twentieth century. All massed-produced tracked machines (whether agricultural, construction, or military) owe a debt to Holt's first experimental steam crawler from late 1904. In historical reviews of important mechanical achievements of the last century, little to no credit has been given to the crawler tractor and its earthmoving relatives. If you were to believe everything you saw on television as the absolute truth, you would fail to realize the far-reaching impact these machines have on our everyday lives.

The creations of Best, Holt, and ultimately Caterpillar have played key roles in almost all of our industrial and urban advancements. Automobiles would not be as advanced if earthmoving equipment hadn't built modern roads and highway systems. Airplanes could not land without wide, smooth runways. From giant skyscrapers, massive dams, and the mining of raw materials, it all had to start somewhere—and chances are, you would find Caterpillar equipment, in one form or another, laying the groundwork for these projects. It's hard to imagine our current lifestyles without them. Earthmoving and agricultural equipment, such as that built by Caterpillar, literally makes the world go 'round. Almost everything in our modern society starts with these machines.

Today, Caterpillar is a true global leader and manufacturer of not only construction and mining equipment, but diesel and turbine engines, large generator sets, agricultural tractors and combines, and forestry equipment. Its customer service and dealership network are envied throughout the industry. But staying number one is not easy. Caterpillar leads in almost every major equipment category. But it never sits back on its laurels. Each product line competes with other companies, in some cases dozens of companies, and some competing companies specialize in only one particular machine. This keeps the pressure on Caterpillar engineers, but it also forces them to produce the best products for its customers.

Caterpillar Chronicle celebrates the fantastic creations of Caterpillar and its founding companies of Best and Holt. From the earliest crawler tractors to the massive mining machines of today, *Chronicle* showcases the best and greatest Caterpillar machinery through the decades. This book is not so much a corporate history of the company, but a close look at the machines and vehicles. As with any project of this size, it would be impossible to include every piece of equipment manufactured by the company. (For the 2000 production year alone, Caterpillar offered over 300 separate pieces of equipment.) Some discretion had to be used when deciding what would be covered in the space allowed. Showcasing many of the company's early tractor and equipment offerings from the 1920s to the 1950s was not a difficult endeavor. But starting in the 1960s, with the release of so many new products, this book concentrates on the key machines. In the late 1970s and continuing through today, the shear number of equipment releases is truly overwhelming, so only the most relevant product lines and key introductions are covered. It's not our intention to emphasize one product line over another but to cover the most popular and recognizable machines, such as earthmoving or agricultural equipment.

Throughout the early chapters of this book, you will notice that in many instances the name or nomenclature for a particular piece of machinery is followed by a series of letters and/or numbers in parentheses. These designations often refer to the model series or type of the machine. As an example, during the early years, Holt built various versions of the "75" gas tractor. These were then issued a model series identification such as T-6 or T-8. In this case, the number and letter designation represents a tractor fitted with a specific engine. Most of these were not known by the general public, except for individuals who serviced and maintained them. The designations are included here to help differentiate one model from another. Starting in 1925, after the formation of Caterpillar Tractor Co., a standard method for identifying the various tractor models was used; a prefix code was listed at the beginning of all new equipment serial numbers. Referred to as the "Serial Number Prefix Code," it identifies the type of tractor model, engine type, track-gauge, transmission, etc., of the unit. This code has been used to identify much of the equipment built from the 1920s through the 1950s that is of most relevance to collectors and enthusiasts. In some cases, this code is the only way to tell one tractor model from another. For the more modern equipment, this code has been listed as a means to help the reader clarify significant model introductions or upgrades. This system of model identification is still in use by the company today.

Caterpillar *was* regarded as one of the leading heavy-equipment manufactures of the twentieth century. But to many, Caterpillar is the leader, period. With its sights set on the future, the company is prepared to continue its leadership position well into the new millennium.

1

"IF THAT DON'T LOOK LIKE A MONSTER CATERPILLAR"

BEST AND HOLT CREATE A PHENOMENON

The 1880s and 1890s were a pivotal time for the American farmer. The Wild West had been tamed, and the California Gold Rush was all but over. The horse-drawn plow, which had served the farmer well, was about to be reinvented, as was the harvesting of the season's bounties from the fields. Two key players in this unfolding drama were Benjamin Holt and Daniel Best. Both men were about to change the direction and history of mechanized agriculture. They would also have as profound an effect on road building and military transport, although they didn't realize it. For Holt and Best, the fertile farming valleys of California in the last decades of the nineteenth century would be their entrance point into an important part of American industrial history.

Benjamin Holt started his career by joining his father's lumber business in Concord, New Hampshire. The business specialized in hardwoods for wagon building. Yet one aspect of the wagon building business gave them trouble. The climate of Concord was poorly suited to seasoning the wood used for wheel fabrication.

In 1869, Benjamin's brother, Charles, started a new company in San Francisco, called C. H. Holt & Company. Charles also dealt in hardwoods, which he purchased from his father's company and sold to various wagon and boat manufacturers in the San Francisco area. The Holts tried seasoning the wood for wheel fabrication in San Francisco, but this proved little better than Concord. San Francisco was often cool and damp. To solve the problem, Charles looked inland to warmer, drier Stockton, California. Stockton was a well-placed town close to the San Joaquin Valley, and the San Joaquin River provided a direct link with San Francisco, making the area a perfect place to set up new manufacturing facilities. In 1883, Charles brought Benjamin in to oversee operations, and together the brothers established the Stockton Wheel Company.

The Holt brothers' interests reached beyond the wagon to other implements of agriculture and progress. One such tool was the combine. Their access to the San Joaquin Valley wheat fields provided

The powerful and imposing Best 110 hp Traction Engine, or "steamer," was a dominant force in the fields of the western United States. Pictured is a 1906 vintage model, No. 175, with the wider drive wheels, belonging to the Joseph A. Heidrick, Sr., Foundation. *ECO*

The Best Combine Harvesters of the 1870s and 1880s were very large machines that required equally large numbers of horses to pull them through the fields. A runaway team with a harvester in tow was a scary and often fatal experience. The steam traction engine would put an end to this dangerous possibility once and for all. *Caterpillar*

them with a very lucrative potential market if they had a combine to sell. They bought a few combine patents and in 1885 started experimental design work on their own model. A year later, in 1886, the company introduced "The Holt Bros. Improved Link Belt Combined Harvester." Their design utilized linked chains and sprockets, instead of conventional belt-driven pulleys. It was less subject to mechanical failure, a problem that could startle the horses and lead to serious injury to the men operating it, as well as damage to the combine.

The Holts had established themselves in the farm machinery business, and they continued to release innovative products. In 1890 they invented the "side-hill" har-

vester (patented in 1892), which helped farmers better utilize all of their available acreage. In this design, the wheels of the machine could be independently adjusted so the header could be matched to the angle of the hillside and the threshing mechanism could be kept level. But even as the side-hill machines were being developed by the company, Benjamin started to take a serious interest in the traction engine. In 1890 he unveiled a steam traction engine of his own design, nicknamed "Old Betsy." This steam-powered machine featured steering clutches, something the other manufacturers of the time did not offer. Ben's innovation of disengaging power to one driving wheel or the other earned him another patent in 1893.

In 1892 the Holt brothers changed the company name from the Stockton Wheel Company to the Holt Manufacturing Company, which better reflected the products being developed and offered for sale by the firm. All of this was to be looked after by Benjamin Holt, who was now the company's president. Daniel Best also had experience in the lumber business, but he came to the industrial manufacturing sector by a more circuitous path. While Benjamin Holt had the family business to occupy his early years, Best was a bit of a wanderer. He left his home in Iowa in his early twenties to go West and seek his fortune. After arriving in Steptoville, Washington, Best sought work at a lumber mill, a trade he knew well from working in the family's sawmill while in his teens. After an unprofitable attempt at running his own mill, Best left for Portland, Oregon, where he found himself working at still another lumber mill. Again, not satisfied with his occupation, he invested with a partner in a gold mine in southern Washington, and had quite a few successful strikes. But just as luck would have it, he lost the entire gold find, and almost his life, when his raft capsized in the rapids of the Snake River. This would have broken a lesser man, but not Best.

Between 1862 and 1869, he worked a variety of mining and lumbering jobs, some profitable and others not. At the end of this period, in 1869, he went to Marysville, California, to work on his older brother Henry's ranch.

While working at the ranch, Best observed that after the grain harvest, his brother, Henry, and all of the surrounding farmers had to transport their grain into town to be cleaned before it could be sold. What was an inconvenience to them seemed an opportunity to Best. He began to think that maybe the key was not to take the grain into town to be cleaned, but to bring the cleaner to the grain instead. This insight would prove most profitable in the months and years to come.

Working through the winter with his brothers Henry and Zachariah, Best prepared to start the testing of his transportable cleaner machines in that year's grain harvest. So successful was the cleaner's performance, that Best applied for and received a patent on his design in April 1871.

But Best was a man ever looking for more profitable excursions. While working on his farming inventions, he made another try at gold mining in 1874, with little to show for it. He even made a design improvement on an existing clothes washing machine, for which he received a patent in April 1877. Around 1880, Best was back in the fields, designing ever larger harvesters for the farmers of California. These machines combined the process of harvesting, cleaning, and bagging all in one unit. Combines

Although not as large or as powerful as the Best 110 hp Traction Engine, the Holt 70 hp Senior Road Engine was the largest offered by the company, and it was a very capable machine. The unit, pictured about 1906, is equipped with a Scotch-Marine boiler and 42-inch-wide main drive wheels, with the provision of adding additional 42-inch high-flotation wheel extensions. *Caterpillar*

with this ability were available in the eastern farmlands, but not on the scale of the Best design.

With his business interests growing, he made the move to a larger manufacturing area in 1886. He named his new operation, in San Leandro, California, "Daniel Best Agricultural Works." To meet farmers' needs, the Best harvesters, like those of other makers, including Holt, were getting quite large. They were so large, in fact, that the horse teams could barely pull them through the fields. Best would soon have the answer to this problem, as it would literally drive by his office windows in 1888.

That spring, Best witnessed a demonstration of a steam traction engine designed by a blacksmith named of Marquis de Lafayette Remington. Remington had built his first steam traction engine in Woodburn, Oregon, in 1885. This first steam tractor was based on a machine designed by Nathaniel Porter Slate of Tangent, Oregon, around 1869. Remington received the rights to the design as payment on a $600 debt owed to him by Slate. By January 1888, the patent office officially recognized his machine design. Two months later, he took his second traction engine to San Leandro for a demonstration in front of Best's office facilities. So impressed was Best with what Remington called the "Rough and Ready," he purchased the rights to build the 30-hp traction engine and sell it on the West Coast, although he agreed not to market it in Remington's home state of Oregon. In all, Remington only built six tractors. Best started work immediately to develop traction engine power for his combine harvester. By February 8, 1889, the first Best traction engine was ready for shipping. It marked the dawn of high-production mechanized farming, and the beginning of the end for the large horse and mule teams.

AN ALLIANCE FORMED AND BROKEN

Heading into the twentieth century, both Holt and Best offered steam traction engines, matched up to combine harvesters of their own designs. Popular models for Holt included the 40-hp Junior Road Engine from 1891, the 60-hp Standard Road Engine from 1895, and the powerful 70-hp Senior Road Engine. Popular Best models included the 50-hp Traction Engine from 1889, and the 110-hp model from 1897. Both the Holt and the Best traction engines were more commonly referred to as "steamers."

Even though the Holt and Best model lines mirrored each other almost product for product, the customers clearly had their favorites. In the field, the Best steamers were more popular because of their more powerful engines. As for the combined harvesters, the public used Holt models in far greater number. By 1912, Best had built and sold some 1,351 steam combines, but Holt had produced about 8,000 of the harvesters in various sizes.

The Best and Holt steam traction engines worked well when the going was on dry and stable ground. But in peat, or other soft soils, these tremendously heavy steamers would get themselves mired down in the fields. A temporary solution to this problem was the fitting of extremely wide rim extensions, which provided better flotation. Both Best and Holt used these on their traction engines, but they still left a lot to be desired. The manufacturers needed another technical breakthrough to solve this problem. That solution came with the introduction of the belted crawler track.

Though Benjamin Holt did not necessarily come up with the concept of a tracked machine, he is responsible for putting the concept into full production as a completely workable tractor. Inspired by some of the early designs of the Lombard Log Hauler, Holt went to work on his own creation. On November 24, 1904, Holt started testing a modified version of his No. 77 wheel-type traction engine on Holt property, near the Stockton city limits. He had the No. 77 steamer's rear wheels removed and replaced with a set of tracks, made from malleable link belts, with wooden blocks attached to act as treads. Early tests were very encouraging. The tracked steamer was run on soft ground to see if the system would provide enough flotation for the heavy unit. It did.

This Holt Tracked Road Engine was the company's first workable prototype machine that used continuous crawler belts instead of round drive wheels. It had originally started life as a 1904 Holt No. 77 round-wheel steamer. The tracked prototype is pictured in March 1905, with Pliny Holt at the controls. This is one of the original three images taken of this unit by company photographer Charles Clements. *Caterpillar*

Originally built in 1908, this 25-hp Holt 40 (No. 1004) was the second gas-powered crawler tractor to be sold by the company. The No. 1003 was the first one sold to a paying customer. This Holt 40 is part of the Joseph A. Heidrick, Sr., Foundation, and is the oldest known surviving Holt crawler tractor in the world. *ECO*

The Northern Holt 45B pictured was one of only two units built by Pliny Holt at the Northern Holt Co. in Minneapolis, Minnesota, in 1909. Two more of this two-wheeled steering design were also built by the Canadian Holt Co. in 1909. This tractor, No. 102, is part of the Fred C. Heidrick Ag History Center and is the only surviving example of this unique design. *Randy Leffingwell*

The first gas tractors built by Clarence Leo Best after he left Holt were round-wheel designs, such as this C.L.B. 80 hp unit, pictured in 1914. It was powered by a massive six-cylinder Buffalo gas engine. Only 38 of this model were built between 1911 and 1916. *Caterpillar*

The C.L.B. 75 Tracklayer was introduced in 1914 and was an improved version of the C.L.B. 70 Tracklayer from late 1912. Weighing in at approximately 28,000 pounds, it actually outweighed the big Holt 120, which tipped the scales at 26,500 pounds. The rare C.L.B. 75 pictured, No. 963, is owned by Laurence Darrach of California, and was originally purchased new by his father in 1919, the last year of production for the big Tracklayer. *ECO*

THE LEGEND IS NAMED

In early 1905, the term "Caterpillar" was first used to refer to Holt's creation. Charles Clements, a company photographer often used by Holt, is credited with coining the name.

In a letter to the company a decade later, written at Holt's request, he described the circumstances at the time:

STOCKTON, CALIFORNIA.
APRIL 30th, 1915.
MR. P. EHRENFELDT, Secretary, The Holt Manufacturing Company
Stockton, California.

Dear Sir:

Complying with your request for a statement as to how and when the word "CATERPILLAR," as applied to the tractor, originated, will say that I am the person who named it, and it happened in this way.

One afternoon in the month of March 1905, I was phoned to get ready to take some photos in the country, destination not stated. Down stairs I found awaiting me Messrs. Benj. Holt and P. E. (Pliny) Holt in an automobile, the latter driving. We traveled West and soon reached Roberts Island. The only information I had had thus far was that an engine was to be photographed. Nearing the Holt Ranch, we perceived a steam traction engine in the distance. Mr. Benjamin Holt stated, "They are not running." Noticing the absence of the big side wheels, I said, "They are broken down," at which Mr. P. E. Holt turned around, looked at me and laughed, but said nothing. Suddenly I noticed that the outfit was moving along, but did not say anything, thinking that the engine was on board a barge going through some canal, seemingly hidden by the heavy crop of volunteer barley. All of this time we were nearing the outfit, when suddenly it came around between us and the crop of barley, and for a moment I was struck dumb with amazement. Jumping upon my feet I exclaimed aloud, "IF THAT DON'T LOOK LIKE A MONSTER CATERPILLAR." Mr. Benj. Holt reddened at the remark and smilingly asked, "What makes you think that?" I answered, "Why, even a child could make no mistake. Just watch the undulating movement as it creeps along" (the original model ran quite slack, the undulation being 12 inches or more when running on the wooden slats).

After inspecting the outfit, Messrs. Benj. Holt and P. E. Holt mounted the engine and made a turn around in the field, Mr. P. E. Holt at the throttle. During this time I exposed three plates on the outfit. Returning to the Works, I developed them and the next morning placed them in envelops(sic.) (which is our usual custom) and marked the name "CATERPILLAR" on them. I told Mr. J. Hardy, the Chief Draftsman at the time, what I had seen the day before, and showed him the negatives, also the name, at which he laughed.

Two days after, Mr. P. E. Holt came to the Drafting Department and asked me if I had prints of the platform wheel engine (it seems by this name it was known during the experiments made with it in our yards). I told him I did not know what he meant, at which he stated, "Why, you photographed the engine day before yesterday at the Ranch." "Oh!, you mean the CATERPILLAR," I remarked. "Well," he stated, "whatever you call it, give me three prints as soon as possible." I filled several more orders after that.

A short time afterwards Mr. P. E. Holt sent a magazine, called the FARM IMPLEMENT NEWS, to me, the front cover of which he wished copied. Having done so, I added this negative to the three above-mentioned plates, all of which are now in our negative files. By the way, the cover copied had a cut or illustration taken from a print made off one of the negatives I had taken at the Holt Ranch, showing, as I stated before, Mr. P. E. Holt at the throttle.

Trusting the above is the desired information, I beg to remain,
Respectfully yours,
(Signed) C. CLEMENTS
Subscribed and sworn to before me this 1st day of May 1915.
(Signed) R. E. MANN,
Notary Public, in and for the County of San Joaquin, State of California

The company tested additional prototype track designs throughout 1905 and 1906. By the end of 1906, the seventh track design, tractor No. 111, referred to as the "Holt Brothers Paddle Wheel Improved Traction Engine," was built and sold to a paying customer, making this the first true production model. Actual delivery of No. 111 was in early 1907. Records are a bit confusing when dealing with the testing of the early track machines. It seems there were seven crawler designs, used on three steam-powered tractor chassis. The seventh design was the one used on No. 111, which was the third complete operable machine.

Another technological advancement that was happening at the same time as the development of the track concept was the gasoline engine. So impressed was Holt with its possibilities that in October 1906, he and one of his nephews, Pliny E. Holt, established another company, the Aurora Engine Company in Stockton, for the continued development of the gas engine concept. Later on in 1913, the Aurora firm would be integrated into Holt Manufacturing.

The original prototype Holt gasoline-powered crawler tractor was first tested in December 1906. In early 1908, the second unit was built. Later in that same year, the third tracked gas tractor, a Holt Model 40 (Serial No. 1003), was shipped in September to a paying customer, making it the

The Holt 18 Midget, introduced in 1914, was the smallest tiller-wheeled gas tractor offered by Holt Manufacturing. It was mainly targeted to orchard and vineyard farmers. Last year of production for the 18 was 1917. The Holt Midget pictured, No. 7079, is part of the Fred C. Heidrick Ag History Center. *Randy Leffingwell*

Introduced in 1912, the Holt Baby 30 looked much like a Holt 40, only in a smaller scale. Built only at the Holt Stockton, California, plant, its production ended in 1916. Pictured is a 1914 vintage model of the Baby 30 from the Joseph A. Heidrick, Sr., Foundation. *ECO*

first gas "Caterpillar" tractor sold. These early Model 40 tractors were powered by a four-cylinder, gas, 6x8-inch bore and stroke, valve-in-head motor, rated at 25 hp. The early tractors were manufactured in Stockton until November 1909, and totaled about 56 units. A second batch of approximately 72 Model 40 T-2 units was built in Peoria in 1913. All of these were powered by a four-cylinder, M-2 gas, 7x8-inch bore and stroke, valve-in-head Peoria motor.

The competition between Holt and Best in the tractor and combine market came to a head in 1905, when Best filed a lawsuit against Holt for patent infringement concerning the power take-off. The case went back and forth in the courts throughout most of 1906 and 1907, but before the court could make a final ruling, Best and Holt agreed to settle outside. They began talks on the feasibility of combining their companies. Daniel Best was now 70 years old, and he thought it might be a good time in his life to sell his interest in Best Manufacturing to Holt. On October 8, 1908, Best sold the business to Benjamin and Charles Holt, but not before making sure that his son, Clarence Leo Best, would be the new president of the Holt Manufacturing Company's San Leandro facilities. It was a key position in the company, but the Holt brothers would still maintain ultimate control of the firm.

Expansion was on the minds of the Holts, with the eastern part of the country as the next most likely area for their products. In 1909, Pliny Holt established the Northern Holt

The Holt 60 was a more powerful version of the original Holt 40/45 gas crawler tractors. Introduced in 1911, it was built in Stockton, as well as in Peoria. The Stockton-built Holt 60 was a Model T-7, while the Peoria tractor was referred to as the Holt 40-60, Model T-4. This immaculate 1913 Holt 60, Model T-7, No. 1838, is owned by Larry Maasdam of Iowa and Ron Miller of Michigan. *ECO*

Company in Minneapolis, Minnesota, but things did not work out as planned. The advantage of tracked machines over wheel-type machines was minimal in the East. Add in the extra cost of the tractors, which was considerable, and you have a recipe for failure. Only two tractors were eventually built, and both of these had special front ends with two steering wheels.

While in Minneapolis, Pliny heard of a facility in Illinois that might suit the company's needs. The Colean Manufacturing Company of East Peoria, Illinois, was in bankruptcy proceedings. Colean's factory was relatively new and had specialized in building threshers and steamers. It was the ideal location for Holt. On October 25, 1909, a deal was finalized that would make Peoria the firm's new headquarters. When the company finally incorporated in Illinois the following January, it carried the new name of The Holt "Caterpillar" Company. But by 1914, it was simply known as The Holt Manufacturing Company, which is what the original Stockton company location was referred to. The "Caterpillar" term had been officially registered as a company trademark in 1910.

Meanwhile, back in San Leandro, C. L. Best was not happy with the way things were working out for him at Holt. Many of his ideas were thwarted by Holt family members who held lesser positions in the company, but had seats on Holt's Board of Directors. Finally Best had had enough, and he left Holt in 1910, as did many key engineers loyal to him. The terms of the original sale of his father's company to Holt in 1908 stipulated that C. L. could not reenter the tractor business for 10 years if he were to leave the firm. Best basically ignored this and started a new enterprise called the C. L. Best Gas Traction Company, located in Elmhurst, California. Like father, like son. The war between Best and Holt was on again.

At first, Best built wheel-type tractors, powered by big "Buffalo" gas engines manufactured by the Buffalo Gasoline Motor Co. of Buffalo, New York. The smallest of these was the C.L.B. 25 hp (Model 25-30) Gas Tractor. Produced from 1910 to 1913, it was powered by a four-cylinder, 6x7 1/2-inch bore and stroke engine. Only 10 were built.

Next came the C.L.B. 40 hp (40-45) made from 1910 to 1915. It was equipped with a larger four-cylinder, 7x9-inch bore and stroke motor. About 17 units of this tractor were assembled. Related to this model was the C.L.B. 54 hp, built from 1911 to 1915. This model shared most of its specifications with the "40 hp" tractor, except it was powered by a 7 1/2x9-inch bore and stroke engine. Only 18 of these ever saw the light of day.

The Holt 75, Model T-8 pictured, was the last series of this type to be built by Holt. Released in 1921 and only built in Stockton, it differed greatly from its predecessors in the design of its radiator and crawler assemblies. When production finally ended in 1924, only 67 units had been manufactured. This extremely rare tractor, serial number S4008, was the eighth one made and is owned by Larry Maasdam of Iowa. *ECO*

The big gas round-wheel tractors built by Best were the C.L.B. 60 hp (60-70) from 1910 to 1916, and the C.L.B. 80 hp, produced from 1911 to 1916. Both of these tractors got their power from sizable six-cylinder Buffalo engines. The major difference between the two models, other than power, was that the 60 hp had a 7x9-inch bore and stroke engine, while the 80-hp utilized a 7 1/2x9-inch model. These were the most successful of the early C. L. Best round-wheel tractors, with 35 of the 60 hp, and 38 of the 80-hp models being built. Best designed a special C.L.B. 90 hp round-wheel tractor in 1912, powered by a massive Buffalo four-cylinder, 10x12-inch bore and stroke, gas motor. But old production records indicate that none were ever sold to the public, if they were built at all.

Another design from that year, however, would prove critical to Best's success. In late 1912, he introduced the company's first tiller-wheel, gas-powered, tracked machine—the C.L.B. 70 hp Tracklayer. Best's 70 Tracklayer incorporated many advanced features not found in the Holt machines, such as the liberal use of high-grade steels. The 70 was powered by a Best-designed four-cylinder, 7 3/4x9-inch bore and stroke, gas engine. In 1914, the 70 became the 75 Tracklayer. Both tractors looked virtually the same except the 75 was a bit more powerful and weighed more. It was a husky-looking machine that proved just as tough as its counterpart, the Holt 75. These tractors became so popular that Best was able to repurchase his father's larger, former plant at San Leandro in mid-1916 (Holt had moved its remaining operations

out around 1913), which increased his manufacturing output considerably. When production ended on the big Tracklayers in 1919, about 734 tractors had been built. A small number of these tractors were built as C.L.B. 75 hp Round-Wheel tractors. This model was basically the Tracklayer version with its tracks removed and replaced with 90-inch diameter wheels.

Other large tiller-wheeled Tracklayers designed by C. L. Best included the C.L.B. 90 hp and the C.L.B. 120 hp. The 90 Tracklayer, a beefed up version of the 75 model introduced in 1916, was powered by a Best four-cylinder, 8x9-inch bore and stroke, gas engine. The track sections on this tractor were a full two-feet longer than the tracks on the 75. These longer tracks were also designed with seven track rollers, as compared to the five found on the shorter-tracked Tracklayer. Production ended on the 90 Tracklayer in 1917, with company records indicating only 39 built. This tractor's big brother was the limited production 120 hp Tracklayer. Very little history survives on these machines. Shipping records indicate that one was built in 1916 and four in 1917. These may have been built as test candidates for a possible heavy military artillery prime mover. None are known to exist today.

While C. L. Best essentially had only two tiller-wheel Tracklayer models to choose from, Holt offered a full line of tiller-wheeled "Caterpillar" tractors. The success of the Holt 40 led directly to the Holt 45 series. Looking much like the earlier 40 tractors, the 45 models were equipped with a different engineflthe four-cylinder, Holt M-1, 6 1/2x8-inch bore and stroke, valve-in-head,

Specially designed as a 20-ton military prime mover, the Holt 120, Model T-9, was the company's most powerful tiller-wheeled tractor. Its legendary ability to pull heavy artillery during World War I is without question. Only a couple of these tractors still exist today, and this 1917 model, which is part of the Fred C. Heidrick Ag History Center, is one of the finest of them all. *Randy Leffingwell*

gas motor. The 45 series tractors were built at both the Stockton and Peoria plants. The tractor from Stockton was known as a Holt 40-45, and was available from 1909 to 1911. The Peoria design, built between 1910 and 1913, was identified as the Holt 30-45 (T-1). In total, about 154 of the Stockton 45 tractors were built, while some 94 units of that model came out of the Peoria factory.

For customers wanting a bit more power, the company offered the Holt 60 Caterpillar, which was built at both Holt plants. In Stockton, it was introduced in May 1911 as the Holt 60 (T-7). This model was equipped with a four-cylinder, Holt M-6, 7x8-inch bore and stroke, valve-in-head, gas motor. The Peoria machine was known as the Holt 40-60 (T-4), and was also from 1911. The 40-60 was equipped with a Holt M-3 gas motor that was the same size as the Stockton machine, but utilized an "Ell-head" valve design. The 60 series proved to be a popular tractor with customers, and the sales were a big improvement over the 45 model line. The T-4 model of the 60 had sold some 260 tractors when production halted in 1916. The T-7 unit accounted for approximately 691 machines before its time came to an end in 1915. Of this total, 63 were for military purposes.

If a customer wanted even more power, the company had just the tractor: the Holt 75. The mighty Holt 75 was the most popular and best selling tiller-wheel–equipped Caterpillar tractor that the company ever made. Its record as a tough farming tractor is well known, but it was also an excellent machine for road-building work. The tractor also found itself in the heat of battle as a heavy artillery prime mover with different armies in Europe during World War I. The 75 was manufactured at both of the Holt factories. The first model to be introduced, in 1913, was the Holt 60-75 (A-NVS). This tractor was built in Stockton and was powered by a four-cylinder, Holt M-7, 7 1/2x8-inch bore and stroke, valve-in-head, gas engine. Starting in 1916, the big tractor, now referred to as the Holt 75 (T-8), was built at both plants in California and Illinois. Most of the production out of the Peoria plant was destined for military duty, which ended in late 1918. These tractors differed from the Stockton-built models in the design of their cooling systems and track assemblies. Engines were the same in the two tractors.

Between 1914 and 1915, the Peoria plant produced a special run of Holt 75 (T-6) tractors, equipped with a Holt M-5 series gas motor. The major design difference between this motor and the one found in the regular 75 was the use of an "Ell-head" valve layout. The success of this design was rather limited because of engine problems, and only 16 were ever produced.

In 1921 the last Stockton design of the Holt 75 tractor was released, with an improved radiator and upgraded track assemblies. This Holt 75 was still considered a T-8 model series when its time in the product line finally came to an end in 1924. Only 67 units of this last Stockton model were produced. In all, there were approximately 4,161 units of the 75 T-8 model series manufactured from both plants. Of this total, 1,810 of these tractors were specified as military orders.

The request for a very heavy-duty artillery tractor in the 20-ton range from the military led to the design of the Holt 120. The first series of this tractor to be tested was the 120 Model A-PEP in 1914. This design utilized a big gas Holt

six-cylinder, 7 1/2x8-inch bore and stroke, "Enclosed" Peoria motor. But problems with this engine design delayed a full-production model until 1915. The tractor, identified as the Holt 120 (T-9), was fitted with a Holt M-8. This engine had the same number of cylinders, as well as the bore and stroke, of the previous model, but in this application was equipped with an Ell-head design. This proved to be the engine the 120 had needed all along. The tractor was rated at 120 brake-horsepower and 70 drawbar-horsepower, with an operating weight of 26,500 pounds. Compare this to C. L. Best's 75 Tracklayer, which had only 75 brake-horsepower to move its 28,000-pound bulk around. When looked at in these terms, the Holt 120 was quite an efficient design, at least as far as a tiller-wheeled tractor was concerned. Almost all of the 120 tractors were built for use by Great Britain and the United States in World War I. All of the Holt 120 tractors were assembled in Peoria, which amounted to about 698 machines when production ended in 1922, though it seems only two were built in that last year. Of this total, 676 were built as military issue. Today, the surviving Holt 120 tractors in the world can be counted on one hand.

During this period, Holt designed and built more than just large tiller-wheeled tractors; it also built some small ones. These were the Holt Baby 30 and the Model 18 Midget. Both of these tractors were aimed at orchard and vineyard farmers who required small, but highly maneuverable tractors to work in the groves. The Holt Baby 30 was first introduced in 1912. It looked like its bigger brothers, but was proportioned smaller for its intended use. The Baby was powered by a Holt four-cylinder, 5 1/4x6-inch bore and stroke, valve-in-head, gas motor. The Holt 18 Midget was released in 1914 with a four-cylinder, 4 1/2x5 1/2-inch bore and stroke, Ell-head motor. Both of these small tractors were considered successes for Holt, with roughly 301 units of the Baby built and about 347 of the Midget. Both of these tractor models were built at the Stockton plant.

All of the above tractors built by Best and Holt steered by means of a front tiller-wheel. This made the turning radius of the tractors often quite large, making work in smaller, tighter places the work of horse and man. If the crawler tractor was ever going to replace animal power completely, it needed to lose that cumbersome tiller-wheel. This would be the next big design advancement on the horizon for Holt's Caterpillars and C. L. Best's Tracklayers.

Introduced in 1915, the Holt 120 (Model T-9) shared many of the components found on the Holt 75 tractors, which were built at the Peoria plant at that time. But the big difference was the tractor's big six-cylinder gas engine. The 75 utilized a four-cylinder unit. All of the Holt 120 tractors were built in Peoria. Last year of production was 1922. *Randy Leffingwell*

2

TOGETHER WE STAND, DIVIDED WE FALL

HOLT AND BEST SPLIT AND MERGE

The renewed competition between Holt and C. L. Best would again push the boundaries of crawler tractor design and development. One major advancement was the elimination of the front steering tiller-wheel from some of the new designs. These tractors, with the nickname muleyfla farmer's term for a cow without hornsflbrought a new class of machines into orchard and vineyard work. Even though the early Holt Baby 30 and Midget 18 and the Best "Humpback" 30 were marketed for this purpose, their maneuverability still left a lot to be desired.

By late 1913, Holt had their first prototype muley tractor without a tiller-wheel called the Holt 20-30 (Model T-5), ready for testing. The 20-30 was powered by a Holt M-4, four-cylinder, 6x7 inch bore and stroke, Tee-Head Doman gas engine, rated at 30 brake-horsepower. But the Holt 20-30 was a bit underdeveloped. Its production total of only eleven tractors built reflected this. But it was a start.

The Holt 20-30 quickly evolved into Holt 45 (T-10), in 1914. The 45 muley was a completely different model type from that of the earlier Holt 45, which utilized a tiller steering wheel. The 45 muley was powered by a gas, four-cylinder Holt M-9 motor, with a 6x7 inch bore and stroke, rated at 45 brake hp. Key to the 45s design features was its use of a rather simple, direct independent drive for each track, allowing for independent control. This enabled the tractor to turn in its own length, a feat that was practically impossible for a tiller-wheeled machine. This allowed the 45 to work in more confined areas that were not possible with a standard tractor of this power output.

The Holt 45 proved to be quite a tough tractor out in the field. But the tractor's success there was only part of the story. The Holt 45 would really prove its worth, not in the farming

Caterpillar replaced its 2-Ton tractor with the model Ten (PT) in 1929. Along with the standard model, orchard and high-clearance versions were also available. Standard track gauge was 37 inches and 44 inches for the wide-gauge version. The Caterpillar Ten (PT4) pictured, part of the Keith Clark Collection, is equipped with optional Bishop citrus fenders, and was the fourth tractor built in the closing days of 1928, even though it is considered a 1929 model. *ECO*

fields of America, but in the battlefields of Europe. Battlefield and supply line conditions called for vehicles that could operate under the most severe conditions imaginable. If you couldn't keep your lines of supply open and your artillery on the move, you were not going to win the war. The answer to these challenges was the tracked artillery tractor.

In November 1915, the U.S. Army put the Holt 45 through a rigorous testing program at Fort Sill and found that the tractor was up to military duty. Overseas, the French military found the Holt 45 to be an ideal medium-sized artillery tractor and prime mover, as did the U.S. Army. To complement this model of the 45, Holt built a special version known as the Model 45 E-HVS (T-12) Armored Artillery Tractor in 1917. This model differed from the standard 45 in that it was covered in armor plating. Also, the frame was of a cast-steel design. The motor was the same as that found in the standard unit. In all, approximately 1,891

The Holt 45 (Model T-10), introduced in 1914 and built in Stockton and Peoria, was a real workhorse for the company. It was a popular military artillery prime mover, as well as a very capable agricultural tractor. The Stockton-built, 1919 vintage 45 pictured, No. 20939, is part of the Bill Santos collection of California. *ECO*

Holt 45 muley tractors were built when production ceased in 1920. Of this total, 42 tractors were of the armored 45 E-HVS variety, which ended production in 1918.

A companion and eventual replacement for the 45 was the faster and more powerful Holt 10-Ton (T-16), which was introduced as the 10-ton Model 55 Artillery Tractor. It was powered by a four-cylinder Holt M-11 gas, 6 1/2x7-inch bore and stroke motor, rated at 55 brake-horsepower and 40 drawbar-horsepower. The Model 55 was covered in full armor plating, and looked much like the previous 45 E-HVS model it replaced, only with a larger motor. The Model 55 was in production from late 1917 to 1919.

While the military versions of the 10-ton were being built, Holt also produced a commercial version of the tractor. The first prototype of the unit was built in 1918, but full production did not commence until 1919. This model, also known internally as a Model T-16, utilized the same type of motor found in the military version. The standard 10-ton was a husky-looking machine, if a bit crude around the edges. In late 1924, the Holt name was cast into both sides of a newly redesigned radiator housing, improving the looks considerably.

To help compete with some of Best's tractors out West, Holt built a special Western 10-Ton model (TS-21) in 1921. The Western differed in design from the normal 10-Ton in quite a few areas. This model used an upgraded Holt M-21, four-cylinder, 6 1/2x7-inch bore and stroke motor, which was built at the Stockton plant, as was the tractor itself. All of the other commercial 10-Ton tractors and their motors were assembled in Peoria. The Western used a modified undercarriage that was shorter than the standard unit, with wider track pads to help reduce ground compaction. The radiator, as well as all of the sheet metal, was of a cleaner, more compact design. Holt's goal with the Western was a field tractor that weighed less than a normal 10-Ton, but packed the necessary horsepower punch for the really big jobs. But in the end, only 152 Western 10-Ton tractors were built by the time production came to a halt in 1923.

The 10-Ton tractor's smaller brother was the Holt 5-Ton (T-11), which was introduced in 1917 as the 5-Ton Artillery Tractor Model 1917, its official military designation. All of these early tractors (except for three by Holt) were built under license agreements from Holt by Maxwell Motor Car Company of Detroit, Michigan, and by Reo Motor Car Co. of Lansing, Michigan. The motor in these tractors was a four-cylinder, Holt M-12 gas, 4 3/4x6-inch bore and stroke engine, rated at 40 brake-horsepower and 25 drawbar-horsepower. Production of these armored versions by Maxwell and Reo would continue through 1918. Most of these tractors would carry the U.S.A. letters on their radiator fronts, instead of the Holt ligature. In all, Maxwell built 2,193 units of the 5-Ton, and Reo produced 1,477.

Factory records indicate that Holt began building production 5-Ton (T-11) tractors in 1919. But the war complicated record keeping. After the armistice was signed, the military started returning 5-Ton tractors to Holt, to be converted into commercial models, complete with new serial numbers. At least 151 tractors in 1919, with an additional 150 units in 1921, are listed this way. With that said, the total number of the T-11 series 5-Tons built by Holt was right around 2,425, not counting the renumbered units.

Starting in 1921, Holt built the first of nine prototype 5-Ton Model T-29 tractors, the eventual replacement of the T-11 series. By mid-1923, the Model T-29 was released for sale. Although the tractor's motor was basically the same as the previous model, including power output, the look was all new, with a newly designed fuel tank mounted ahead of the operator, integrated into the overall sheet metal of the front end. The undercarriage track frame was a riveted fabrication. These early T-29 tractors, with the riveted frames, were all built at the Stockton factory between 1923 and 1924, with total output of approximately 212 units. In late 1924, a revised version with a cast-steel track frame was introduced as the New 5-Ton Caterpillar Tractor, Model T-29. Along with the new undercarriage, the Holt name was cast into the radiator sides, while the previous Stockton-built machines had the letters as a stencil cut-out.

The Holt 10-Ton (Model T-16) tractor would eventually take the place of the Holt 45 "muley," though both models were produced at the same time for a few years. The commercial version of the T-16 was introduced in 1918 and was built in Peoria, before being discontinued as a Caterpillar model at the end of 1925. Pictured is the 1922 vintage 10-Ton of the Joseph A. Heidrick, Sr., Foundation. *ECO*

Between 1920 and 1921, tractors built at the Holt Peoria plant included the 120 (T-9), the 10-Ton (T-16), and the 5-Ton (T-11). *Caterpillar*

The smallest tractor in the Holt product line in the early 1920s was the 2-Ton Model T-35. Introduced in 1921, the 2-Ton was powered by a Holt M-35, four-cylinder, 4x5 1/2-inch bore and stroke motor, rated at 15 draw-bar-horsepower and 25 belt-horsepower. The original model released used an undercarriage and track frames that were riveted together. In 1924 a new cast-steel fabrication was introduced, which was far stronger than the riveted design. Later that same year, the radiator housing now had the Holt name cast on the sides, replacing the previous stencil cut-out design. The 2-Ton Model T-35 looked very much like the 5-Ton Model T-29 in a smaller package. According to the records, about 1,350 units of the riveted frame version of the 2-Ton had been built when production ended on it in 1924. The newer model would continue on as part of the Caterpillar Tractor Co.

Not long after Holt introduced its first muley tractor, Best would counter the innovation with a design of its own. One of the first tillerless tractors offered was the C. L.

Introduced in late 1918, the Best 25 was added to the product line in the hopes of expanding the popularity of the "muley" tractors offered by the company. Production ended in 1920, with some 300 units shown as being built. Pictured is Bill Santos' Best 25 (No. 165) from 1919, and in the background, its eventual replacement, a Best 30 from 1921. *ECO*

Best 40 Tracklayer. Introduced in late 1914, it was in direct competition with the Holt 45. Even though it was down 5 brake-horsepower from the Holt, it made up for it with its overall lighter working weight. Around 1918, a more powerful version was shown of this model called the C. L. Best 45. It looked just like the 40, but with an increase of 5 horsepower. Records seem to indicate that only one of these special models was ever built. When the Best 40 ended production in 1919, approximately 747 had been manufactured for commercial use.

The medium-sized Best muley tractor found a good reception in the marketplace. This cannot be said, though, for two smaller tillerless crawler models that followed the release of the 40. In 1916 the small C. L. Best 16 Pony Tracklayer was introduced to the farming market. The Pony, also known as the 8-16, was powered by a four-cylinder, Best 4 3/8x5 1/4-inch bore and stroke, gas engine, rated at 8 drawbar-horsepower and 16 belt-horsepower. Primarily intended for orchard work, it failed to see any real production because of a lack of steel in the marketplace, due to military demands for the war. Old production records indicate that only three Pony 16 tractors were built, two in 1916 and one in 1917. This model was then followed by the C. L. Best 30 Tracklayer in 1917. But this 30 was not the same as a model that would come out in just a few years. In many respects, this tractor was the false start for the Best 30 from 1921. The model from 1917 was powered by a four-cylinder, 5 1/4x6 1/4-inch bore and stroke, gas motor, with power ratings of 16 drawbar-horsepower and 30 belt-horsepower. Only 15 units of this original Model 30 ever saw the light of day, all in 1917.

Up until now, the sales numbers that Best was posting were quite small when compared to the quantities being built by Holt for military production needs. But in 1919, Best introduced what would become one of the greatest crawler tractor models ever to pull a plow through fertile soil—the Best 60 Tracklayer.

The Best 60 marked a significant turning point in the evolution of the crawler tractor. Some of the features that made the 60 such a standout performer were its oscillating track roller frames, the use of some 36 bearings to reduce friction and wear in key mechanical areas, and a steering system that utilized roller-bearing–mounted, multiple-disc–enclosed friction clutches. The motor in the tractor was a big four-cylinder, Best 6 1/2x8 1/2-inch bore and stroke, gas engine, capable of 35 drawbar-horsepower and 60 belt-horsepower. But by 1922, power output had increased to 40 drawbar-horsepower. The Best 60 was a reliable and extremely tough tractor out in the field. For its time, this crawler tractor was simply the finest large muley money could buy. In a few years, it would also become the backbone of the Caterpillar Tractor Company's new tractor product line, not as a Best 60, but as the legendary Caterpillar Sixty.

The Best 60 pretty much replaced the 40 in the company's crawler tractor lineup. In 1921 the Best 25 tractor's replacement was finally ready for introduction as the Best 30 Tracklayer. The Best 30 was based on the design principles of the popular 60 model, but approximately half the power. It was equipped with a four-cylinder, Best 4 3/4x6 1/2-inch bore and stroke motor, rated at 20 drawbar-horsepower and 30 belt-horsepower. Like the 60, the 30 was one tough little crawler, and it proved to be a very popular tractor in the marketplace.

CATERPILLAR TRACTOR COMPANY

In many respects, it was the war in Europe that would shape the future for the Best and Holt companies, though they didn't know it at the time. During the years from about 1915 to 1919, almost all of the tractor design and production by Holt was for some type of military application. Just about everything that came out of its plants was dictated by the U.S. Ordnance Department. At the time, Holt had no reason to worry, since they were building tractors at record numbers. Holt could hardly meet demands, and issued licenses to various other manufacturers to help increase production.

On the other hand, the C. L. Best Gas Traction Co. had obtained assurances from the government that it could

Pictured is the first Best 60 Tracklayer tractor, No. 101A, from 1919. From the start, the 60 was a very popular tractor, known for its power and reliability in the field. *ECO Collection*

The Best 60, from the Joseph A. Heidrick, Sr., Foundation, is an early 1919 vintage model and is completely restored. These early models were rated at 35 drawbar-horsepower and 60 belt-horsepower. Working weight was right around 17,500 pounds. *ECO*

The most popular of all Best tractors, at least as far as numbers produced are concerned, was the Best 30, from 1921. It shared many of the design innovations of its bigger brother, the 60, but in a smaller package. Pictured is a 1922 version (S.N. S1514) belonging to Doug Veerkamp of California. *ECO*

This Holt 5-Ton (Model T-29) tractor of the Joseph A. Heidrick, Sr., Foundation is unique because of its riveted track frame and undercarriage. Introduced in 1923, it was only built in this configuration at the Stockton plant. Production ended on this riveted-built design in 1924. The tractor pictured is a 1924 model, Serial Number S-50099. *ECO*

continue farm crawler tractor production. Best would supply tractors to the farmers, while Holt would see to the military's needs. This arrangement gave the Best company a distinct advantage in designing and building a tractor that was well suited to work on the farm. The Best 60 and 30 were clear evidence of this. But once the war was over, situations started to arise that neither company was really prepared to deal with on its own.

After the armistice was signed in November 1918, one of the first things to start flowing into Holt's company offices was a stream of canceled tractor orders from the U.S. Ordnance Department. At the beginning of the war, the military had asked Holt and the licensed manufacturers for 24,791 track-type tractors, including the 2 1/2-ton, 5-ton, 10-ton, 15-ton, and 20-ton models. But by the end of the war, only 9,771 tractors had actually been built and delivered. This created many internal problems for Holt, since its factory war expansions were based on production at a much larger level of tractors being built.

The end of the war would hurt Holt in many ways. With no more war to fight, the government had no need for new tractors; nor did it need many of the tractors the military already had. The military gave many of these units to the Bureau of Public Roads. From there, they were shipped throughout the United States. What the government didn't give away, it sold for pennies on the dollar as Army surplus. Farmers had little incentive to buy a new Holt when they could purchase a government model, some practically brand new, for next to nothing. It did not take the farmers and contractors long to do the math. The more they saved, the more Holt lost out in potential sales.

Even though Best didn't have to contend with the factory conversion from military to commercial development that Holt did, it too was hurt by the flood of used tractors in the marketplace. During the early 1920s, the C. L. Best Tractor Co., its new name as of 1920, was very well suited for the farming market, while the Holt tractors, based on government requests, were a bit on the heavy side. But Best was not a large enough company to weather such a sales downturn in the industry. After so much early success, both companies now faced the possibility of failure. It was time, they realized, to rekindle an old relationship.

On April 15, 1925, a five-page document was filed by the law firm of Chickering & Gregory of San Francisco, with the office of Secretary of State of California, identified as document number 113767, the Articles of Incorporation of Caterpillar Tractor Company. This established the new company and its main purposes: "To manufacture, produce, buy, sell, import, export, or otherwise acquire, dispose of, or deal in tractors, harvesters, machinery, agricultural implements, and vehicles of every kind and character." In the coming months, after approval of both companies' shareholders, the Superior Court of the State of California ordered the voluntary dissolution of the two companies. The names of The Holt Manufacturing Company and The

C. L. Best Tractor Company were now history. In their place was a single, stronger, combined corporation: the new Caterpillar Tractor Company.

The company's first order of business was to eliminate any duplicate procedures between the two former manufacturing entities. The number of employees was reduced, as was the dealer network, since in most major markets, there was a Best and a Holt dealer. Now there would be a need for only one.

At first, the Caterpillar Tractor Company's product line consisted of both of the Best tractors, along with the three offerings from Holt. The Best 60 and 30 would now be referred to as the Caterpillar Sixty and Thirty. The Holt tractors were simply called the Caterpillar 2-Ton, 5-Ton, and 10-Ton, just as before. The colors chosen for the company's products were gray, with red trim. The old Best colors of black, gold, and red were now history.

The company started to take a much closer look at reducing its overall manufacturing costs. One of the first casualties of this process was the Cat 10-Ton tractor. Although reliable and well liked, it just was not in the same league as the Sixty. Since both tractors were essentially competing for the same customers, the 10-Ton got the ax. Its overly complicated undercarriage and the number of individual parts in the tractor made it a more expensive unit to produce. During the eight months it was in production as a Caterpillar product in 1925, approximately 454 units had been built. In all, some 6,938 Holt/Cat 10-Ton T-16 tractors were manufactured. Of this total, 2,803 were built as Artillery Tractors, including 700 units assembled by the Chandler Motor Car Company of Cleveland, Ohio, under license from Holt. The total number of tractors built does not include Serial Numbers 68192 through 68241, since these 50 machines were returned by the government Ordnance Dept. in 1921 and issued new identification numbers after being converted to commercial use.

The product line was further trimmed in 1926, when the word was given to halt production on the 5-Ton tractor. Even though the tractor sold reasonably well, its older mechanical design was not in keeping with the Thirty and Sixty models. The elimination of the 5-Ton line would open up needed manufacturing space for the Thirty tractor, which was now also being produced in Peoria. From mid-April 1925 through 1926, about 1,147 units of the 5-Ton were assembled carrying the Caterpillar Tractor Co. markings. Some 1,500 of the Peoria-built Holt New 5-Ton/Cat 5-ton tractors were built in all.

The largest tractor in the Caterpillar model line was the Sixty, the former Best 60. After the merger and a color change, this tractor continued to post impressive sales. Production of the Sixty continued in San Leandro through 1930. A second production line had been started in late 1925 at the Peoria plant, which continued building the Sixty through 1931 (though one tractor was listed as being built in 1932). The tractors built at the two different plant locations each used a specific serial number identification.

To compete with the Best 60 tractor in the western part of the United States, Holt built a special tractor model referred to as the Western 10-Ton (Model TS-21). Introduced in 1921, it was built exclusively at the Stockton plant, while regular production 10-Ton tractors were assembled in Peoria. Production on the Western ended in 1923. *ECO Collection*

The Sixty tractors built in San Leandro started production in 1919 with the number 101A. The units assembled in Peoria starting in 1925 were issued a beginning number of PA1. In all, some 18,932 Best 60/Cat Sixty tractors were eventually built.

The Caterpillar Thirty was also produced at the two different plant locations during its life in the product line. The tractors built in San Leandro from 1921 to 1930 carried a beginning serial number of S1001, while the models assembled in Peoria between 1926 and 1932 began with a number designation of PS1. All of the Thirty tractors were painted gray with red trim, except for the units produced

The Stockton-built Holt 5-Ton (T-29) was replaced by a Peoria-built model in late 1924, and was referred to as the Holt New 5-Ton "Caterpillar" Tractor, Model T-29. Its undercarriage was of a cast-steel design, not riveted. This model became the Caterpillar 5-Ton in 1925. Pictured is a Caterpillar 5-Ton (S.N. 44487) version from 1926, which is part of the Keith Clark Collection. *ECO*

The 2-Ton (Model T-35) was the smallest of the regular production "muley" tractors built by Holt. Introduced in 1921, early models utilized riveted track frames. In 1924, cast-steel assemblies became standard. This pristine Holt 2-Ton (S.N. S26267) model from the Keith Clark Collection is a 1923 Stockton-built version with the riveted undercarriage. *ECO*

The Holt 2-Ton (T-35) became the Caterpillar 2-Ton in 1925. Other than a casting change on the sides of the radiator housing, the tractor continued on as is. The Caterpillar 2-Ton, as well as all of the cast-steel track-frame Holt versions, were manufactured in Peoria. The 1928 vintage 2-Ton (S.N. 75575) belongs to Ron Miller of Michigan. *ECO*

after December 7, 1931. These were painted Caterpillar Hi-Way Yellow with black trim. Total production of the Thirty from both factories from 1921 to 1932 added up to approximately 23,739 tractors, by far the most popular crawler tractor for the company up until that time.

The little Caterpillar 2-Ton was the smallest tractor in the early Caterpillar line and the longest running of the Holt designs to remain in production. For the most part, this model was left virtually unchanged from late 1924. After the merger, a new casting for the radiator housing was made with the Holt name removed and replaced by 2 TON. This model proved to be very popular with orchard and vineyard farmers, which accounts for the rather large number of tractors sold in such a short time. Although this version of the 2-Ton was only produced from 1924 to 1928, some 8,989 units were built.

The 2-Ton was replaced in December 1928 by the Caterpillar Ten (PT) model line. First full year of production for the Ten is listed as 1929, since only four tractors were

indicated as being built in the closing days of 1928. The Cat Ten was powered by a four-cylinder, 3 3/8x4-inch bore and stroke, gas motor, rated at 15.15 drawbar-horsepower and 18.72 belt-horsepower. By the numbers, the Ten was a bit smaller and less powerful than the 2-Ton. The Ten weighed in at 4,420 pounds, while the old 2-Ton tipped the scales at about 5,300 pounds. But the Ten was an all-new design, in keeping with the Model Twenty that was released over a year earlier. A high-clearance model was also offered for row crop work. The Ten was well liked in the marketplace, especially by orchard farmers, where the tractor's size allowed it to maneuver effortlessly between the groves of trees. Its biggest complaint from the field was its reputation to vapor-lock on a hot day, because of the fuel tank being mounted on top of the engine. This allowed the gas in the tank to get too hot and to create vapor locks in the fuel line, which stopped the flow to the carburetor. It would take Caterpillar engineers a few years to get the message and move the tank away from the top of the engine in future designs. Even with these little quirks, about 4,929 were built by the time the tractor was replaced in 1932.

In the Caterpillar product line in the late 1920s and early 1930s were three separate model lines, which were referred to as Model Fifteen tractors. The first of the Caterpillar Fifteen (PV) tractors was introduced in 1929. The PV series Fifteen tractors were powered by a four-cylinder, Cat 3 3/4x5-inch bore and stroke, gas engine, rated at 22.77 drawbar-horsepower and 25.94 belt-horsepower. In all, some 7,559 tractors were produced by the time the model line ended in 1932.

In 1932 two more models of Caterpillar Fifteen tractors were introduced. These were the little, or small, Fifteen (7C) and the Fifteen High-Clearance (1D). These new Model Fifteens were not the replacement tractors for the discontinued PV Fifteen series. Rather, they were the new replacement designs for the PT series Ten model line. Both of these tractor models were powered by a four-cylinder, Cat 3 3/8x4-inch bore and stroke motor, rated at 18.03 drawbar-horsepower and 21.63 belt-horsepower. The improvements over the old Ten were quite substantial, especially the relocating of the fuel tank from on top of the engine to in front of the operator. No more vapor-lock problems. But by now, potential customers of the Fifteen had already moved on to more powerful tractor choices. This would help explain why only 307 units of the small 7C Fifteen were built. The 1D Fifteen High-Clearance was only good for 95 tractors. Caterpillar quickly realized the change in the marketplace and pulled the plug on both Fifteens in 1933.

The Caterpillar Twenty (L) model series was first introduced in late 1927. Its main historical significance is that it was the first tractor model designed by the company that did not rely on a previous Holt or Best creation. These first tractors were built in San Leandro. But starting in 1928, a second assembly line was started in Peoria for the Model Twenty (PL). Both the L and PL series of Twenty tractors were the same, although their point of origin was different. The engine found in both models was a four-cylinder, Cat 4x5 1/2-inch bore and stroke, gas motor, rated at 28.03 drawbar-horsepower and 31.16 belt-horsepower. This series of Model Twenty tractors would establish the design look for many future Caterpillar tractors. Production on the San Leandro–built L series would end

The Best 30 became the Caterpillar Thirty in 1925. The Caterpillar Thirty was built at two locations. The San Leandro plant had serial numbers beginning with "S," and the Peoria plant had "PS" preceding the serial number. This is a Peoria-built Caterpillar Thirty (PS6362), from the Keith Clark Collection, and it is a 1929 version equipped with a hood bonnet, which was optional and part of the Cold Weather Package. *ECO*

in late 1929, while the Peoria production run would continue until late 1931. In all, 1,970 units of the Twenty (L) were built in San Leandro, while Peoria produced 6,331 Twenty (PL) tractors.

The year 1932 saw the introduction of the Caterpillar "small" Twenty (8C) model line. This tractor had nothing to do with the previous Twenty L and PL series. It was instead the replacement for the Cat Fifteen (PV) model. Many of the design shortfalls found in the PV series Fifteen tractor were remedied in this new Twenty 8C series version. The sheet metal was also all new, as was the seating area. The tractor utilized the same bore and stroke motor found in the PV Fifteen, but with additional improvements that helped reliability considerably. Power was up a bit, with a listed rating of 23.69 drawbar-horsepower and 28.39 belt-horsepower. But the market only gave homes to 652 of the 8C series Twenty. In the first weeks of 1934, Caterpillar ended production of the little tractor.

In 1925 the popular Best 60 became the Caterpillar Sixty. And like the Thirty, the Sixty was manufactured at San Leandro (serial numbers ending with "A") and Peoria (numbers beginning with "PA"). The San Leandro–built Caterpillar Sixty (3324A) pictured is a 1926 model from the Keith Clark Collection. The canopy framework is painted red; though not original specification, it does not detract from the overall look of the restoration. *ECO*

After numerous attempts at marketing a smaller gas-powered tractor, Caterpillar finally hit a home run with its Model Twenty-Two in early 1934. The Twenty-Two (2F) was the successor to the Twenty (8C). The Twenty-Two utilized a four-cylinder, Cat 4x5-inch bore and stroke, gasoline motor, rated at 25.77 drawbar-horsepower and 31.54 belt-horsepower. The Twenty-Two was also offered

The Caterpillar Sixty is one of the company's most endearing gas tractor models from its past. It was popular in its day, and many units have survived the test of time to be restored to like-new condition. One of these Sixty tractors is this immaculate San Leandro–built, 1926 model, serial number 3331A, owned by Dave Smith of Oregon. *ECO*

in an optional High-Clearance configuration. This tractor was just about as bulletproof as small crawler units can be. Customers simply loved its simple but reliable design. Caterpillar was greatly rewarded in turn, with sales measuring in the thousands. In fact, some 9,999 tractors of the original 2F series were built between 1934 and 1937. An additional 5,157 units of the Twenty-Two (1J) model were built between 1937 and 1939. The 1J series was basically the same as the 2F versions. Most of the changes mainly revolved around improvements of the manufacturing process of the tractors.

The Caterpillar Twenty-Five (3C) was introduced in December 1931, as the replacement for the Model Twenty (PL). For the most part, the 3C series Twenty-Five was the same as the PL series Twenty. All of the major components and specifications remained virtually the same. The power ratings were a bit higher at 28.63 drawbar-horsepower and 35.18 belt-horsepower, but this has more to do with how the engine power ratings were being measured at the time. Production started on the Twenty-Five at the same time the company announced a change to the new Caterpillar Hi-Way Yellow (see next chapter) and a new logo design. But at the time, a number of unsold PL series Twenty tractors, painted gray, were still in the factory yard. Word has it from some retired Caterpillar executives that these tractors had all of their serial numbers and radiator sides changed to conform with the new Twenty-Five nomenclature. The old gray color was removed and repainted in the Hi-Way Yellow, with black trim. Yet these tractors retained the old style Caterpillar wavy or crawling logo on the front of the radiator top tank. Another fact that seems to back up this account is the manufacturing totals of the model line itself. While the Twenty-Five was in production from

The Caterpillar Fifteen (PV) and "small" Fifteen (7C) were totally different model lines. The PV series was introduced in 1929 in standard 40-inch and 50-inch wide-gauge track layouts. The 7C was actually the replacement model for the Ten (PT) tractor in 1932. Track gauge for the 7C series was the same as the Model Ten. Pictured from the Keith Clark Collection is a 1929 Fifteen (PV2491 WG) on the left, and a 1933 "small" Fifteen (7C271 WG) on the right. *ECO*

The Caterpillar "small" Fifteen High-Clearance (1D) tractor was introduced at the same time as the regular model in 1932. Available in only in a 44-inch track gauge, it was designed for orchard and nursery work. When it was discontinued in 1933, only 95 tractors had been built. This extremely rare 1932 vintage tractor, Serial Number 1D11, is part of the Keith Clark Collection. *ECO*

The Caterpillar Twenty (L and PL) and "small" Twenty (8C) shared a common model designation but were completely different machines. The Twenty series "L" (San Leandro) and "PL" (Peoria) were introduced in 1927 and 1928, respectively, and were available in standard 42-inch and 55-inch wide-gauge track layouts. Its engine was of an overhead valve design. The "small" Twenty (8C) replaced the old Fifteen (PV) in 1932. Track gauges were the same as the old series also. The engine in the C series was of a flathead design. Pictured from the Keith Clark Collection is a 1929 Twenty (PL2217 WG) on the left, and on the right is a 1933 "small" Twenty (8C617) orchard seat tractor. *ECO*

Introduced in 1934 as the replacement for the "small" Twenty (8C), the Caterpillar Twenty-Two (2F) was an extremely popular tractor. Standard 40-inch or 50-inch wide-gauge track layouts were offered, as was an optional high-clearance set-up. The tractor pictured is an upgraded Twenty-Two (1J1507) model from 1937, owned by Marv Fery of Oregon. *ECO*

December 1931 to 1933, only 638 tractors are listed as being sold. Of that total, between 251 and 268 units are listed as being built in the last three weeks of December, which also includes Christmas shutdown. This is just too great a number of tractors to be built in such a short time, considering the Twenty-Five's final production totals. Most of these units from December, one can surmise, were the Twentys converted from inventory.

The Caterpillar Twenty-Five evolved into the improved Twenty-Eight (4F) in 1933. The Twenty-Eight utilized a slightly larger four-cylinder, Cat 4 3/16x5 1/2-inch bore and stroke, gasoline engine. This gave the model an increase in power to 30.49 drawbar-horsepower and 37.47 belt-horsepower. The Twenty-Eight looked pretty much like the later models of the Twenty-Five. In the end, only 1,171 tractors had been built when production ended

The Caterpillar Twenty-Five (3C) was released in December 1931 as the replacement for the old model Twenty (PL), though it still shared most of its bits and pieces, including the track-gauges, with that tractor. The tractor shown is a very early model Twenty-Five (3C173) from 1931, and is part of the Keith Clark Collection. *ECO*

The Caterpillar Twenty-Eight (4F) replaced the model Twenty-Five in 1933. This tractor brought the evolution of the series "L" and "PL" Twenty and the 3C Twenty-Five to a close, when production ended in 1935. The perfectly preserved 1935 Twenty-Eight (4F786 SP WG) shown is also part of the Keith Clark Collection. *ECO*

in late 1935. The number of units of this model sold has less to do with how well the tractor performed, and more to do with the steady changeover by customers to diesel-powered machines. It's a shame really, since the Twenty-Eight was quite a well-designed tractor. The end of the Twenty-Eight also marked the end of the evolution of the L and PL series Twenty, and the Twenty-Five.

In 1935, Caterpillar introduced the model Thirty (6G) tractor. The Thirty designation had been absent from the Caterpillar line since 1932, when the old PS series Thirty was retired. The 6G series Thirty was a totally new design, with features that would show up in many Cat tractors, both gas and diesel. The 6G series was powered by a four-cylinder, Cat 4 1/4x5 1/2-inch bore and stroke, gasoline engine, rated at 35 drawbar-horsepower and 41 belt-horsepower. But this Thirty had the disadvantage of coming into a marketplace in which the diesel tractor was taking more and more sales away from traditional gas-powered units. The 6G series Thirty was in production until early 1938, when it was renamed the model R-4, detailed in a later chapter.

During the 1920s and 1930s, Caterpillar released quite a few models that differed only slightly in horsepower ratings. Many of these models were put into direct competition against another popular crawler tractor manufacturer at the time by the name of Cletrac (an acronym for Cleveland Tractor Company). Cletrac's earliest tractor designs were in fact based partly on the C. L. Best 8-16 Pony. As the years went by, the company gained a solid reputation as a builder of tough and very reliable crawler tractors. What really put the pressure on Caterpillar was Cletrac's pricing,

considerably lower than Caterpillar. And for some customers, the bottom line was all important. But Caterpillar was soon going to break away from the old way of thinking about crawler tractors as only gasoline-powered machines. Soon the company was to embark on an entirely new generation of tractor designs that would offer its customers greater production, with lower fuel bills than they had ever imagined. The era of the diesel-powered tractor was about to begin.

Released in 1935, the Caterpillar Thirty (6G) was a totally new design and not based in any way on the old PS series Thirty, which was retired in 1932. Available in standard 44-inch and wide-gauge 60-inch track widths, it was renamed the Caterpillar R-4 in early 1938. The tractor pictured belongs to the Joseph A. Heidrick, Sr., Foundation. *Randy Leffingwell*

3

DIESEL ENGINE ADVENT

A New Breed of Caterpillar

During the mid-1920s, Caterpillar research engineers started to take a more serious look at the benefits that could be gained from the diesel engine design, as compared to the industry-accepted gas engine. The diesel engine was nothing new. The extremely high compression, sparkless engine was conceived decades earlier by a German inventor named Rudolf Diesel. In 1893 he published a research paper on his design theory, for which he was granted a German patent. By 1895 he had the first prototype up and running. In October 1897, Diesel signed a contract with the well-known beer brewer Adolphus Busch, of St. Louis, Missouri, which gave Busch the right to build his engine design for the licensing fee of $1 million. This was an incredibly huge sum of money for this time, but one that the wealthy Busch didn't seem to mind paying. By 1898, Busch began producing the first diesel engine design in the United States.

But the diesel engine didn't grow tracks overnight. The early uses for the engine centered around marine and stationary engine applications. Although both Best and Holt had looked into the diesel's use as a future power source for tractors, it was not until the companies merged into the Caterpillar Tractor Company that the idea gained momentum. Caterpillar's research into diesel technology increased greatly after a tractor equipped with a Benz diesel beat a Caterpillar Sixty gas tractor in an overseas comparative equipment demonstration in 1927, plowing a cotton field in the Gezira Plains, in the Anglo-Egyptian Sudan. Caterpillar almost immediately purchased one of the Benz diesels and had it shipped to its research department for further inspection. The Benz design was a good one, but Cat felt that if it was going to develop a diesel that would perform reliably on a moving tractor, out in the elements, it would have to be of its own design.

During 1932, the Caterpillar Diesel Sixty started to be referred to as the Diesel Sixty-Five, to better reflect its true drawbar-horsepower output. The Diesel Sixty/Sixty-Five model was only offered in one standard track gauge of 72 inches, the same as the gasoline-powered Sixty tractors. The Diesel Sixty-Five (1C51) pictured is owned by Ted Halton of the Halton Co. and Dave Smith of Oregon. *ECO*

A young Caterpillar engineer by the name of Arthur Rosen is probably the man most responsible for the design of the first Cat diesel engine. Working out of the San Leandro plant, Rosen and his team built a prototype four-cylinder diesel testing unit. The information gained from this unit was then applied to building full-size production engines. Two test diesels were initially built and placed in Cat Sixty–type crawler chassis, with heavier reinforced frames and a special geared-down version of the transmission used in the gas version. By September 1931, the first of a new breed of Caterpillar tractors, the Diesel Sixty, was ready to be delivered to customers.

The first production Diesel Sixty tractor delivered was unit Serial Number 1C2, which was shipped from the San Leandro plant and delivered on September 14, 1931, to the W. C. Schuder farm in Woodland, California. The first Diesel Sixty built, 1C1, was held back by Caterpillar for further testing before being delivered to its first home, California Equities Co., Ltd., in Stockton, California, on November 7, 1931. Only the first two Diesel Sixty tractors were built at the older San Leandro plant, and both were painted in the original Caterpillar Gray color scheme. Starting with 1C3, all of the rest of the production run was built at the East Peoria, Illinois, facilities. All of these tractors were painted in the new Cat Hi-Way Yellow paint. This was officially made the standard color on December 7, 1931 (by order of J. D. Fletcher, Caterpillar Export Sales Manager, Circular Letter No. 53), though a Cat Silver Gray, trimmed in black option, was also offered at no extra cost to those customers who just couldn't accept a yellow Cat. Tractor 1C3, which was the first Diesel Sixty to come

off the assembly line in late October at the East Peoria plant was delivered on November 7, 1931, to Oahu Sugar Company, Waipahu, Oahu.

The main advantages of the diesel engine over a gas unit were its tremendous low-end torque curve and its superior fuel economy. The Cat D9900, four-cylinder, 6 1/8x9 1/4-inch bore and stroke engine in the Diesel Sixty was a real stump puller. Maximum power was available over a much wider working range than a gas unit, and the gas engine couldn't touch the diesel when it came to economy of operation. This point was well proven in 1932, when Diesel Sixty 1C12 set a new world's record for nonstop plowing.

Tractor 1C12 was delivered on February 29, 1932, to Mark V. Weatherford's Fairview Ranch, located in Arlington, Oregon. Between March 4 and April 27, 1932, the tractor plowed a total of 6,880 acres, with a total operating cost of only 7.78 cents an acre. Four impartial judges were there to oversee the testing. Three of the judges were professors of agricultural engineering from Oregon State College, Washington State College, and the University of Idaho. The fourth was a farmer and Caterpillar owner who assisted in the testing procedures. Fred Lewis, a Caterpillar field engineer for the Service Department, described 1C12 in action during the test in his March 10, 1932, service report: All plowing is done in high gear, except a few steep pitches in the field, on which it is necessary to shift to second gear. The engine seemed to handle the load with ease, and smoked only slightly when on a steep pitch.

The record-setting 1C12 diesel would eventually be sold in 1935, to Elwood and Harold Hartfield, also of

The first production Caterpillar Diesel Sixty tractor was this unit, Serial Number 1C1, pictured in the summer of 1931. The 1C1 and 1C2, were the only Diesel Sixty units built at the San Leandro plant in California. Note the old-style "crawly" Caterpillar logo on the front radiator tank. It is believed that only the first two production units had this casting. *Caterpillar*

Arlington. It was during this time that the tractor picked up the nickname of Tusko, named after an elephant at the Portland Zoo.

Caterpillar thought that with these early achievements of the Diesel Sixty in 1932, customers would be knocking the door down to get to them, but that was not the case. The Great Depression was taking its toll on the nation's farmers. They were not about to risk what little money they did have on some newly introduced, and in their minds still unproved, diesel-powered tractor creation. And there were problems with the early Cat diesels—though most of these were due to the inconsistent make-up of diesel fuels across the nation. Many farmers wrongly assumed that the early diesels could run on just about anything. Caterpillar recognized this problem early on and spearheaded the research into the formulation of more consistent diesel fuels.

Also of some concern was the lack of suitable lubricating oils that could stand up to diesel engine use. Caterpillar's shared research with some of the major oil producers led to

the development of the first detergent, multicompound oil, called Delo. But getting the proper distribution for the oil proved rather difficult. A solution was finally found when Caterpillar started supplying single-cylinder test engines to the oil suppliers, so they could fully develop and test lubricants that would eventually be marketed as suitable for use in Caterpillar diesels.

Even with these early problems, the Diesel Sixty stands as one of the most important tractor milestones in Caterpillar history. With no real sheet metal to speak of, the D9900 diesel was there for all the world to see. The engine layout and dimensions made for a very compact and clean design, especially when viewed from the right side. Mounted on the left side was a small Cat, two-cylinder, gas pony motor. This was used to start the big diesel. Once the main engine fired up, the pony engine was disengaged and shut off. As mentioned, the Diesel Sixty was more than just a gas Sixty with a diesel engine strapped on. Along with the beefed up frame, the radiator was modified.

The most famous Caterpillar Diesel tractor ever built is this Diesel Sixty (1C12), better known as "Old Tusko." Named after a cantankerous elephant at the Portland Zoo in Oregon, it set world records for nonstop plowing in March and April of 1932. Old Tusko is currently owned by Allen F. Anderson of Oregon. *ECO*

35

157 tractors were built; 1C1 through 1C14 were manufactured in 1931, and 1C15 through 1C157 were produced in 1932. Most of the early models in 1931 had SIXTY cast on the radiator sides, but a couple had the word DIESEL. This happened sporadically in the early part of 1932, before the DIESEL nomenclature became the only casting made.

The gas-engined Caterpillar tractors were not about to go quietly into the night. Caterpillar continued releasing new models, but in many model lines, the same tractor was offered in both a gas and a diesel version.

During the 1932 to 1937 period, however, Caterpillar was going through a metamorphosis. Its old, high-powered gas engines for crawler tractors were being shed, as the use of the diesel engine started to bloom. At the same time, new sheet-metal designs now covered tractors that for years left most of their engines out in the open. Fresh designs, with the new Hi-Way Yellow color, helped to kick-start a stagnant farming industry that had been racked by the Great Depression. Still, many of the models during this time period were produced in relatively low numbers, as farmers and contractors had little money to spend on new equipment. But as the decade progressed, money started to flow back into farmers' and contractors' pockets, and the tractors they most wanted were the ones built in East Peoria, Illinois.

In 1932, Caterpillar introduced the Thirty-Five (5C) tractor, which now occupied the spot in the product vacated by the former model Thirty (PS). The Thirty-Five was powered by a Cat 6000G, four-cylinder, 4 7/8x6 1/2-inch bore and stroke, gasoline engine, rated at 37 drawbar-horsepower and 41 belt-horsepower. This tractor's diesel counterpart was the Diesel Thirty-Five (6E). This unit was equipped with the Cat D6100, three-cylinder, 5 1/4x8-inch bore and stroke, diesel engine, which carried a power rating of 38.65 drawbar-horsepower and 46.08 belt-horsepower. The gas Thirty-Five was in production from 1932 to 1934, while the Diesel Thirty-Five was only built from 1933 to 1934. Both tractors were covered in newly designed sheet metal that hid all the important bits, as opposed to the old Thirty that left nothing to the imagination. Louvered engine bay side-curtains were standard on the gas model, while the diesel version went without. All in all, tractors in the Thirty-Five series were smart-looking machines. In total, 1,730 of the gas 5C versions were built, while the diesel 6E model took a slight sales advantage lead with 1,999 units.

Caterpillar replaced both versions of the Thirty-Five in 1934 with the model Forty (5G) and the Diesel Forty (3G). The Forty was powered by a Cat 6500G, four-cylinder, 5 1/8x6 1/2-inch bore and stroke, gasoline engine, capable of 42 drawbar-horsepower and 48 belt-horsepower. The Diesel Forty made do with a Cat D6100, three-cylinder, 5 1/4x8-inch bore and stroke, diesel engine, rated at 44 drawbar-horsepower and 49 belt-horsepower. Aesthetically, the Forty series pretty much looked like the Thirty-Five series, when the gas and diesel versions were compared side-by-side. Some manufacturing changes were made to the undercarriage, but these really didn't change the look of the tractors in any measurable way. Sales of the gas-powered 5G model totaled only 584, while the diesel 3G production run produced 1,971 machines.

The Caterpillar Fifty (5A) gas-engined model actually preceded the introduction of the Thirty-Five when it was introduced in 1931. The look of the Thirty-Five and Forty

Pictured working in April 1956 in Arlington, Oregon, is the Caterpillar Diesel Sixty 1C12, "Tusko." (The "Old" was added some years later.) Harold W. Hartfield, at the controls, became the second owner of 1C12 in 1935, and was the uncle of the present owner, Allen F. Anderson of Oregon. *Anderson Collection*

Also, a heavy equalizer spring replaced the previous equalizer bar. Tracks were 34-section links, with tandem-type recoil springs on the undercarriage. Power output for the early units was listed in September 1931 as 63 drawbar-horsepower and 75 belt-horsepower. By February 1932, these figures had risen to 68 drawbar-horsepower and 79 belt-horsepower. By the end of the production run in late 1932, power ratings were listed at 70.25 drawbar-horsepower and 83.86 belt-horsepower.

There has always been some controversy over the designation of the 1C diesel tractors. In the beginning they were referred to as the Diesel Sixty; in the middle of the run they were simply called the Caterpillar Diesel; at the end of the production run, they were known as the Diesel Sixty-Five. The problem is there is no discernible break in the serial numbers to indicate what happened where and when. In all,

From any angle, the Caterpillar Diesel Sixty-Five was a well-proportioned tractor. Its frame and undercarriage were based partially on the designs of the gas Sixty, but contained many upgrades and improvements to make it suitable for the massive amounts of torque the big D9900 diesel engine could produce. *ECO*

tractors was heavily based on the early sheet-metal designs of the Fifty. When the tractor was originally introduced, its nomenclature, FIFTY, was cast on the sides of the radiator housing. But by 1933, the name casting was removed from the sides and placed on the front of the top tank of the radiator. By late 1933, the fuel tank was relocated from in front of the operator to a position behind the seat. Also, the firewall and instrument panel were changed significantly. Even though these design modifications would eventually find their way onto larger Cat tractors, the smaller Thirty-Five and Forty models, including the diesels, would be passed over.

The gas Fifty was powered by a Cat 7500G, four-cylinder, 5 1/2x6 1/2-inch bore and stroke, gasoline engine, rated at 50 drawbar-horsepower and 55 belt-horsepower, though these figures increased to 52.65 and 60.13, respectively, by 1933. Its alternative fueled brother, the Diesel Fifty (1E), which wasn't released until 1933, was equipped with a Cat D7700, four-cylinder, 5 1/4x8-inch bore and stroke, diesel engine, which produced 56.03 drawbar-horsepower and 65.60 belt-horsepower. When the gas-powered Fifty ended production in 1937, approximately 1,808 units had been built. The Diesel Fifty ended its run in 1936. But even though the diesel version had one less year of production under its belt, it outpaced the gas version with 2,065 machines. This was clear evidence that the diesel engine was starting to take charge in all horsepower categories in the crawler tractor product lines.

In 1932, Caterpillar officially introduced the model Sixty-Five (2D) as the replacement unit for the gas Sixty, the tractor that had really put the company on the map. The Sixty-Five looked nothing like its predecessor. The sheet-metal design for this tractor was unique in the Caterpillar lineup. It may have been a bit too unique for its own good. With its high mounted and rounded hood, and tall-looking radiator, the Sixty-Five sort of resembled a mechanical

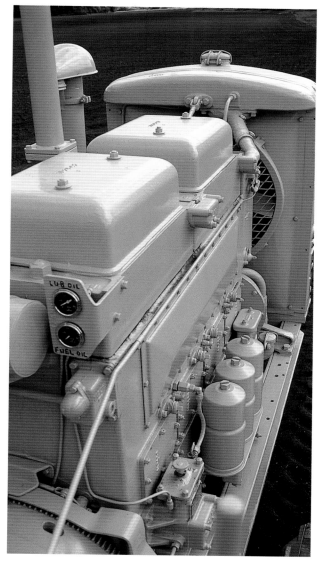

From the right side of the operator's seat, one easily sees the big and brawny D9900 diesel engine of the Caterpillar Diesel Sixty-Five. Compared to large gas engines, the D9900 was an extremely well-designed, clutter-free unit on the outside. But it's what's underneath that counts, and with the diesel's big fat torque curve, power was always readily at hand. *ECO*

The gasoline-powered Caterpillar Thirty-Five (5C) was introduced in 1932, and was available in a standard 53-inch track gauge and a 74-inch wide-gauge version. It was replaced by the Forty (5G), which was available in standard 56-inch and 74-inch wide-gauge track layouts in late 1934. Pictured from the Keith Clark Collection is a 1935 Forty (5G130 SP) on the left and a 1932 Thirty-Five (5C515) on the right. *ECO*

Introduced in 1933, the Caterpillar Diesel Thirty-Five (6E) was the counterpart to the gas-engined Caterpillar Thirty. It was originally released with a standard 53-inch track gauge, which was increased to 56 inches in 1934. The wide-gauge 74-inch version remained consistent through the model run. The rare orchard seat, 1933 Diesel Thirty-Five (6E820) pictured is part of the Keith Clark Collection. *ECO*

pachyderm. This metalwork housed a Cat 9000G, four-cylinder, 7x8 1/2-inch bore and stroke, gasoline engine, rated at 68 drawbar-horsepower and 79 belt-horsepower. The frame and undercarriage of the tractor were based largely on the Diesel Sixty/Sixty-Five design, and were not just a straight carry-over from the gas Sixty. The biggest modification was in shortening of the frame rails for the more compact gas engine installation. The gas Sixty-Five was a solid performer in its brief production life, which ended in mid-1933, with only 521 tractors seeing the light of day. The tractor's outside appearance was just too radical a design departure for its time. Customers basically thought the tractor looked ugly, and who wanted to own an ugly tractor? Today, the look of this model is not all that bad. A bit ungainly, yes, but surely one of the more interesting tractor sheet-metal designs in the company's history.

The Caterpillar Diesel Forty (3G) was introduced in late 1934 and was sold alongside the gasoline-powered Forty model. Track gauges were the same as the last versions of the Diesel Thirty-Five, the model the Diesel Forty replaced. The vintage 1934 Diesel Forty pictured, Serial Number 3G14, belongs to the Joseph A. Heidrick, Sr., Foundation. *ECO*

For Caterpillar, the Seventy (8D) and Diesel Seventy (3E) were the starting point for a very successful line of large tractors that would change the way these machines would be perceived in the future. Both of these models were introduced in early 1933, and for the most part used the same sheet-metal design, except for different patterns in the hood for air cleaner and exhaust openings. The real story was their engines. The gas Seventy utilized a big Cat 9500G, four-cylinder, 7x8 1/2-inch bore and stroke, gasoline engine, rated at 76 drawbar-horsepower and 87 belt-horsepower, figures that were soon increased to 77.07 and 89.43 respectively. The Diesel Seventy was equipped with essentially the same engine found in the original Diesel Sixty tractor, the four-cylinder D9900, but with a little more grunt dialed in, with 76 drawbar-horsepower and 87 belt-horsepower. On paper, both of these tractors looked like sure winners. But the tight money situation in the economy, and ever quickening engineering advances being made by Cat, would quickly take the luster off of the big tractors in the marketplace. In the end, only 266 gas Seventy tractors were built when production ended in 1937, which signaled the end of the big gasoline engine in large Caterpillar tractors. As for the Diesel Seventy, only 51 units of this model were built before its time came in 1933, after only a few months of production. The low production numbers hid the importance

Introduced in late 1931, the Caterpillar Fifty (5A) was first released with the "FIFTY" nomenclature cast on the sides of the radiator housing and had the fuel tank in front of the operator. By 1933 the designation was moved to the front of the radiator, and the fuel tank was moved to behind the operator's seat. *ECO Collection*

Compared to the original Caterpillar Fifty of 1931, which had the fuel tank in front of the operator, this 1934 model has the fuel tank relocated to the back of the seating area. This particular Fifty (5A1006) is part of the Keith Clark Collection. *ECO*

of Cat's move into big tractors. It was simply time for the tractor platform to evolve, because Caterpillar had a new, more powerful diesel engine design ready to replace its groundbreaking D9900.

Caterpillar started to get real serious about large diesel tractors in mid-1933, when it introduced the Diesel Seventy-Five (2E), the replacement for the Diesel Seventy. As large government works projects helped to get America back to work, contractors needed bigger iron to accomplish large-scale earthmoving projects. At the same time, R. G. LeTourneau, a builder of tractor equipment attachments and accessories, was introducing larger earthmoving devices, such as pull-scrapers, rooters, and bulldozing blades. The Diesel Seventy-Five was tailor-made to work with these large bulldozer blades and pull-scrapers, and quickly found its place in large production earthmoving and mining operations across the country. Under the hood of the tractor beat the heart of the new Cat D11000, six-cylinder, 5 1/4x8-inch bore and stroke, diesel engine. Power output from this engine was listed at 83.23 drawbar-horsepower and 98.01 belt-horsepower. The new model utilized basically the same undercarriage and track gauge as the Seventy series, though the frame was modified for the installation of the six-cylinder diesel. By the time the Diesel Seventy-Five's run was over in 1935, approximately 1,078 units had found their way into the marketplace.

The Caterpillar Diesel Fifty (1E) was first released in 1933 and was sold alongside the gas-powered Fifty version. Both tractor models were offered in standard 60-inch or 74-inch wide-gauge track widths. The 1934 Diesel Fifty (1E1159) pictured belongs to George E. Logue of Pennsylvania. *ECO*

The Caterpillar Sixty-Five (2D) bears the distinction as the only model in the company's history ever to wear this type of "rounded" sheet metal. Introduced in 1932, only 521 units were built before it was discontinued in mid-1933. The 1932 vintage gas Sixty-Five (2D453) pictured, equipped with full engine covers and a logging bumper, is part of the Keith Clark Collection. *ECO*

THE AUTO PATROL

In 1928, Caterpillar made a major step forward into the realm of road construction machinery when it purchased the Russell Grading Manufacturing Co. of Minneapolis, Minnesota. Long considered a leading company in the building of road maintenance equipment, its products complemented Caterpillar's tractors perfectly.

The Russell company was originally founded in 1903 by Richard Russell and C. K. Stockland in Stephen, Minnesota. Russell's first major product release was a horse-drawn elevating type of grader, with a gas engine-driven conveyer. In the beginning, the building of the new machine was farmed out to the makers of the conveyor system, but to help control the grader's cost, all manufacturing was brought in-house in 1906. After additional financing was secured, a new factory location was found in Minneapolis, which greatly increased the company's manufacturing capabilities.

The financial troubles and delays encountered in the development of the elevating grader were more than offset by Russell's other reputable product offerings. These included blade graders, drag and wheel scrapers, and

plows. The first of these implements, a small two-horse road maintenance grader, was introduced in 1908. After this came the first eight-horse Simplex Road Machine. This was followed by the Traction Special, a grader specifically built for use with a tractor. Both of these graders were also released in 1908, making it a very busy year for Russell. Other popular Russell blade graders would soon emerge, carrying such names as the Standard (1912), the Mogul (1913), the Super-Mogul (1922), the Reliance (1915), the Super-Reliance (1923), the Special (1912), and the Super-Special (1924). All were designed to be pulled by a tractor.

The next big step in fabricating road maintenance machines occurred in 1919, when the company built its first self-propelled grader, in prototype form. The little invention consisted of a single axle, two-wheeled Allis-Chalmers tractor in the front, with a grader unit attached in the rear. This concept was officially introduced in 1920 as the Russell Motor Hi-Way Patrol No. 1. Interest in the marketplace was high, but when Allis-Chalmers ran into a patent dispute involving that particular tractor model, it had to be withdrawn from the market. The Russell self-

This picturesque Caterpillar Sixty-Five (1D) is part of the Max Tyler Collection. This rare tractor, Serial Number 2D358, is a 1932 model, equipped with the optional heavy-duty crankcase guard and front pull hook. The undercarriage of the gas Sixty-Five was based largely on the Diesel Sixty/Sixty-Five model and *not* on the old gas Sixty unit. Track-gauge width was 72 inches. *ECO*

Introduced in early 1933, the gasoline-powered Caterpillar Seventy (8D) would set the design look for the company's big crawler tractors throughout the 1930s. This was the largest gas-powered tractor Caterpillar ever produced; it ended production in 1937, with only 266 units built. Pictured is a 1934 Seventy (8D158) belonging to Don Dougherty of California. *ECO*

The Caterpillar Diesel Seventy (3E) was introduced at the same time as its gas Seventy sibling in early 1933, but production only lasted to the fall of that year. The D9900 diesel engine in this model was always a bit on the finicky side, so Caterpillar decided to replace the tractor with the Diesel Seventy-Five, which had the new D11000 diesel motor. Only 51 Diesel Seventy tractors were ever produced. *ECO Collection*

propelled grader has to be put on hold, until another suitable tractor power source could be found.

In 1925, Russell released a new model of the self-propelled grader design called the Motor Patrol No. 2. Utilizing a Fordson tractor in the rear this time, the grader attachment was now in the front. Unfortunately, Fordson showed little interest in developing the project further with Russell, so the model was eventually dropped after only a couple of years of production. But the design of the grader with the tractor in the rear was sound. Other Russell designs in this configuration included the Motor Patrol No. 3 in late 1925, which was based on McCormick-Deering's Model 10-20. The Motor Patrol No. 4 from late 1926 was based on a Caterpillar 2-Ton crawler tractor. In 1927, Motor Patrol No. 5 was offered with a Cletrac K-20 crawler tractor, and in 1928, the Motor Patrol No. 6 was released, which was based on the Caterpillar Twenty.

The success of this type of motor grader, especially the Motor Patrol No. 4 with the Cat 2-Ton tractor, had convinced Caterpillar officials that the Russell grader product line needed to be under a new roof. After some early meetings between the two companies, a deal was formally reached in August 1928, in which Caterpillar would purchase the Russell Grader Manufacturing Co. as a whole unit. After the purchase, Caterpillar went to work in shaping the new product lines to fit its own offerings. The company quickly sold off product lines that did not have a direct bearing on the sale of Caterpillar track-type tractors, such as the gravel equipment and scraper designs. Any Motor Patrol model that did not utilize a Caterpillar tractor was likewise history. Product lines retained included self-propelled, tractor-pulled, and elevating graders.

The new Caterpillar self-propelled graders consisted of the Motor Patrol No. 10, with a Cat Ten tractor (1929); the No. 15, with the Cat Fifteen (1929); and the No. 20, with the Cat Twenty, which was formerly known as a Motor Patrol No. 6 (1928). The last of this type of design to be released by Caterpillar was the Motor Patrol model No. 28 (1933), which utilized a Cat Twenty-Eight tractor.

The older type of tractor-pulled road graders were retained for the time being, with models such as the Caterpillar Ten, Fifteen, Twenty, Twenty-Five, Fifty, and Sixty Leaning-Wheel Graders. Starting in 1930, the company started to bring the old Russell designs up to Caterpillar standards. These included the models No. 77 in 1930; the No. 66 in 1932; the No. 44 in 1930; the No. 33 in 1931; and the No. 22 in 1936. Small Cat graders during this time included the Trailer Patrol in 1929 and the No. 4 Hi-Way Patrol in 1932.

The large elevating graders also had fairly long lives in the grader product line. The Caterpillar Sixty Elevating Grader took the place of the old Russell 42-C in late 1929.

It was replaced by the Caterpillar No. 48 in early 1933. In 1935, Caterpillar offered a slightly smaller model in the No. 42. Both the No. 48 and No. 42 elevating graders stopped production in 1942.

But the real change to Caterpillar's graders occurred in 1931, when it introduced the new Auto Patrol—the industry's first, true rubber-tired, self-propelled, production motor grader. Unlike the earlier Motor Patrols, with which the grader was simply a front-end attachment to an existing crawler unit, the Auto Patrol had its own engine placed high and in the rear of the machine. This kept the engine in a cleaner work environment, improved operator visibility, and increased traction on the drive-axle. So solid was the design concept, it would form the basis for all motor graders yet to come in the industry.

At first, Caterpillar's new grader was simply referred to as an Auto Patrol. But by the end of 1931, it received the designation of the model No. 9 (8A). The No. 9 was powered by a modest Cat 4200G gasoline engine, rated at 36.2 brake-horsepower. In early 1932, a slightly lighter-weight

This rare, first-year 1933 Caterpillar No. 48 (4E17) Elevating Grader is fully operable and is owned by George E. Logue. Although originally equipped with a gasoline 5500G motor, it was upgraded at some time in its working life with a Cat D4400 diesel engine. This diesel motor was not made factory available in this grader model until late 1936. Production ended on the No. 48 in 1942. *ECO*

Unveiled in 1931, the Caterpillar Auto Patrol would establish the overall design layout for motor graders for years to come. Except for the use of articulated frames and tandem rear drive axles, today's modern machines do not look radically different from the very first Auto Patrol shown. *Caterpillar*

version of the motor grader was introduced called the No. 7. (6D). It was equipped with the same engine and power output as the No. 9. Production on these first two Auto Patrols ended in early 1933.

Caterpillar was quick to add new and improved Auto Patrols, starting in late 1932 with the No. 11 (7D). This was followed by the No. 10 (7E) in 1933. Both were gasoline-powered motor graders, with a single rear-drive axle. Starting in 1934, Caterpillar introduced the Diesel Auto Patrol (7F). This model, equipped with the Cat D6100 diesel, was the first Auto Patrol to be equipped with this type of power plant. The year 1934 also marks the first time that the company offered tandem-drive rear axles on all of its Auto Patrol models, which helped relieve the bouncing or loping ride that affected the single rear-axle graders. Starting in mid-1936, the Diesel Auto Patrol became the Diesel No. 11. Also added to the lineup was a Diesel No. 10 version with a D4400 diesel. Both models were available in single or tandem-drive configurations, just as in the gasoline-powered versions. An option for leaning front wheels was also made available in 1937.

In mid-1938, Caterpillar released its most popular and famous motor grader of all time–the incredible model No. 12 (9K). Key to the No. 12's success was its triple-box section main frame, which was far more rigid and stronger

than that of the old twin-beam designs found in previous Auto Patrols. But of greater importance was the ability of the front wheels to lean, which made turns shorter and counteracted side-draft caused by grading forces at the blade were made standard. The original model, which was referred to as a No. 12 Auto Patrol in its first year only, was powered by a Cat D4600 diesel engine, rated at 66 brake-horsepower. A gasoline-powered version was also offered as an alternative, but was dropped by 1942. Tandem rear-axle drive was the only choice. In 1947 the No. 12 received a new D318 diesel, which carried a power rating of 100 brake-horsepower.

The No. 11 and No. 10 Auto Patrols were finally replaced in mid-1939 by the No. 112 and No. 212 motor graders. Even though these models technically took the place of the older Auto Patrols, the last of the earlier machines was still produced as late as early 1940, to use up parts inventories. Both of the new models were basically smaller versions of the No. 12, with the No. 112 being the larger of the two. Both of these models were offered in diesel and gas engine forms, as well as single and tandem-axle rear-drive layouts. Production temporarily came to a stop on the No. 112 in 1942 and the No. 212 in 1943, due to wartime demands. Production resumed after the war for the No. 212 in 1946 and the No. 112 in 1947, though in diesel form only.

All three of Caterpillar's motor graders continued on through the 1940s and 1950s, with the No. 12 becoming the No. 12E in 1959 and the No. 112 evolving into the No. 112E, also in that year. But the odd man out was the No. 212, whose production life came to an end in 1957.

Released at the same time as the Diesel No. 10, the Caterpillar Diesel No. 11 Auto Patrol was the new designation given to the Diesel Auto Patrol, introduced in 1934. When production ended on this model line (1939 for the single drive and early 1940 for tandem drive), approximately 56 of the 5K series single drive and 1,261 of the 6K tandem drive diesels had been built. The Diesel No. 11 shown belongs to George E. Logue. *ECO*

4

PROGRESSION OF POWER

EARTHMOVER PRODUCTION SKYROCKETS

The 1930s marked the beginning of the end of gasoline-powered heavy equipment from Caterpillar. Some of the last gas tractor models to survive the 1930s and make it into the early 1940s were those in the R series. These tractors were often earmarked for government use, such as with various military branches or the forestry service. But many would also find homes in the private sector as well. Five models of R-series gas-engined models were built at various times between 1934 and 1944. These were the R-2, R-3, R-4, R-5, and R-6.

The Caterpillar R-2 (5E3501), which was introduced in late 1934, was the first of three different serial numbered model lines to be released. This R-2 was powered by a Cat four-cylinder, 4x5-inch bore and stroke, gas motor, rated at 28.2 drawbar-horsepower and 32.1 belt-horsepower. Production ended on this R-2 model in 1937, with 83 units manufactured in total.

Following the 5E series came the 4J and 6J variations of the R-2 tractor. Based largely on the D2 diesel tractor chassis, the engines were really the only things different between the two model lines. Both were powered by Cat 3400G, four-cylinder, 3 3/4x5-inch bore and stroke, gas engines, rated at 25.5 drawbar-horsepower and 31.5 belt-horsepower. Both of these R-2 tractors were built from 1938 to 1942. After this date, no more R-2 tractors were manufactured. Of the total count of these R-2 models produced, 1,185 were of the 4J series, while some 1,150 were of the 6J variety.

Between 1934 and 1935, Caterpillar offered an R-3 (5E2501) tractor that closely resembled its model Twenty-Eight. But the R-3, with its more powerful Cat 5500G, four-cylinder, 4 1/2x5 1/2-inch bore and stroke, gas motor, carried ratings of 36.64 drawbar-horsepower and 43.88 belt-horsepower.

Caterpillar's big earthmoving power brokers in the 1930s were the Diesel Seventy-Five and the RD-8. Compared next to each other, the 110 belt-horsepower–rated D13000 diesel of the RD-8 looks very similar to its predecessor, the 98 belt-horsepower D11000 of the Diesel Seventy-Five. Both of these tractors are part of the Max Tyler Collection. *ECO*

The Caterpillar R-2 tractor line was introduced in late 1934, and over its lifetime, would be released in three serial number runs. The first 5E3501 series R-2 was a 50-inch track gauge layout. In 1938 two new R-2 models were released based on the chassis of the D2. The 4J series utilized a 40-inch track gauge and the 6J series was a 50-inch gauge model. This authentic 1937 military issue R-2 (5E3561) belongs to Marv Fery of Oregon. *ECO*

Introduced in early 1938, the Caterpillar R-4 (6G) model line was actually a continuation of the Cat Thirty (6G) tractor from late 1935. Only the nomenclature was different. The gas-powered R-4 was available in a standard track gauge of 44 inches or a wide-gauge version of 60 inches. The 1939 vintage R-4 (6G955) shown with an R. G. LeTourneau C4 Angledozer belongs to Don Dougherty of California. *ECO*

Only 60 of the R-3 tractors were built, with most going to government agencies, especially the forestry service.

The Caterpillar R-4 (6G) was the last of the gas-engined tractors to be offered commercially by the company. Introduced in early 1938, the R-4 was actually the Cat Thirty (6G), only with different nomenclature. All mechanicals were virtually the same, including power output. When the R-4 model line came to an end in 1944, some 5,383 tractors of the 6G series had been built.

Introduced in 1934, the Caterpillar R-5 model lines shared many components with the Cat Thirty-Five and Forty. But the R-5 was not the same as either of these tractors. The R-5 was released in three production batches. The first series, starting with Serial Number 5E3001, was in production until 1936. In that same year, R-5 units, starting with Serial Number 4H501, started production. These lasted up to 1940, until the last group, the 3R machines,

started rolling off the line. In all, 500 of the 5E series, 1,000 of the 4H, and 49 of the 3R tractors were built. All of the 3R units were assembled in 1940. All three series shared the same Cat 7500G, four-cylinder, 5 1/2x6 1/2-inch bore and stroke, gas engine, rated at 53.37 drawbar-horsepower and 64.06 belt-horsepower (54.99 drawbar and 64.28 belt starting in 1937).

Of all the gas-engined Caterpillar tractors built or offered by the company, the R-6 is probably the rarest one of all. Introduced in 1941, the R-6 was basically a Model D6 chassis, equipped with a Cat 4600G, six-cylinder, 4 1/4x5 1/2-inch bore and stroke, gasoline-powered engine. Power output was listed at 55 drawbar-horsepower and 65 belt-horsepower. It was offered in a standard 60-inch track gauge or a 74-inch wide-gauge version. Surviving records on this particular model are scarce to say the least. It is thought that no more than

Produced between 1934 and 1935, with only 60 tractors being built, the gas-powered Caterpillar R-3 (5E2501) is considered an extremely rare machine. The R-3 was available in a 55-inch track gauge only. The immaculate early 1935 vintage R-3 (5E2532 SP) shown is part of the Max Tyler Collection. *ECO*

five tractors were ever assembled. To complicate matters, the R-6 was introduced in the same year as America went to war with Japan. Many of the manufacturing records at that time were removed from Peoria and stored in off-site locations for safekeeping, due to governmental manufacturing de-centralization requests. After the war, some of these records were shipped back to Peoria, while some were not. It would make things easier if the serial numbers on an R-6 could be compared to surviving manufacturing records, but this is all but impossible, since no examples of the model are known to exist today.

As the spark-ignition, gasoline-powered Cat engines started to enter their twilight years during the 1930s, other changes were also taking place that would have significant meaning for the company for years to come. The introduction of the diesel engine and the Auto Patrol were the first steps toward the reversal of the company's primary and secondary markets. Agriculture, so long Caterpillar's dominant market, would be eclipsed by construction earthmoving.

Major works programs initiated by the government to help get America out of its worst economic depression increased the demand for heavy construction equipment. Even though Caterpillar tractors used all sorts of auxiliary equipment from various allied equipment manufacturers, such as bulldozing blades and pull-scrapers, one supplier stood higher than all the rest. A man and a company by the name of R. G. LeTourneau would help complete the transformation of Caterpillar to the foremost builder and supplier of earthmoving construction and mining equipment in the world.

In the earthmoving industry, R. G. LeTourneau was considered one of the foremost experts at producing cost-effective dirt-moving equipment. His designs regularly proved cheaper to use than those of other manufacturers. Products such as his straight and angle dozing blades and power control units (PCU), Carryall pull-scrapers, rooters, and rock-buggies were used by all of the major track-type tractor builders, including Cletrac, Allis-Chalmers, and, of course, Caterpillar. But the relationship with Caterpillar tractors was the one that would really put the company on the map. The growing company, with headquarters in Stockton, California, had a good sales force but lacked a large dealer network. This changed in 1934, when an agreement was reached with Caterpillar Tractor for it to carry the full line of R. G. LeTourneau earth-moving equipment at all of its domestic dealerships. This did not include all of the foreign Cat dealer franchises, but many of them also opted for the LeTourneau machines. This agreement did not limit Caterpillar dealers from carrying other similarly built allied equipment. But the combination of Caterpillar and LeTourneau equipment was without a doubt one of the greatest alliances in earthmoving history.

To help in the delivery and production of equipment, LeTourneau enlarged its manufacturing capacity by establishing a large factory in Peoria, Illinois, in 1935. Located in the northeast section of town, it was just down the street

An improved Caterpillar D2 (4U, 40-inch gauge; 5U, 50-inch gauge) released in 1947 featured the Cat D311 diesel, replacing the previous model's D3400 unit. The D2 (5U15493) shown is a 1955 vintage wide-gauge model, equipped with factory direct electric start, owned by Dave Smith of Oregon. *ECO*

The very popular diesel-powered Caterpillar D2 tractor was introduced in early 1938, and was available in a 3J series with a standard 40-inch track gauge and a 5J series with a wide-gauge 50-inch layout. This is a 1939 vintage D2 (3J3433 SP), with fender-mounted fuel tank, belonging to Tom Novak of Ohio. *ECO*

The Caterpillar diesel-powered RD-4 (4G), officially released in 1936, was based heavily on the gas-engined R-4 model line, but with the diesel engine. Track gauge versions offered included a standard 44-inch and a 60-inch wide-gauge. This RD-4 (4G3726), fitted with an R. G. LeTourneau C4 Angledozer, is a 1937 model belonging to Wayne Swart of California. *ECO*

The original D5 (9M) series from 1939 is a very rare Caterpillar tractor model line. Built in that year only, just 46 were produced. The tractor was essentially a D6 unit fitted with a special D4 chassis with five track rollers. It was only available in a 60-inch track gauge width. This rare D5 (9M28) belongs to Paul Kirsch of Oregon. *ECO*

and across the Illinois River from East Peoria, the home of Caterpillar Tractor. This, of course, was no accident. By having both manufacturers so close, Caterpillar tractors could be shipped directly to LeTourneau for an extremely small fee, be equipped with bulldozing blades, PCUs, etc., and be on their way by truck, rail, or ship. This would prove of an immense importance during World War II, when the government required almost all of the equipment the two companies could produce for the war effort. It was a common sight around the world for service personnel, many of whom had worked for the two companies in peace-time, to be fighting and working side by side with Caterpillar tractors equipped with bulldozers and pull-scrapers built by R. G. LeTourneau. They were truly an unstoppable force. About the only thing that could derail them was themselves, and that's just what happened.

After months of speculation, LeTourneau officially announced in February 1944 that the alliance of the two earthmoving powerhouses was at an end. Then in May 1944, Caterpillar announced that it was going to start production of bulldozers, PCUs, pull-scrapers, and rooters of its

own design. One reason for the split was surely the introduction in 1938 of the Tournapull. The LeTourneau Tournapull was the industry's first true, self-propelled and self-loading, rubber-tired scraper. Even though the early Tournapulls were powered by a Cat diesel engine, its threat to the latter company's product line was clear. With every sale of a

The RD-4 tractor's nomenclature changed to the model D4 in late 1937. Shown is a restored 1945 military issue D4 (5T1886) tractor with a standard 44-inch gauge, equipped with an R. G. LeTourneau D Carryall scraper, which is owned by Ed Akin of California. *ECO*

The RD-6 tractor's big brother was the RD-7, introduced in 1935. The first 5E7501 series only saw 25 units built before being replaced by the 9G series later that first year. Two track gauges were offered, in widths of 60 and 74 inches. This 1936 vintage RD-7 (9G1972 SP) is part of the Max Tyler Collection. *ECO*

Caterpillar introduced its very popular diesel-powered RD-6 model series in 1935. The first 5E8501 series only saw five tractors built before being replaced by the 2H series in that same year. Tractors in this series were offered in 56-inch standard and 74-inch wide-gauge track widths. The 1935 vintage RD-6 (2H221W) pictured was restored by Dave Smith of Oregon and is now on permanent display at Caterpillar's East Peoria CV Building. *Randy Leffingwell*

The Caterpillar RD-7, with its torquey D8800 diesel engine, was a favorite high-production dozer for its day, especially when equipped with an R. G. LeTourneau A7TW Angledozer, such as this unit in 1939. *ECO Collection*

Tournapull, a possible Caterpillar crawler tractor sale was lost. As early as 1941, Caterpillar had introduced a rubber-tired, high-speed tractor in the form of the DW10, specially designed for scraper and bottom-dump use. It was clear the two companies were now starting to compete with each other, rather than aid each other. If it were not for the war effort at the time, the agreement between the two companies probably would have ended much sooner than it did.

During the time of the relationship with LeTourneau, Caterpillar diesel crawler tractor development was in high gear. As the older gasoline-powered models were retired, new diesel-engined ones were introduced to take their place in the product line. The first of the small diesel tractors was the D2. Introduced in 1938, the Cat D2 (3J/5J) continued in the tradition of the company's past farming tractors. It was marketed as a small, economical agricultural tractor, as well as a contractor's machine. The D2 was an extremely reliable and thrifty diesel tractor. The 3J and 5J series were powered by a Cat D3400, four-cylinder, 3 3/4x5-inch bore and stroke, diesel engine, rated at 25.5 drawbar-horsepower and 31.5 belt-horsepower. In 1947 the D2 (4U/5U) was upgraded with a D311, four-cylinder, 4x5-inch bore and stroke motor, with an increased power output of 32 drawbar-horsepower and 38 belt-horsepower. The front radiator housing design was also significantly changed from the previous model. The tough little diesel tractor would remain in the Caterpillar lineup all the way up to 1957, when the model line was retired.

Next closest in size to the D2 was the RD-4, which was introduced in 1936. The Caterpillar RD-4 (4G) was based heavily on the R-4 spark-ignition gas tractor, but without the engine. The RD-4 was powered by a Cat D4400, four-cylinder, 4 1/4x5 1/2-inch bore and stroke diesel, producing 35 drawbar-horsepower and 41 belt-horsepower.

In late 1937, the nomenclature for the RD-4 was changed simply to D4 to simplify matters. Everything else with the tractor remained virtually unchanged, except the radiator, which was revised slightly and the change from two carrier track rollers to one. Other model introductions of this D4 design were the 7J series from 1939 to 1943, the 2T series from 1943 to 1945, and the 5T series from 1945 to 1947. All were powered by the D4400 diesel. In 1947 a revised D4 (6U/7U) model was introduced equipped with the Cat D315, four-cylinder, 4 1/2x5 1/2-inch bore and stroke diesel, rated at 43 drawbar-horsepower and 48 belt-horsepower. Both of these variations on the D4 proved very popular in the marketplace, and with regular updates in horsepower, continued in the product line all the way up to 1959.

In 1939 the first Caterpillar D5 (9M) model series made its appearance, if only briefly. This D5 was a special run of only 46 units, all built in 1939. The 9M series D5 was powered by a Cat D4600, six-cylinder, 4 1/4x5 1/2-inch bore and stroke, diesel engine, rated at 45 drawbar-horsepower and 52 belt-horsepower. The tractor was basically a D6 unit fitted with a special five track roller D4 chassis. After this model, the D5 disappeared from the product line. Finally in 1967, the D5 was again made available as an entirely new model line.

The Caterpillar RD-6 was a standout, all-around performer in the product line. The RD-6 (5E8501), introduced in 1935, was basically a more powerful version of the Diesel Forty. Only the name was different. But just five units were built with this prefix number, before being replaced by the 2H

series RD-6 in that same year. The new RD-6 was powered by the Cat D6600, three-cylinder, 5 3/4x8-inch bore and stroke diesel (5 1/4-inch bore in the 5E series), rated at 45.38 drawbar-horsepower and 51.86 belt-horsepower. In late 1937, the nomenclature of the RD-6 changed to the D6. The appearance of the tractor was unaltered from the original RD-6 model line.

In 1941 an entirely new D6 (4R/5R) model line was introduced. This D6 was a very handsome-looking machine when viewed from any angle. The front end was

The Caterpillar D7 (3T) tractor was a perfect match to the No. 70 pull-scraper. The 3T series of this model was originally released in 1944, and was available only in a 74-inch track gauge. The 3T series was replaced by the 17A series D7C in 1955. This is a 1949 model D7 (3T9505), which is owned by Bob Russell of California. *ECO*

A D8 tractor starts to come together at the end of the assembly line at Caterpillar's East Peoria Plant during March 1942. This D8 is an 8R series with a 78-inch track gauge. Power output for this model was 113.14 drawbar-horsepower and 131 belt-horsepower. The 8R series was superseded by the 2U series in late 1945. *Caterpillar*

especially nice, with its rounded edges and tapered lines. This D6 model line was powered by the Cat D4600 diesel, the same engine as installed in the original D5 (9M), but with a higher power output of 55 drawbar-horsepower and 65 belt-horsepower. The 4R and 5R series of the D6 would continue on in production until 1947, when they were upgraded into the 8U series and the 9U series. Both of these models would stay in the product line until 1959. The big news with these tractors was their use of the Cat D318, six-cylinder, 4 1/2x5 1/2-inch bore and stroke, diesel engine, rated at 66 drawbar-horsepower and 76 belt-horsepower. Also, the front radiator and hood sheet-metal designs were altered from the previous rounded look to one that was a bit more conservative.

The Caterpillar RD-7 was everything the RD-6 was, but only in a larger and more powerful form. Introduced

in 1935, the first RD-7 (5E7501) model line was essentially a renamed Cat Diesel Fifty with more horsepower. Only 25 of these tractors were built. The RD-7 came into its own with the release of the 9G series in late 1935. The 9G series was powered by a Cat D8800, four-cylinder, 5 3/4x8-inch bore and stroke, diesel engine, rated at 61 drawbar-horsepower and 70 belt-horsepower. In late 1937, the R was dropped from the nomenclature, just as in previous model lines, and it was now simply referred to as the D7. The 9G series was produced until 1940, when it was replaced by the 7M series D7 in that same year. The 7M series introduced the nicely rounded front end and hood sheet metal that was also found on the D6 of this same vintage. The same D8800 diesel was under the hood, but now tuned for more power, with 75 drawbar-horsepower and 87 belt-horsepower on hand. By the end of the year, this had

The RD-8 was introduced in 1935 and was renamed the D8 in late 1937. This is a very early 1935 RD-8 (1H49), with a No. 48 Elevating Grader in tow. Both units are part of the George E. Logue Collection. *ECO*

When the Caterpillar D8 was teamed with an R. G. LeTourneau D8 Angledozer, as in this unit from April 1939, it was an unbeatable dozing machine for its day. *ECO Collection*

A 1941 D8 (1H8370 SP) owned and operated by Dick Railing of California is pictured in 1999. With literally decades of hard use under its belt, this D8, equipped with an R. G. LeTourneau K8 Bulldozer, can still put in a good day's work. *ECO*

In 1945, Caterpillar started releasing its own bulldozing blades, after the termination of the joint marketing agreement with R. G. LeTourneau in 1944. Pictured is a 1945 model D8 (8R7574 SP) equipped with a Cat No. 8S Bulldozer and No. 24 front Cable Control. The towed ripper is a LeTourneau unit. This D8 belongs to Ed Akin of California. *ECO*

increased to 80 and 90 horsepower respectively.

The 9G series of the D7 model was built until 1944, when the 3T series took its place in that same year. The 3T series was a more mechanically refined version of the previous model. On the outside, they were practically identical. The 3T series remained in production until 1955, when it was replaced by the much improved D7C (17A). The D7C was powered by the Cat D339, four-cylinder, 5 3/4x8-inch bore and stroke diesel, rated at 102 drawbar-horsepower and 128 flywheel-horsepower. The D7C was in production until late 1958, and was replaced by the D7D in early 1959.

During 1944 and 1945, two special series of D7 tractors were built by Caterpillar equipped for use by the Army Corps of Engineers. These were the 4T series, built from 1944 to 1945, and the 6T series, manufactured only in 1945. Basically the same as the standard D7 tractor at the time, they had special mechanical changes to help them cope with the shipping and working environments they were likely to see in overseas operations.

The largest of the RD series of releases by Caterpillar was the RD-8. Introduced in 1935, the RD-8 (5E8001) was pretty much just a Diesel Seventy-Five with a little more power. Only 35 of these tractors were built. The next model of the RD-8 (1H) had a lot more to talk about than just a name change. Under the hood of the big tractor was the Cat D13000, six-cylinder, 5 3/4x8-inch bore and stroke diesel, producing a healthy 95 drawbar-horsepower and 110 belt-horsepower. Even though the RD-8 and the Diesel Seventy-Five looked almost the same, the refinement of the D13000 Diesel made the tractor truly one of the all-time greats. By the time the 1H series came to an end in 1941, power had been increased to 113.14 drawbar-horsepower and 131 belt-horsepower. As with the RD series of tractors, the RD-8 became the D8 in late 1937 and continued on until late 1941, when its replacement, the 8R series, was introduced. The 8R series D8 was a more mechanically refined brute, but on the outside, looked pretty much like its predecessor. This model was replaced in late 1945 by the 2U series D8. More grunt was now available from the bulletproof D13000, with a power output of 130 drawbar-horsepower and 148 belt-horsepower indicated. Early 1950 saw the introduction of a new radiator grill front-end design that established the look of the D8 for years to come. The last model of D8 tractors to

follow in the 2U series design footsteps was the 13A series D8 from 1953 to 1955. This tractor would eventually see its power ratings surpass its predecessors with a listed output of 150 drawbar-horsepower and 185 flywheel-horsepower.

In 1955, Caterpillar offered two models of the D8 tractor. The 15A series D8D was equipped with torque converter drive, while the 14A series D8E utilized a direct drive system. Both models were now powered by the Cat D342, six-cylinder, 5 3/4x8-inch bore and stroke, diesel engine. Both tractors were rated at 155 drawbar-horsepower and 191 flywheel-horsepower. In 1956 the D8D unit became the D8G, and the D8E became the D8F, though the series prefix numbers remained unchanged. Production on both models ended in late 1958, when they were superseded by the D8H model line.

The D8 was a great tractor for Caterpillar. But an even larger model built by the company in the 1950s would be the stuff of legends. This tractor was the mighty D9. Of the early large track-type tractors designed by Caterpillar, the D9 is unique in that it was literally designed from the ground up and not based on a previous model. The D9 did not evolve from, nor was it a souped-up version of, the D8 tractor line.

As the D8 model line continued on in the 1950s, it was updated and improved with periodic horsepower increases. This 1954 vintage D8 (13A2485 SP) tractor has a big Cat No. 80 (2D) scraper in tow. This model of the D8, originally released in late 1953, was rated at 150 drawbar-horsepower and 185 flywheel-horsepower. Capacity of the scraper was 13.5 cubic yards struck and 17.5 heaped. Both units are owned by Ed Akin. *ECO*

The history of the development of the D9 dates back to September 1946, when the company first tested a large prototype tractor that featured many design elements not found in Caterpillar designs of the time. Most notable was the mounting of the radiators at the rear of the unit, which helped shorten the hood and front-end area surrounding the engine bay. But management decided this design concept was too radical to put into production. Also, the machine tool technology to mass build such a big unit economically was not yet available.

During the early 1950s, Caterpillar started to get serious again about a larger tractor. It had been component testing for quite a while in various D8 test units. In 1952 management approved construction of two prototype units that would form the basis for the D9 tractor program. Information gathered from the proving ground testing of these two units led Caterpillar to build 10 more tractors in 1954, incorporating extensive design changes. These units were known as the D9X tractors. All of these units were put into field testing use, both at the proving grounds and at selected working sites where contractors could put the machines through real world working conditions. One of the first complaints was that the tractors were not powerful enough for the weight of the units. The D9X tractors were initially powered by the new Cat D353, six-cylinder, 6 1/4x8-inch bore and stroke, diesel engine, with a power rating of around 200 flywheel-horsepower. To solve this power problem, engineers added turbochargers to the test units, which gave an instant boost in horsepower. After a few more mechanical changes, the D9X was certified as

This is one of the 10 D9X pilot dozers built for field evaluation in May 1954. At this point in the dozer's design phase, its Cat D353 diesel is not turbocharged. Full production would get under way on a turbocharged D9D model by mid-1955. *ECO Collection*

This is a 335-flywheel-horsepower Caterpillar D9E model series dozer working in May 1960. The E-series machines were introduced in mid-1959, and were in production until 1961, when they were replaced by the D9G. This tractor is equipped with a No. 9C cushion Bulldozer and the No. 184 Hydraulic Control, a first for the D9 model series. *Caterpillar*

In late 1940, Caterpillar unveiled its first two-axle tractor built for scraper and bottom-dump work, the DW10. When the first DW10 (1N) went into full production in 1941, it was routinely paired up with scraper models from LaPlant-Choate and LeTourneau, or a Cat-designed W10 Wagon bottom-dump. This is a 1946 vintage DW10 (6V), which is part of the George E. Logue Collection. *George E. Logue*

This very early Caterpillar No. 70 (8C) towed scraper unit was photographed in June 1946. Capacity rating for the No. 70 was 8.7 cubic yards struck and 11 heaped. This model, and the No. 60 and the No. 80, were the first of the company's scraper designs to be released, all in 1946. *ECO Collection*

ready for production. By mid-1955, the new tractor was officially released for sale as the D9D.

The Caterpillar D9D was a big tractor. It was the ideal machine for heavy dozing and ripping work, such as that found in mining operations. The D9D was released in two versions: the 18A series with direct drive and the 19A series with torque converter drive. Power ratings for the first series of tractors was 230 drawbar-horsepower and 286 flywheel-horsepower. In 1956 power ratings for the D9D were increased to 260 drawbar-horsepower and 320 flywheel-horsepower.

The next version to follow the D9D was the Model D9E in mid-1959. The D9E was available in three drive versions. The 34A series used the new powershift drive, the 49A had direct drive, and the 50A utilized torque converter drive. Power was also increased on the D9E, with 268 drawbar-horsepower and 335 flywheel-horsepower now available from the turbocharged D353 diesel. Other improvements mainly revolved around a bigger and stronger undercarriage with a new equalizer bar, better and longer lasting tracks, and the option of the Cat No. 184 Hydraulic Control for use with hydraulically operated bulldozersfla first for the D9 model line. The D9E was a more refined version of the original model, but even bigger changes were in store for Cat's big dozer in 1961, when the company officially introduced the incredibly popular G model series.

NEW PRODUCT LINES

After the termination of the sales agreement with R. G. LeTourneau in 1944, Caterpillar was free to design and build its own product lines of bulldozer blades and power control units, pull-scrapers and rippers. The company started to release its first bulldozing straight blades and cable power control units in 1945, with angling blades the following year. Hydraulic blade controls were introduced in early 1947. As for pull-rippers, these made the product line in 1947 as the Cat No. 18 and the No. 28. The first pull-scrapers made the lineup in 1946. All of these new products complemented the company's tractor line perfectly and would establish these machines as the premiere earthmoving equipment available in the world.

Caterpillar's introduction of its new scraper models really put the company in head-to-head combat with LeTourneau for scraper market share. The first of the cable-controlled pull-scrapers Caterpillar introduced were the No. 60, No. 70, and No. 80, all released in 1946. A smaller model No. 40 hydraulic-controlled unit made the scene in 1949. A larger model No. 90 was also eventually released in 1951.

The smallest of these pull-scrapers was the No. 40, a hydraulically operated unit meant for use behind a D4 tractor, equipped with the No. 44 Hydraulic Control option. Capacity of the scraper was 3.6 cubic yards struck and 4.5 heaped.

The next size up from the No. 40 was the No. 60, which was rated as a 6-cubic-yard-struck and 7.5 heaped unit. The No. 60 was designed for use with the model D6 tractor. The operations of the scraper were all by cable, controlled from the D6 when equipped with a power cable control unit.

Up next was the slightly larger No. 70 pull-scraper. This model was designed for use behind the D7 tractor, and like the No. 60, was cable controlled. Capacity for this unit was rated at 8.7 cubic yards struck and 11 heaped.

The Caterpillar No. 80 and No. 90 were the largest cable-operated scrapers in this model series. Both of these units were designed to be matched to the D8 tractor. The No. 80 had a rated payload capacity of 13.5 cubic yards struck and 17.5 heaped. The No. 90 was rated as a 21.2-cubic-yard scraper struck and 27 heaped. With 15-inch sideboard extensions, capacity was increased to 25.5 cubic yards struck and 31 heaped.

The original rear-end design of the No. 60, 70, and 80 scrapers was considerably altered in later years. The new design featured straddle-mounted, adjustable rear axles that kept the cutting edge level when tire diameters differed slightly. The updated No. 60 was released in 1952. Its capacity was now rated at 7 cubic yards struck and 9 heaped. The No. 70 was first seen in 1951 with a rating of 10 cubic yards struck and 12.5 heaped (12 and 15 cubic yards with sideboards). The No. 80 was the first to be updated when it was released in 1950. Its capacity had risen to 15 cubic yards struck and 19.5 heaped (18 and 22.5 cubic yards with sideboards). The No. 90 already had the new design when it was first released in 1951.

Starting in the mid-1950s, the company made numerous changes to the pull-scraper model lines, including new product designations. In 1955 the No. 80 was replaced by the No. 463. The following year the No. 70 became the

Caterpillar updated its DW10 model in 1947. Gone were the rounded sheet-metal designs, now replaced by more traditional looking fabrications. Power had been increased in the new model from 100 horsepower to 115. The DW10 (1V131) shown is a 1947 model equipped with an R. G. LeTourneau LP Carryall scraper. Both of these machines are also owned by Ed Akin of California. *ECO*

Introduced in the fall of 1950, the Caterpillar DW20 (21C) three-axle scraper, with its Cat D337 diesel, was a real "screamer" at full throttle out in the field. Shown at work in June 1954 is a DW20 with the No. 20 scraper unit. Capacity for this scraper was 15 cubic yards struck and 20 heaped. *ECO Collection*

A DW20 tractor equipped with an optional Athey PD20 side-dump trailer receives a bucket load from an excavator. Capacity for the PD20 was 30 tons. Other Athey trailers built for the DW20 also included the 40-ton capacity PH20 coal hauler. *Caterpillar*

No. 435, and the No. 90 was replaced by the No. 491. The No. 40 and the No. 60 were not changed.

Caterpillar started to establish a basis for a self-propelled scraper outfit in late 1940 with its DW10 (1N), rubber-tired, two-axle tractor, with full production beginning in 1941. The original DW10 was powered by a Cat D4600, six-cylinder diesel engine, rated at 90 gross horsepower, though this was increased to 98 horsepower within months of its release. The look of the tractor reflected the truck designs of the time, mainly in the rounded shapes of the front fenders with integrated headlight housings. Because of wartime supply needs, the production of the DW10 was suspended in 1943 and 1944 to make more assembly line space available for military production. The DW10 (6V) would again resurface in 1945. It had a bit more power at 100 horsepower, and the sheet-metal design of the rounded fenders was simplified, with the headlights now attached by a bracket assembly. Air brakes and rear fenders were also made standard items at this time. In mid-1947, an updated model was introduced with considerable changes. This DW10 (1V) was powered by the Cat D318, six-cylinder diesel, now rated at 115 horsepower. The front fender and radiator housing assemblies were simplified to lower manufacturing costs. This pretty much eliminated all of the rounded shapes of the earlier models. This design would carry over until approximately February 1954, when the model was removed from the product line and replaced with the larger DW15 tractor.

The DW10 was first marketed by the company pulling the LaPlant-Choate CW-10 Carrymor, or the LeTourneau Model LS Carryall scrapers, or the Athey PD10 side-dumping trailer and the Caterpillar-designed W10 Wagon bottom-dump hauler. The first scraper attachment designed and built by Caterpillar for its small tractor was the No. 10, introduced in 1947 for use behind the more powerful DW10 (1V) model series. The No. 10 scraper was rated at 8.7 cubic yards struck and 11 heaped. In late 1951, a slightly larger No. 15 unit was added with capacity ratings of 10 cubic yards struck and 13 heaped.

As mentioned, the model DW15 took the place of the DW10 tractor in early 1954. The DW15 rubber-tired tractor was powered by a Cat D326, six-cylinder diesel engine, carrying a power rating of 150 flywheel-horsepower. The DW15 looked much like the last series of the DW10, just a little larger overall. In 1955 a DW15C model was introduced with an improved D326F diesel, rated at 186 gross horsepower. This was increased to 200 gross horsepower and 172 flywheel-horsepower in the DW15E model in early 1957. Caterpillar made the last model of the series, the short-lived DW15F, in 1958. It was discontinued in 1959. Scrapers designed for use with the DW15 model line were the Caterpillar No. 15, and its replacement, the No. 428, along with the older model No. 10. The No. 15 was replaced by the No. 428 in late 1956.

For the big jobs, Caterpillar's top-of-the-line, rubber-tired, self-propelled scrapers for the 1950s were its immensely popular DW20 and DW21 model lines. These models were really Caterpillar's answer to LeTourneau's big Tournapull scrapers, especially the DW21. Both the DW20 and DW21 were designed at the same time and shared most of their major components,

The Caterpillar No. 668 Series C model line was basically a four-wheel-drive version of the DW20 tractor, built for general equipment sales and not marketed as a military item. The military four-wheel-drive DW20 (50C) was built from 1954 to 1955. The No. 668 was produced from 1956 to 1957. The unit shown is equipped with a No. 668S Bulldozer, No. 46 Hydraulic Control, and logging arch. *ECO Collection*

including the engine. The main difference was in the design of the tractors. The DW20 was based on a two-axle, four wheel layout. The DW21 utilized a tractor with a single axle and two wheels.

Caterpillar unveiled the DW20 and DW21 scrapers at the construction equipment Road Show, held in Chicago in August 1948. But it was not until about September 1950 that both models became available to the marketplace, with 1951 being the first full year of production. The DW20 (21C for scraper/6W for W20 Wagon use) was powered by a newly designed Cat D337, Rootes supercharged, six-cylinder diesel engine, rated at 275 gross horsepower and 225 flywheel-horsepower. Its main job was to pull the No. 20 scraper unit, which carried 15 cubic yards struck and 20 heaped, and the W20 Wagon bottom-dump trailer, rated at 14 cubic yards struck and 22 heaped. Later versions carried larger 20-cubic-yard struck and 30 heaped capacities, as the DW20 increased in horsepower.

Early on, annoying design gremlins kept popping up with the D337 diesel engine, which affected the overall reliability of the DW20. Caterpillar was quick to address these problems with the introduction of an upgraded turbocharged D337F diesel engine, with an increased power rating of 300 gross horsepower. The DW20E from 1955 was the first to get the new engine package. With this added power came a revised scraper unit in the form of the No. 456 in mid-1955. This unit was capable of carrying 18 cubic yards struck and 25 heaped. Other models of the tractor included the DW20F in 1958 with 320 gross horsepower

Released at the same time as the DW20, the Caterpillar DW21 was the company's first self-propelled, two-axle scraper design. The DW21C with the No. 470 scraper unit is ready for shipping from the Decatur Assembly Plant in 1957. This model was powered by the turbocharged D337F diesel, which was introduced in this model series in mid-1955. *ECO Collection*

and the DW20G with 345 gross horsepower in 1959. The scraper units used on the DW20G series was the No. 456B, rated at 19.5 cubic yards struck and 27 heaped, and the new No. 482B with 24 cubic yards struck and 34 heaped.

The history of the DW21 model line somewhat mirrored that of its sister machine, the DW20, and what was said of that unit can be said of this one as well. The DW21 (8W) was introduced at the same time as the DW20, and was powered by the same D337 diesel engine. The rear No. 21 scraper was almost identical to the No. 20 used in conjunction with the DW20, except that the design of the scraper's neck and the way it attached to the single-axle tractor were different. Capacities were in line with those of that unit as well. In mid-1955, the DW21 was upgraded into the DW21C model series, as was the scraper unit, now referred to as the No. 470. The DW21C was equipped with the turbocharged D337F diesel, rated at 300 gross horsepower. The No. 470 scraper was rated the same as the No. 456 unit used on the DW20. In 1958 the DW21D was released with 320 gross horsepower on tap. And in 1959, the most powerful version of the scraper to be built, the DW21G, was put to work, now attached to an enlarged No. 470B unit. Capacity of the No. 470B was the same as the DW20 model's No. 456B scraper unit. The DW21G had no counterpart to the much larger No. 482B scraper, the

The Trackson Company started supplying its first "Traxcavator" shovel attachments to Caterpillar in 1937. These 3/4-cubic-yard-capacity, cable elevator-type loaders were originally marketed for the Cat Thirty (6G) tractor. This is one of the first Thirty models equipped with the Trackson Shovel option, pictured in November 1937. *Marv Fery Collection*

Largest of all the early Trackson Traxcavator cable elevator-type loaders was its T7. The T7 loader attachment was designed for use with the Caterpillar D7 tractor. The T7 was rated as a 2 1/2-cubic-yard shovel. After Caterpillar bought Trackson in December 1951, the big Traxcavator was added to the product line as the Caterpillar T7 (34C), if only briefly. *ECO Collection*

model used with the DW20G. In early 1961, the DW21, as well as the DW20 model lines, finally came to an end, but not without establishing Caterpillar as one of the market leaders in the manufacturing of self-propelled scrapers.

Another special variation of the DW20 was the 50C series four-wheel-drive tractor built mainly as an aircraft tug for the U.S. military. The company made this DW20 model only in 1954 and 1955, manufacturing 170 units. The civilian variation on this model was the Caterpillar No. 668C wheel tractor built in 1956 to early 1957. The No. 668C was a four-wheel-drive tractor, powered by a turbocharged Cat D337F diesel, rated at 300 gross horsepower. The tractor was available with the No. 668S Bulldozer Blade, controlled either by the No. 46 Hydraulic Control, or with the No. 27 Cable Control. The unit was also offered in plain tractor form for pulling the No. 456 scraper, but because of severe front wheel shimmy at traveling speed, the scraper option was quickly dropped. The No. 668C suffered from a problematic four-wheel-drive system, which was the main reason the model was only available for such a short time. With very little play in the drive system, the tractor had a habit of throwing its driveshaft when dozing on hard ground. But units working in coal stockpiling did not suffer from this problem, since the soft material allowed the wheels to slip under load, which reduced the strain on the system. In the end, however, only 48 units of the No. 668C were ever built.

Other important model lines added to Caterpillar's product offerings in the 1950s were track loaders and pipelayers. Both of these product introductions started out life as accessory options built for Caterpillar tractors by the Trackson Company, located in Milwaukee, Wisconsin. Established in 1922, the company started supplying Caterpillar with pipelaying attachments for various tractors in 1936. In 1937 the company supplied its first Traxcavator vertical elevator front loader attachment to Caterpillar for use with the model Thirty (6G) crawler tractor. Other models would eventually follow. By the late 1940s, four models of Trackson tractor loader attachments were offered for Caterpillar equipment. These included the Traxcavator T2 for a Cat D2, the T4 for the D4, the T6 for the D6, and the largest, the T7, which went on the D7. In 1950 a new design called the HT4 was introduced. The HT4 was meant for use with the D4, but the design of the loader assembly was completely new. The vertical cable-lift loader design was replaced by a completely hydraulic cylinder controlled unit. The look was completely modern for its day and made the other model designs look archaic in comparison.

Caterpillar liked the Traxcavator tracked tractors so much that in December 1951 the company purchased the Trackson Company outright and made it a subsidiary. By late 1952, the Trackson name was eliminated altogether. All of the current loaders, as well as the pipelayers, became part of the official product line. Traxcavator models included the T2 (31C), the T4 (32C), the T6 (33C), the T7 (34C), the HT4 (35C), and the TracLoader L2 (36C) and the LW2 (37C wide-gauge). Pipelayer models included the PD4 (38C), the MD6 (39C), the MD7 (40C), the MD8 (41C), and the hydraulically counterweight controlled MDW8 (42C).

By the end of 1952, the T2, T4, T6, and T7 were history. But on a positive note, Caterpillar introduced an all-new model, the No. 6 (10A) Traxcavator Shovel. What

This 1948 vintage Trackson "Traxcavator" T2 shovel attachment is mounted on a Caterpillar D2 (5U1797). This 3/4-cubic-yard machine was completely restored in 1999, and is part of the Historical Construction Equipment Association. This model became a Caterpillar T2 (31C) in December 1951. *ECO*

Trackson's first hydraulic loader design was the HT4, introduced in 1950. The HT4 was a 1 1/4-cubic-yard-capacity loader, mounted on a Caterpillar D4 crawler tractor. This model became the Caterpillar HT4 (35C) in December 1951. It remained in production until mid-1955, when it was replaced by the Cat No. 955C. *ECO Collection*

The Caterpillar No. 6 Traxcavator Shovel was replaced by the newly designed No. 977D in late 1955. The No. 977D (20A) was the largest of the new 900 series track loaders, which also included the No. 933C (11A) and the No. 955C (12A). Capacity for the No. 977D was the same as the old No. 6 model. This Cat 977H (53A) model series, which was first released as a replacement for the E series, was photographed in 1960. *Caterpillar*

made the No. 6 so special was that it was the company's first fully integrated track loader, designed from day one with the loader assembly and tractor built as a single unit. It was considered the first such design in the industry. The No. 6 was powered by a Cat D318 diesel, rated at 66 drawbar-horsepower and 76 belt-horsepower. Capacity for the loader was 2 cubic yards. By late 1954, power and capacity had risen to 100 flywheel-horsepower and 2 1/4 cubic yards.

Keeping the No. 6 company in the revamped tractor-shovel line was the old HT4 and the not-long-for-this-world L2 and LW2, whose end came in late 1953. The HT4, which was based on the D4 tractor at the time, remained in front-line duty until 1955, when Caterpillar wiped the slate clean and introduced all-new Traxcavator track loaders.

In 1955, Caterpillar released its new 900-series Traxcavator loaders. The smallest, the No. 933C, was introduced in mid-1955, as was the next size up, the No. 955C. The No. 6 shovel's replacement was the No. 977D, which took center stage as the largest in the group in late 1955. All were new designs that built on the success of the No. 6 machine. All of these models continued into the 1960s in upgraded series with more horsepower and larger capacity buckets.

The pipelayers also went through some model changes, starting in 1955, with the introduction of the No. 583C. The No. 583C was based on the use of the D8 tractor and was intended as the replacement for the older MD8 and MDW8 designs. In 1957 the D7-based No. 572C was introduced. This model was a heavier duty pipelayer than the MD7, with greater lifting capacity. But for the time being, both D7 based pipelayers shared space in the model line. In late 1959, the No. 561B model was introduced as the D6 tractor-based replacement for the MD6. By 1961 the last of the old guard, the MD7, was finally replaced by the D7-based No. 571.

The Caterpillar No. 6 "Traxcavator" Shovel was the industry's first true hydraulic track loader with the shovel assembly designed as an integrated part of the tractor design. Released in late 1952, the original No. 6 (10A) was a 2-cubic-yard machine, powered by a Cat D318, rated at 76 belt-horsepower. By late 1954, these figures had increased to 2 1/4 cubic yards and 100 flywheel-horsepower. *Caterpillar*

5

ENGINEERING IRON MUSCLE

MACHINE CAPACITY TAKES A QUANTUM LEAP

The 1960s was a period of unprecedented growth in the design and production of larger and more powerful earthmoving equipment. Massive construction projects throughout the world, but especially in North America, fueled the need for the most productive machines available. The expanding superhighway systems stretching across the nation, as well as dams, aqueducts, and many other large-scale construction projects, demanded the most powerful and effective machinery. Mining for raw materials such as gold, copper, iron ores, and coal was also pushing the demand for equipment to levels never before seen in the industry. Orders for machines, not just from Caterpillar, but for almost all of the other heavy equipment manufacturers, were at all-time highs. During this period, Caterpillar expanded its existing product lines with larger and more powerful models, in addition to adding several new lines, which broadened the company's sales into new territories. Also during this time, the company put greater emphasis on research and development of new products to help keep pace with the needs of customers in the years to come.

THE 600-SERIES SCRAPERS

In the 1960s, Caterpillar reinvented its scraper product lines to keep pace with the more than 40,000 miles of new interstate highway projects that had been started in the late 1950s. The company embarked on a total redesign of its self-propelled scrapers starting in 1958, with the testing of three experimental prototypes—the DW16, DW25, and DW26. The two-axle DW16 was the smallest of the three. The DW25 was a much larger three-axle unit with a two-axle tractor. The DW26, like the DW16, was a two-axle scraper, with a single-axle tractor unit. Caterpillar engineers used these prototypes to test various experimental tractor/scraper designs, both in the field and at

Although its power was the same as the 657, the twin-engined Model 666 carried a much larger payload. The 666 was a three-axle scraper model intended for high-speed earthmoving work. This unit belongs to Osborne & Sons Construction of Gillette, Wyoming. *ECO*

the company proving grounds. None of these models would make it into production. Yet design elements from all three would form the basis of the new scraper models the company was about to start introducing.

To make a firm break with the past, the DW model nomenclature was replaced with the new 600-series product line designation. The first of the new line to be introduced in 1959 was the Caterpillar 619B two-axle scraper. The 619B single-axle tractor was mated to a cable-operated No. 442B scraper unit rated at 14 cubic yards struck and 18 heaped. The 619B was powered by a turbocharged, six-cylinder Cat

Equipped with a more powerful 250-fhp Cat D340 diesel and the availability of a powershift transmission, the Caterpillar 619C replaced the 619B model in 1960. Capacity of the scraper was 14 cubic yards struck and 18 heaped. *Caterpillar*

D337F diesel engine, rated at 225 gross horsepower. The 619B was the direct result of the DW16 prototype test program. Both units had similar dimensions and layouts. But the 619B was a little larger in capacity, with a completely new radiator housing for the tractor. The engine used in the DW16 was the one initially installed in the 619B. If there was a weak spot in the design of the new scraper, this was probably it. The economy of the original engine was not very good for a scraper of this size. The horsepower output was nothing to write home about either. Cat engineers put everything to right in 1960 with the upgraded 619C. The 619C was now powered by a much-improved Cat D340, four-cylinder, turbocharged diesel, rated at 280 gross horsepower and 250 flywheel-horsepower. A powershift model version was also offered, which was an instant success.

In 1960, Caterpillar introduced the next two models in the new series in the form of the 630A and 631A. The 630A was a three-axle design, with two axles for the tractor and one for the rear scraper unit. The 631A was a two-axle scraper design, with one for the tractor and one for the scraper unit. They were very similar in appearance to the test DW25 and DW26, but the mechanicals of the prototypes differed greatly from what finally went into production. Both the 630A and the 631A were powered by six-cylinder Cat D343 diesels, rated at 420 gross horsepower and 335 flywheel-horsepower. Capacity of the scrapers was the same, at 21 cubic yards struck and 28 heaped. Both units also share the distinction of being the last cable-operated, self-propelled scraper units to be introduced by the company. After this, all of the self-propelled units would be fully hydraulically controlled. In 1962 both models were upgraded to the 630B and the 631B. In 1963 a 631B Special Application (SA) model was introduced for extreme service use. By 1966 power had increased to 400 flywheel-horsepower for both versions of the 631B.

Caterpillar had confidence in the 600-series line. What began with a trickle of models in 1959 became a flood of new machines by 1962. The company had been a little slow in getting into some of the more sophisticated scraper designs that were being offered by other manufacturers, especially Euclid. But now Caterpillar was making up for it in a big way. No less than seven new models came charging into Cat dealers around the country. These machines were some of the largest, most powerful, and most advanced conventional scrapers to be built at that time. For two-axle scraper designs, Caterpillar introduced the models 641, 651, and the twin-engined 657. And it unveiled no fewer than four new three-axle machines, the models 632, 650, 660, and the largest of all the offerings, the 666.

The Caterpillar 641 scraper from 1962 was the next size up from the model 631B at the time. The 641 was powered by the eight-cylinder Cat D346 diesel, rated at 560 gross horsepower and 450 flywheel-horsepower. Capacity of the scraper unit was 28 cubic yards struck and 38 heaped. In 1963 a 641 Special Applications model was added to the line for use in severe loading conditions. For 1965 power was increased on both offerings to 500 flywheel-horsepower. In 1968 a revised 641 SA model was briefly fielded before being upgraded to a B series in late 1968. The 641B SA and the standard 641B had their power output raised to 550 flywheel-horsepower. Capacity of all models remained consistent with the original introduction machine.

In 1960 the Caterpillar 631A made its first appearance in the earthmoving industry. Rated as a 21-cubic-yard struck and 28 heaped scraper, it was a fairly large machine. Power for the 631A came from a 335-fhp Cat D343 diesel. The scraper bowl on this model was cable controlled. It became completely hydraulic with the 631B in 1962. *Caterpillar*

The larger 651 scraper utilized the same engine as that found in the 641, and carried the same power output ratings. The 651 could handle 32 cubic yards struck and 44 heaped in its large scraper bowl. As with the 641, the 651 got a boost in power in 1965 to 500 flywheel-horsepower. In 1968 the 651B was released with power increased to 550 flywheel-horsepower.

The top dog in the two-axle Caterpillar lineup was the twin-engined 657. The 657 was the company's first two-axle scraper model to utilize a front and rear engine, which provided drive to all wheels. This concept was introduced by Euclid in 1949. What made Euclid's scraper possible was the use of Allison Torqmatic transmissions, which let the front and rear units work together in synchronization. But Caterpillar did not have its own fully automatic transmission. That changed when it introduced its powershift transmission with the 600 series. Now a twin-powered scraper was possible. The 657 used the same diesel in the front tractor as was found in the 651. The rear scraper unit was powered by a six-cylinder Cat D343A diesel, rated at 420 gross horsepower and 335 flywheel-horsepower. Combined with the front engine, total power figures hit 980 gross horsepower and 785 flywheel-horsepower. Scraper capacity was the same as the 651 model. In 1965 power was increased to 860 flywheel-horsepower, 500 for the front engine and 360 for the rear. Then again in 1966, Cat engineers found still more ways to squeeze 400 flywheel-horsepower from the rear powerplant, bringing the output to a sizable 900 flywheel-horsepower. Special 657 units, introduced in 1968, came factory ready with all the necessary equipment for a push-pull setup, in which both scrapers could hook together for increased loading efficiency. In late 1968, the regular model was upgraded to the 657B series, with an increase in power output to 950 flywheel-horsepower. The following year, the push-pull 657B was released.

Customers who wanted the high-speed stability of a three-axle scraper needed look no further than the new 600 series offerings. The Caterpillar 632 utilized the same tractor found on the 630B. The engine was also the same diesel D343, rated at 420 gross horsepower and 335 flywheel-horsepower. The main difference between the two models was the size of the 632 model's scraper, which could hold 28 cubic yards struck and 38 heaped. In 1963 a 632 SA version was made available. Then in 1964, power for both variations was raised to 360 flywheel-horsepower. But the marketplace seemed to favor the larger three-axle scrapers built by the company. Also in its size class, the two-axle 641 model was the preferred type machine to have at the job site. This helps explain why the 632 only lasted in production until 1965.

Caterpillar's big three-axle scrapers were its 650, 660, and 666. All three of these models shared components in one way or another, especially the 660 and 666. The 650 was powered by the Cat D346 diesel, rated at 560 gross horsepower and 450 flywheel-horsepower. This was also the standard tractor engine in the 660 and 666. The 650 scraper was capable of handling 32 cubic yards struck and 44 heaped, the same as the two-axle 651 and 657 models.

The Caterpillar 660 and 666 were the largest capacity earthmoving scrapers ever factory-produced by the company. Both units were rated at 40 cubic yards struck and 54 heaped. The 660 depended on at least two D9 dozers to help push-load the unit to achieve full loads in a respectable time. The 666 could get by with just one D9 because it utilized two engines, front and rear, like the 657. The rear scraper's engine

was also the same unit found in the 657—the D343A, rated at 420 gross horsepower and 335 flywheel-horsepower. Total power output for the 666 was 980 gross horsepower and 785 flywheel-horsepower. In 1963 the tractors on the 650, 660, and 666 were all made the same series. Only the decals on the sides of the tractors were different. In 1964 power was increased to 500 flywheel-horsepower for all three units, and in 1965, the rear engine output in the 666 was raised to 360 flywheel-horsepower, making that unit capable of 860 flywheel-horsepower. The power on the rear engine jumped again in 1966 to 400 flywheel-horsepower, bringing the total output on the 666 to 900 flywheel-horsepower. Finally in 1969, all three scrapers became B models. The 650B, 660B, and 666B all were now rated with 550 flywheel-horsepower tractors. This raised the total output of the 666B to 950 flywheel-horsepower. This would be the last major change in the three-axle scraper lineup these models would see. The 650B officially came to an end in 1972, while the 666B soldiered on until 1978. The last of the big three-axle scrapers built was a model 660B. On February 7, 1979, the last 660B tractor rolled off Caterpillar's Decatur Plant's assembly line.

The Model 630B was the three-axle scraper counterpart to the two-axle 631B in Caterpillar's product line. Both models were introduced in 1962, and essentially used the same scraper designs. Only the "goosenecks" and hitches were different, and capacity for both scrapers was 21 cubic yards struck and 30 heaped. *ECO Collection*

The first twin-engined, two-axle scraper model to be introduced by Caterpillar was its Model 657 in 1962. The 657, pictured in August 1964, was basically a Model 651 with a rear drivetrain for the scraper unit. Both models were rated at 32 cubic yards struck and 44 heaped. The 651's power output was 450 fhp, while the 657, housing an extra engine, produced a total of 785 fhp. *Caterpillar*

The three-axle model 666 and the two-axle 657 were both released in 1962. Capacity for the 666 was rated at 40 cubic yards struck and 54 heaped. Power output was originally rated at 785 fhp but had risen to 900 fhp by 1966. The 666 earned the distinction as the largest "standard" production scraper ever offered by the company. *ECO*

For big coal stockpiling operations, Caterpillar produced a very limited special order model at its Decatur Plant, comprising of a 657 tractor and a 666 high-sided scraper unit. The first of these limited factory 657/666 Coal Scrapers was produced in June 1967. This 657B/666B, shown at the factory in April 1972, was one of the last factory units produced. With 950 fhp and a capacity of over 70 cubic yards heaped, the scraper was a real monster. This special unit was never advertised by the company for general sale. *ECO Collection*

After this, Caterpillar closed the book on three-axle scraper production of any kind.

After the landslide of scraper introductions made in 1962, Caterpillar would only add a few more new models in the 1960s. One of these was the model 621, which was introduced in mid-1965 as the replacement for the 619C scraper. The 621 scraper, however, had fully hydraulic controls, as opposed to the cable controls on the old 619C unit. The 621 was powered by an eight-cylinder Cat D336 diesel, rated at 300 flywheel-horsepower. Load capacity for the scraper bowl was just a bit more than the 619C, with ratings of 14 cubic yards struck and 20 heaped.

In 1968, Caterpillar released its very popular twin-engined 627 model line. This was the third model to utilize two drivetrains, just like the previously released 657 and 666 machines. The 627 was a completely new design and was not based on an upgrade from a prior model. Its engines were the six-cylinder Cat D333T diesels, front and rear. Total output was 450 flywheel-horsepower, or 225 flywheel-horsepower from each unit. Capacity rating for the 627 was 14 cubic yards struck and 20 heaped, the same as the model 621. In 1969 the 627 push-pull model was officially released. Much like a regular 627, it was factory equipped with the necessary front and rear equipment to allow both units to be hooked together for faster loading cycles.

To add further dimension to its scraper offerings, Caterpillar introduced the J619 elevating scraper in 1964. The J619 utilized a hydraulically powered, elevator type design for the scraper unit built by the Johnson Manufacturing Co. The self-loading ability of this unit did not require the help of push-dozers. It would load material in a paddle-wheel fashion. Capacity for the model was 20 cubic yards heaped. The tractor front of the J619 was the same as the regular 619C scraper. In mid-1965 the J619 was

replaced by the improved model J621. The J621 utilized the same tractor as the normal 621. Its Johnson elevating scraper was capable of handling 21.5 cubic yards heaped.

In 1966, Caterpillar made a big increase in the capacity of its self-loading elevating scrapers when it released the model 633. The 633 tractor was based on the standard 631B unit and was powered by a six-cylinder Cat D343 diesel, rated at 400 flywheel-horsepower. The scraper utilized a four-speed elevator that was driven by a single hydraulic motor mounted at the top of the elevator mechanism. Capacity for the 633 was 32 cubic yards heaped.

The midsize twin-engined Caterpillar 627 scraper was introduced in 1968 and has been in the product line ever since. With 450 fhp on hand, the 627 was capable of handling 14 cubic yards struck and 20 heaped. This 627, pictured in 1967, is one of the first preproduction units undergoing field testing. *ECO Collection*

The Caterpillar J621 elevating scraper replaced the former model J619 in mid-1965 and utilized the same tractor as that of the standard 621 scraper. The hydraulically driven elevator-type scraper was built by the Johnson Manufacturing Co. and was rated at 21.5 cubic yards heaped. The tractor was powered by a Cat D336 diesel, rated at 300 fhp. *Caterpillar*

The Model 944A Traxcavator was Caterpillar's first wheel loader design to be marketed by the company in 1959. It was originally offered with either a Cat Diesel or a Continental gasoline engine and capacity was about 2 cubic yards. The rigid frame 944 loader ended production in 1968. *Caterpillar*

The 633 was the ideal machine for short haul work. As the loading distances increased in length, the 633 would slow down under the additional weight and increased resistance. At this point, standard scrapers were the equipment of choice. Either way, Caterpillar had all the bases covered.

Following in the tire tracks of the largest Caterpillar elevating grader was the smallest model offered by the company, the 613, in 1969. The 613 was sized to operate in tight working conditions. Its size and weight also allowed it to be legally roadable, which would benefit the contractor with two or more job sites in close proximity. The little 613 was powered by an eight-cylinder Cat 3160 diesel, rated at 150 flywheel-horsepower. Capacity for its self-loading elevator scraper was 11 cubic yards heaped.

In 1960, Caterpillar introduced two more rigid frame wheel loaders identified as the 966A and 922A. The 966A was the largest of the early loader designs and was rated as a 2 3/4-cubic-yard machine. Only a Cat Diesel engine was offered in the 966A. In mid-1963, the loader was upgraded into the 966B with an articulated steering frame. *Caterpillar*

The 988 Traxcavator, released in early 1963, was the first wheel loader design offered by Caterpillar to feature an articulated frame. The 988 was a fairly large loader for its day and was powered by a Cat D343 diesel, rated at 300 fhp. Bucket capacity was rated at 5 cubic yards, and working weight was about 56,400 pounds. *ECO Collection*

NEW PRODUCT LINES

Caterpillar made big moves in expanding its heavy equipment product lines in the 1960s with the introduction of numerous new rubber-tired wheel loaders and dozers, and the release of the company's first rigid, rear-dump haul trucks. These new products would go a long way in making Caterpillar dealers true one-stop suppliers of heavy equipment to meet all of their customers' needs.

Caterpillar first entered the rubber-tired wheel loader market in 1959, when it released its 944A Traxcavator. Although the term Traxcavator was used for the crawler track-loaders, it also referred to the early rubber-tired loaders. The 944 prototype was unveiled by the company in early 1956. This prototype was powered by a 100 flywheel-horsepower D315 diesel engine. But this was not the engine of choice for the production unit released in 1959. That model was powered by a four-cylinder Cat D330 diesel, rated at 135 gross horsepower and 105 flywheel-horsepower. A six-cylinder Continental Model B427 gasoline-powered version was also available. Capacity of the loader was 2 cubic yards. The 944 utilized a rigid chassis and was steered by its rear wheels. At this time, articulated steering for Caterpillar loaders was still a few years down the road.

In 1960, Caterpillar added two more wheel loader models to complement the 944A. These were the 922A and the 966A. The 922A was powered by a Cat D320 diesel, rated at 80 flywheel-horsepower, with a Continental Model M330 gasoline-engined version as an alternative with the same power output. Bucket capacity was rated at 1 1/4 cubic yards. Its big brother, the 966A, was rated as a 2 3/4-cubic-yard machine.

The first production 992 wheel loader is pictured in 1968 at Caterpillar's Aurora Assembly Plant in Illinois. This loader would soon be shipped to the Duval Mines in Twin Buttes, Arizona, in October 1968. *ECO Collection*

The 992 loader was rated as a 10-cubic-yard-capacity machine, with a 30,000-pound load limit. Power was supplied by a 550 fhp Cat D348 diesel, and overall working weight of the early 992 was 120,500 pounds. *Caterpillar*

For customers wanting a large rubber-tired wheel dozer, Caterpillar had just the machine for them—the model 834. Introduced in 1963, the articulated frame steering wheel dozer was powered by a Cat D343 diesel, rated at 360 fhp. A smaller model 824 wheel dozer was released at the same time as the 834. *ECO Collection*

The 966A was powered by a six-cylinder Cat D333 diesel, rated at 140 flywheel-horsepower. A gasoline engine option was not made available for the larger loader.

As demand for Caterpillar wheel loaders increased, production was stepped up at its Aurora Assembly Plant in Illinois. In early 1963, the first 988 articulated steering Caterpillar wheel loader came off the assembly line. The 988 was powered by a six-cylinder Cat D343 diesel, rated at 375 gross horsepower and 300 flywheel-horsepower. Bucket capacity for the loader was 5 cubic yards. The 988 would get mechanical upgrades all throughout the 1960s to improve its performance and reliability. In 1968 the loader received a power increase to 325 flywheel-horsepower. Standard bucket capacity also was up marginally to 6 cubic yards.

Caterpillar introduced other small to midsize wheel loaders during the 1960s, including the 922B in 1962, the 950 in 1964, the 980 in 1966, the 930 in 1968, and the 920 in 1969. All of these loaders were of an articulated steering design except the 922B. The 922B and the 944 were the last rigid frame loaders built. They stayed in this configuration until both were discontinued in 1968.

Of all the company's wheel loaders that saw the light of day in this decade, the Caterpillar 992 was without a doubt the greatest of them all. Simply put, the 992 was the largest and most powerful wheel loader the company would produce in the 1960s. The loader was first seen in prototype form in late 1965. At this point in the design, the 992X1, as it was known, was powered by an eight-cylinder Cat D346 diesel, rated at 500 flywheel-horsepower. Capacity of the first pilot machine was 8 1/2 cubic yards. In January 1966, the 992X1 was shipped to Clarkson Construction Co. in St. Louis, Missouri, to start its field testing trials. After months of design evaluations, a second prototype, 992X2, was built in December 1966. This unit was now powered by a more robust Cat D348 V-12 diesel engine, rated at 550 flywheel-horsepower. This would be the engine of choice when the loader was finally released for sale in 1968. The 992 was rated as a 10-cubic-yard machine, with a bucket payload capacity of 30,000 pounds. The first production 992 loader went into service at the Duval Mines in Twin Buttes, located south of Tucson, Arizona, around October 1968.

A close cousin to the wheel loaders were the articulated rubber-tired wheel dozers that Caterpillar introduced in 1963. The model 834 was the largest, followed by the model 824. Both wheel dozers were powered by Cat D343 diesels. The 834 was rated at 420 gross horsepower and 360 flywheel-horsepower, while the 824 had a bit less to play with at 280 gross horsepower and 250 flywheel-horsepower.

Both models received periodic power increases throughout the decade. The 834 was increased to 400 flywheel-horsepower in 1966. The small dozer became the 824B in 1965, with power bumped up to 275 flywheel-horsepower, which was followed by another increase in 1969 to 300 flywheel-horsepower. Both the 834 and 824 model lines were available as tamping foot compactors, when equipped with heavy-duty sheepsfoot or tamping foot steel wheels. These compactors became separate model lines starting in 1969, first with the 825B, followed by the 835 in 1970.

Athey Products Corp. of Chicago built a large assortment of rear- and bottom-dump trailers for Caterpillar's one- and two-axle tractors that were commonly used in scraper applications. A DW21 Series C, equipped with an Athey PRB21 rear-dump bauxite trailer, is pictured. It is heated by the tractor's exhaust to break the seal of sticky ore during dumping. *Caterpillar*

Pictured in July 1959 is the first pilot rear-dump hauler that would eventually become the model 769. Features of the prototype included large single rear tires, air-oil strut suspension system, and a 28-ton capacity. *Larry Clancy Collection*

Fitted with front-end body sections made out of hand-laid fiberglass, the 769X3 started testing in January 1962. Only one prototype was built with this type of radiator shroud. The particular 769X3 is pictured here in October 1962. *Caterpillar*

Another product line first for Caterpillar in the 1960s was the introduction of the company's first true off-highway truck, the model 769. A type of hauler trailer, often referred to as a rocker, had been offered by Caterpillar for use behind many of its one- and two-axle scraper tractors. These trailers were built and supplied by the Athey Products Corp. of Chicago. The tractor/trailer combinations worked well enough, but they were no substitute for a true self-contained, rear-dump truck.

The 769 truck program actually got under way in May 1956. At this point, an initial study was made of all haul trucks currently on the market. After the study was completed, the company decided to build a concept hauler based on a 28-ton load capacity. The pilot 769X1 was built in July 1959, with large single rear tires. Not long after this prototype was completed, a 769X2 version was built without a rear suspension, in the hope that the tires would provide sufficient spring-rate for an adequate ride. Although this would have saved money, it didn't work. The next effort was the 769X3 in January 1962. This model was getting close to the final design. Capacity for this version had also been increased to 35 tons to keep pace with haulers being put on the market by the competition in that size class. November 1962 would see 769X4, which is the design that finally went into production. Full production finally got

The Caterpillar 769X4 prototype, captured in a moment of rest in November 1962, was the design that went into full production starting in January 1963. The 769 was powered by a 375-fhp Cat D343 diesel and had a payload capacity of 35 tons. *Caterpillar*

under way at the Decatur Assembly Plant in January 1963. The production 769 was powered by a six-cylinder Cat D343 diesel engine, rated at 420 gross horsepower and 375 flywheel-horsepower. Important design features of the truck included independent, pneumatic-oil suspension system, and oil-cooled disc brakes on the rear drive wheels.

The 769 went through some irritating growing pains during its first few months of production. Reliability concerns and a few design shortcomings quickly surfaced on the first trucks in the field. But this was not entirely unexpected by Cat engineers. The 769 was the company's first

haul truck, designed from the ground up and not based on an existing model platform. In comparison, the major off-highway truck competitors to Caterpillar's hauler had literally decades of production experience in their designs to draw from. But Caterpillar was in it for the long haul. The company stood behind each and every 769 truck sold, until each problem was remedied to the customer's satisfaction. Upgrades were made to the 769 as the model platform started to mature. In 1964 power was increased to 400 flywheel-horsepower. Then in late 1966, the hauler was upgraded into an improved 769B model series. Most

The limited production, 85-ton capacity, diesel-electric-drive 779 and the 35-ton, mechanical drivetrain based 769B are shown here in February 1968. The inner rear tires on the 779 were not installed until the hauler was transported to its final destination. *ECO Collection*

With working conditions like these, only a track-type tractor will do. Although the work isn't glamorous, this direct-drive Caterpillar D7E, pictured in 1962, makes it look easy. With its 160-fhp Cat D339 diesel, it was the perfect large construction dozing machine. *Caterpillar*

What's better than a Caterpillar D8H? Well, two, of course. These D8H dozers, shown working in January 1964, are both powershift models and are driven by turbocharged 235-fhp Cat D342 diesels. The engine's power output increased to 270 fhp in 1965. *Caterpillar*

notable was the redesign of the dump box to a V-bottom design, which helped eliminate rear-end spillage on haul roads and allowed the use of larger tires. Power output was also increased marginally to 415 flywheel-horsepower. A further redesigned dual-slope dump body was fitted in 1970.

Around 1961, Caterpillar engineers started to set their sights on a much larger haul truck intended for use in hard rock mining applications, since the smaller 769 was basically designed for use in large construction and quarry operations. To help put the project into high gear, the company hired Ralph H. Kress, the former manager of truck development for LeTourneau-Westinghouse and designer of the first trend-setting Haulpak truck in 1962. Kress was made manager of truck development for the Research and Engineering Department of Caterpillar Tractor. After numerous market studies, management decided to make the hauler a diesel-electric-drive truck with a targeted 75-ton capacity.

For the really big jobs, there just wasn't any substitute for the power of a Caterpillar D9G. Introduced in 1961, its toughness and superior reliability made it world famous. A 385-fhp turbocharged Cat D353 diesel provided the muscle. Only the powershift transmission was offered for such a powerful dozer. *Caterpillar*

The D9G made an excellent tractor for pull-scraper work, as shown by this unit with a No. 463F in tow. Released in 1960, the No. 463F carried a rated capacity of 21 cubic yards struck and 28 heaped. *ECO*

This hauler became the model 779. The 779 was designed and built alongside two other experimental prototype hauler concepts, models 783 and 786, that also utilized the electric-drive system found in the 75-ton truck. The 779 was powered by a twin-turbocharged and aftercooled Cat D348 V-12 diesel engine, rated at 1,000 gross horsepower and 960 flywheel-horsepower. Cat designed and built the electric-drive system, employing an engine-driven traction generator, which supplied direct current to two traction motors mounted in the rear axle, one for each drive wheel. The suspension used a larger and more advanced pneumatic-oil cylinder system than that found on the 769. And like that truck, the 779 utilized Cat-designed oil-cooled disc brakes, both front and rear.

By mid-1965, the first rear-dump pilot 779 was ready to start prototype testing. It was delivered to the Cleveland Cliffs Iron Company's Republic Mine, near Marquette, Michigan, for a battery of grueling haul tests. By October 1966, management gave the 779 the go-ahead for full production at the Decatur Assembly Plant. But early problems with the model kept delaying production. The 779 frame was displaying numerous stress fractures in the field. The truck's frame was fabricated from high strength steel, which is very strong and lightweight. But repairs to this kind of steel are extremely difficult. Welding of the frames was all but impossible at mining sites, especially in remote locations during cold conditions, without changing the metallurgy of the steel itself. On the other hand, the 769 utilized mild steel, which was a bit heavier, but was much easier to weld at job locations. After a redesign of the frame, the 779 was officially released for sale in July 1967. At this point, the truck was still rated as a 75-ton-capacity hauler, but in 1968, after further upgrades including a redesigned dump box, payload rating was increased to 85 tons.

The only pipelayer model to be based on the early D9 tractor series was the 594. Introduced in 1965, the model 594 was based on the D9G and was capable of lifting 200,000 pounds on its 28-foot side-boom. Counterweight controls were all fully hydraulic. The 594 became the model 594H in 1974. Production ended on this model line in 1982. *Caterpillar*

The Caterpillar 983 track loader was the largest front-engined Traxcavator model ever produced by the company. Officially launched in 1969, the model 983 was powered by a 275-fhp Cat D343 diesel and had a bucket capacity of 4.5 cubic yards. In late 1978, the tracked loader was replaced by the 983B. *Caterpillar*

But the problems with the hauler kept on coming. The frame, the electric drive, and the suspension system were key sore points. To show how much more steel reinforcement the truck had required since its introduction, you need just look at the weight. In 1965 the 779 weighed in empty at 96,600 pounds. By 1968 it had gained over 10 tons, reaching 118,900 pounds! Finally, Caterpillar officials had had enough, and to cut any further losses, they canceled the 779, along with all of the other electric-drive trucks. The last 779 came off the assembly line in May 1969. In all 41 production 779 haulers were built, though this total does not include pilot trucks. To eliminate any warranty or liability problems with the trucks, all of the 779 haulers in the field were reacquired by Caterpillar starting in late 1969 and throughout 1970. All were then dismantled so that none survive today. Even though the model disappeared, Cat engineering gained

a tremendous amount of information concerning the building of mining trucks from the diesel-electric program. Having freed its engineers from the 779 program, Caterpillar turned its resources to the company's next hauler project, the 50-ton-capacity model 773, which came out in 1970.

THE ESTABLISHED LINES

The 1960s saw Caterpillar releasing numerous new models in its established track-type tractor, Traxcavator, and motor grader lines. These models, along with the new product lines, firmly established the company as the Number One producer of heavy earth-moving equipment in the world.

For the track-type tractors, the company introduced upgraded models over the entire line, from the smallest to the largest. All would become more powerful and productive. Starting with the small end of the product line, Caterpillar

introduced the D4C in late 1959. In 1963 this model was replaced by the D4D. In 1959 an improved D6B model was released. This model was actually replaced by the reintroduction of the D5 model line in 1967. While the D6B was in production, Caterpillar also marketed the D6C model in 1963. The D6C model line remained in production until 1976.

The larger D7 model line became the D7D in early 1959. The D7D was equipped with the turbocharged Cat D339 diesel engine, which produced 140 flywheel-horsepower. The D7D was the first of the D7 model series to utilize a turbocharger for increased power output. But the life of the D7D tractor would be short. In 1961 it was replaced by the model D7E. The D7E utilized the same engine as the previous D series, but now had 160 flywheel-horsepower to play with. In late 1965, this figure increased again to 180 flywheel-horsepower. By late 1969, the model D7F was introduced with the D333 diesel. Power remained consistent at 180 flywheel-horsepower.

The Caterpillar D8H was released in late 1958 and was available in three model series—the 36A series with direct drive in 1958, the 35A series with torque converter drive in 1959, and the 46A series with powershift drive, also in 1959. The big D8H was powered by a Cat D342 diesel, rated at 235 fhp. In late 1965, the tractor received a boost in power to 270 fhp. The D8H was a real performer, so much so that it would continue in the product line until 1974, when it was finally replaced by the 300 fhp model D8K.

At the top end of the track-type tractor line was the mighty D9G, which was introduced in 1961. The D9G model series is considered one of the greatest crawler tractors ever built. With its power, weight, and reliability, its overall productivity was second to none in the 1960s. There might have been a couple of tractors that produced more horsepower than the D9G, namely the Euclid TC-12/Terex 82-80 and the Allis-Chalmers HD-41, but their overall job availability and reliability fell far short of the big Cats. The D9G was powered by the Cat D353, which pumped out 385 fhp. The D9G also featured a larger and heavier duty undercarriage than its predecessors. For the drive system, only the powershift transmission was now offered. Production on the D9G would make its way to the fall of 1974, when it was upgraded into the 410 fhp model D9H.

The 1960s also saw a flood of new Traxcavator track loaders muscle their way into the product line as well. From smallest to largest, these models included the Model 933F in 1958, the 933G in 1965, the 941 in 1968, the 951A (which was built in the United Kingdom) in 1964, the 951B in 1967, and the 955H in 1960, which became the 955K in 1966. For larger jobs, Caterpillar offered the 977E Traxcavator, which had been introduced in 1958. It was replaced by the 977H in 1960, which was superseded by the 977K in 1966. This model continued until 1971, at which time it was upgraded into the 977L.

The largest of all of the front-engined track loaders built by Caterpillar was its 983, which was unveiled in 1969. The 983 was powered by the popular Cat D343 diesel, rated at 275 fhp. Load capacity for the big Traxcavator was 4 1/2 cubic yards. The model 983 found great success in the marketplace and was available with a large variety of bucket options to fit specific job requirements. The 983 made it all the way up to late 1978, before being upgraded to a B model status.

The second oldest Caterpillar product line, next to the track-type tractors, was the motor graders. During the 1960s, these machines, sometimes referred to as blades, also got their fair share of improvements and updates. The company aggressively pursued this market, offering a model size to fit each niche in the earthmoving industry.

The ever popular No. 12 motor grader series became the No. 12E in 1959. This was followed by the No. 12F in 1965. All of these models were rated at 115 fhp. In 1959 the No. 112E motor grader, rated at 85 fhp, was released. In 1960 the No. 112F, with 100 fhp, was introduced at the same time as the No. 112E.

For contractors looking for a slightly more powerful motor grader, Caterpillar offered the No. 120 in 1964 with 115 fhp. This was increased to 125 fhp in 1967. If even more power were needed, Caterpillar served up the No. 14D in 1961. With a power output of 150 fhp, it was an excellent choice for demanding road work. Other models that followed included the No. 14E series in 1965.

But for the really big jobs, only one model would do. That was Caterpillar's mighty No. 16 motor grader. When introduced in early 1963, the No. 16 was the biggest and most powerful blade offered by the company. The No. 16 was powered by the reliable Cat D343 diesel, rated at 225 fhp. The moldboard was 14 feet in length, and customers had the option of a 16-foot blade. A Caterpillar first on this unit was the use of hydraulic-mechanical controls for manipulating the blade functions. Before this, all of the company's graders used mechanical controls. With its full powershift transmission, the No. 16 was the ideal machine for large highway projects, as well as the perfect solution for cutting and blading haul roads in mining operations. The No. 16 was all but unstoppable. Caterpillar increased the grader's appeal still further in 1973, when it was replaced by the 250 fhp model 16G. The 16G was Caterpillar's first articulated frame grader, which improved maneuverability greatly. This model would also see the 16-foot moldboard blade become standard issue, instead of just an option as on the previous model.

Introduced in 1961, the Caterpillar No. 14D motor grader was positioned at the top of the company's grader product line, at least as far as power output was concerned. The No. 14D received 150 fhp from the Cat D333 diesel it housed. Eventually, the No. 14D relinquished its title and became the second-most powerful motor grader for Cat after the release of the 225-fhp No. 16 in early 1963. *Caterpillar*

6

THE WEST COAST CONNECTION

THE CATERPILLAR/PETERSON ENGINEERING ALLIANCE

Engineering innovations in the business of building world-class earthmoving machines has always been a recognized hallmark of Caterpillar. But some of these designs actually came in the back door through a long-time engineering and working relationship with one of Cat's premier dealerships in California, the Peterson Tractor Company.

Peterson Tractor & Equipment Co. was established in 1936 by Howard Peterson in San Francisco. He was just 30 years old at the time. But he had cut his teeth in the earthmoving business by working alongside one of the pioneering greats in the field, Robert Gilmour LeTourneau. In fact, R. G. LeTourneau became Howard's brother-in-law after he married Howard's sister, Evelyn, in 1917. Howard started working for LeTourneau after school in the 1920s. In 1936, Howard cashed in his LeTourneau stock shares and headed down to San Francisco from Stockton to take over the Caterpillar dealership in the Bay Area. There were no hard feelings between Howard and R. G., since the Caterpillar dealer network at the time also represented and sold LeTourneau equipment.

In 1943, Howard's younger brother, Robert A. Peterson (Buster), joined the company, and in 1948 he became a partner in the business. Buster had previously worked for LeTourneau before joining his older brother. Buster had a keen engineering sense, but with only an eighth-grade education, his engineering skills were self-taught. But he refined and broadened his engineering skills during his years with LeTourneau. Soon Buster brought his talents to bear creating incredible innovations for Caterpillar equipment.

Things started to get a bit more interesting in 1948, after Peterson Tractor relocated to its new, much larger facility in San Leandro, California. A new division within the company, Special Equipment Services, headed by Buster, now had the manufacturing space to take on very large engineer-

With two big screaming Cat D353 diesel engines, four driving tracks, and 770 flywheel-horsepower, no scraper was too large for the Peterson Quad-Trac D9G. After Buster sold his patents on the Quad-Trac design to Caterpillar, an official factory version was released in 1968, referred to as the DD9G. This is a Peterson Quad-Trac D9G photographed in March 1964. *ECO Collection*

This Twin Cat D8 tractor was the third and last one built by Peterson in late 1950, using tractors 2U12911 and 2U12912. This was the only Twin D8 to be designed in a "high-clearance" layout. It was shipped to the Holt Company of San Antonio, Texas, in 1951, for land-clearing work at the King Ranch. *Peterson*

ing concept and modification work for its customers. Special Equipment Services' motto was pretty simple—"If it's good for the customer, then it's good for Peterson."

Many of the designs that Buster came up with were the direct result of hours of job-site observations. Other projects were the result of a direct request from a customer, whose special job requirements could not be met with available equipment. And still other designs were produced in conjunction with Caterpillar research engineers who would often call on Buster's special skills for concepts they wanted to "put into iron" quickly. With Buster's involvement, special projects that would take Caterpillar months to get started would now take only weeks. So close was the working relationship between Peterson's Special Equipment Services and Caterpillar Research that the group's engineering and design protocols were made the same as Cat's. This allowed the seamless transfer of drawings and information back and fourth between the two research groups.

One of the first commercially successful equipment designs produced by Buster was the "U Dozer" blade. The

One of Buster Peterson's best-known tractor design modifications was the Quad-Trac Caterpillar D9G. The first unit built, shown here in January 1964, with Buster at the controls, demonstrates the overall maneuverability of the big unit. *Peterson*

The Peterson Quad-Trac D9G tractor sets were used mainly as push-dozers for scrapers. But a few were set up as high-powered "ripping" quads, such as this unit from June 1966, equipped with massive heavy-duty dual ripping shanks. *ECO Collection*

U blade combined the best elements of a straight blade with that of an angle blade. This design allowed the blade to carry and control a larger amount of material during dozing operations. In October 1949, Buster was granted a patent on the design of the U blade. So impressed was Caterpillar with the design of the U blade that the company eventually wound up buying the patent rights from Buster directly and incorporating it fully into its product lines. This was the first of 34 patented designs that Cat would purchase from Buster between 1949 and 1973. Many of the designs found their way onto production equipment, but there were a few that, for one reason or another, just never worked out. Still, Buster's designs influenced Cat research engineers more than any other single outside source during the 1950s and 1960s.

The special equipment designs produced during the 1950s and 1960s were quite varied, to say the least. One of these was the Sno Cat D7 tractors built for the Army Corps of Engineers in 1953 and 1954. Other special equipment designs worthy of mention from Peterson were the Offset Cat D8 Pipelayer, the Demolition Clam Bucket, the Cat 988 Bonus Bucket, the Inside Arm Dozer, massive 15-, 17-, and 28-ton towed rippers, 56-ton heavy-duty rollers, and numerous tractor attachments, such as the Peterson Cable Layer, Asparagus Chopper, and Post Hole Digger. But some of Buster's design programs, especially those involving scrapers and multiple crawler tractors, took on a life of their own, winning for Buster and his engineering group enduring recognition and acclaim from both its customers and Caterpillar Research.

TWIN D8

Buster Peterson's first major engineering creation to attract national attention in the earthmoving industry was the Twin D8. The Twin D8 consisted of two Caterpillar D8 tractors that were essentially made into a single unit. Unlike the side-by-side D9 dozers of the 1960s, the D8s were joined together after their inner track assemblies were removed. Dual controls for both the engines and their drives were mounted in front of the operator and offset to the right of center. The operator sat on the right half of the machine, and the unit could be split apart quickly for over-the-road transport. Buster had originally tried this concept out on a pair of Allis-Chalmers dozers to see if it was viable and worth the engineering effort and money in modifying the D8 units. Early tests of the "Siamese Twin" Allis-Chalmers confirmed that the design had merit, so the go ahead was given to re-engineer the D8 tractors in 1948. With 288 belt-horsepower and 270 drawbar-horsepower, the Twin D8 was considered a very powerful tractor for the late 1940s.

The first Twin D8 went through various tests equipped with a 23-cubic-yard pull-scraper and with a 16-foot-wide bulldozing blade. It got its first true test in late 1948 working on the Hungry Horse Dam project in Montana, equipped with a 22-foot-wide blade with rooter teeth for knocking down and clearing timber on more than 7,800 acres. In this type of application, nothing could stop the big twin Cat.

Peterson went on to build two more Twin D8 tractors. In 1950 they supplied a unit (consisting of tractors 2U-9800 and 2U-10438) to the large earthmoving contractor of Morrison-Knudsen Farmington, which was equipped with a Euclid Loader drawbar, and blower-type fans. The other unit, built in late 1950 (tractors 2U-12911 and 2U-12912), was shipped to the Holt Company in San Antonio, Texas in 1951, for continuous land-clearing duties at the King Ranch. The special high-clearance Twin D8 was equipped with a 16-foot-wide Holt Funnel Dozer and a rear-mounted Holt Root Plow. Weighing in at 52 tons, the dozer was capable of knocking down 40-foot mesquite trees, uprooting massive stumps, and dozing down heavy brush.

Even though Buster designed and offered many other variations and modifications, such as more powerful engines and low gear kits, to soup up the Cat D8 for customers, the

The origin of the original Caterpillar side-by-side dozer, the SxS D9G, has for some years been in question. Was it a Buster Peterson creation or a Caterpillar design? In fact, it was both. In late 1964, Caterpillar Research approached Peterson with the proposal to build the unit. After the first prototype was assembled in late 1966, Caterpillar Research took over the project. The first unit (pictured) undergoes testing at Peterson Tractor in San Leandro, California. *Caterpillar*

Twin D8 modifications were by far the most complex and famous. On January 18, 1951, Buster applied for a patent on the design, known as the Tractor with Twin Power Plants, which was granted to him on May 11, 1954.

QUAD-TRAC D9G

In the late 1950s and early 1960s, manufacturers were designing and building ever larger scrapers, many of them with dual engine configurations. For maximum productivity, push dozers were usually required to assist in the loading of these massive units. With the largest of these scrapers, it was quite common to find two Cat D9s dedicated to push loading a single unit at a time. It required skilled operators to get the two dozers in position and to match the speed of the scraper in a timely manner. But time was always lost maneuvering two independently operated dozers in behind the scraper. Buster thought there must be a better, more productive way of push loading these units. He wondered whether both tractors could be hooked together, so their performance capabilities could be better controlled. Enter the Quad-Trac.

Pictured testing in November 1969 is the first production Caterpillar SxS D9G. Equipped with a massive 24-foot-wide bulldozing blade, the unit was ideally suited for large mining reclamation projects, or coal stripping and stockpiling applications. With 770 flywheel-horsepower available, the SxS D9G was never lacking in power. *Caterpillar*

Buster started to experiment with two Cat tractors, hooked together by a ball-and-socket type hitch, in the late 1950s. But this unit still required two operators to control the tractors. He wanted a better system that would eliminate the need for the second operator.

During this time period, Caterpillar was releasing new, more powerful and larger capacity scrapers into the marketplace. Models such as the 650, 651, 657, and the 666 were in big demand throughout the country. To push-load them, only the biggest tractors would do, and more often than not, it was the mighty Cat D9. Buster zeroed in on this model for his Quad-Trac.

Buster had the first prototype Quad-Trac D9G up and running in late 1963. Two D9G units were hooked together by a ball-and-socket hitch arrangement, with both tractors controlled by a single operator from the front unit. Air-over-hydraulic control lines from the lead D9G tractor controlled all the operating functions of the rear unit. The operator's seat on the front tractor was mounted at a 45 degree angle to the right, making it easy for the driver to view the rear D9G without craning his neck. The front tractor utilized a cushioned Inside Arm Dozer blade for pushing the scrapers. This blade, designed by Buster and

Peterson modified quite a few Cat DW20 scraper models throughout the 1950s. Shown is a specially modified DW20G tractor attached to No. 482 Series B scraper in 1959, which has been stretched 18 inches and equipped with sideboards. This increased its capacity to 34 cubic yards struck and 42 heaped. This Cat/Peterson unit was referred to as the 482-P. It also has another Cat No. 463 scraper in tow, whose cable controls are power-driven by a gasoline engine mounted on the back of the No. 482B unit. *Peterson*

In mid-1974, when the regular Caterpillar D9G became the D9H model series, the special dual and side-by-side units were also likewise upgraded. The SxS D9H was now rated at a whopping 820 flywheel-horsepower. In fact, this was the most powerful dozer offered by the company until the unveiling of the D11R CD Carrydozer, rated at 850 flywheel-horsepower, at the September 1996 MINExpo. Production ended on the SxS D9H in 1977, after the announcement of the mighty D10. *ECO*

Peterson engineer Fred Stevens, was patented in 1972 and later purchased by Caterpillar. With 770 flywheel-horsepower on tap, the Quad-Trac was all but unstoppable. In the past, the scraper operator would start his cycle by taking a shallow cut, and then increasing the bite as he felt the two independent tractors making contact in the rear. The dual D9G unit could apply full power immediately at the beginning of the pushing cycle, allowing the scraper to start off with a full bite, and shortening the amount of time it took to get a full load. After preliminary testing working at Guy F. Atkinson's Briones Dam project near Orinda, California, in late 1963 and early 1964, the Quad-Trac D9G was deemed a complete success. This first unit was then sold to S. J. Groves in West Virginia in 1964.

Caterpillar was highly impressed with the performance of the Quad-Trac. Starting in late 1964, Cat offered the unit in its product line, relying on Peterson for fabrication. Peterson built 10 sets of dual D9Gs between late 1963 and early 1967. Unit numbers 9-9-103 and 9-9-107 were originally purchased by Caterpillar Research, but Peterson bought them back and then resold them. A small but unspecified quantity of do-it-yourself field conversion kits was also produced and sold.

Buster was granted patents in August 1966 on the Draft Assembly for Tandem Tractors and on the Steering Controls for Tandem Tractors. Not long after this, he sold

Buster Peterson's first dual scraper unit to feature his newly designed multiple engine and steering control systems was this Tandem Caterpillar 657 unit. The unit is shown undergoing testing at a construction site near the San Leandro dealership in October 1964. *Peterson*

After the successful testing of the Tandem 657, Buster built the mother of all Caterpillar scrapers—the awesome Triple 657. Delivered in February 1965 to Peter Kiewit's earthmoving contract location of the San Luis Canal aqueduct project, the Peterson Triple Caterpillar 657 was capable of handling 150 cubic yards per trip. *ECO Collection*

the patent rights to Caterpillar, and in 1968, Cat began producing and selling the unit as the D9G. Caterpillar also issued new serial number prefix codes for the unit, 90J for the front tractor and 91J for the rear. All of the Peterson-fabricated sets utilized D9G (66A) units.

In 1974, Caterpillar released an upgraded DD9H (97V front/98V rear) model of the big quad set. The DD9H incorporated all of the improvements of the regular D9H model, but with two tractors combined, power output was a mighty impressive 820 flywheel-horsepower. This unit stayed in the product line until 1980. In all, 10 Peterson Quad-Trac D9Gs, 51 Cat DD9Gs, and 7 Cat DD9H sets were produced.

SIDE-BY-SIDE DOZER

Caterpillar had been impressed with the overall design execution of the Peterson Quad-Trac conversions, especially Buster's multiple engine and maneuvering air controls for a single operator. When Caterpillar was considering a high-production dozer, made up of two D9G tractors connected side by side, they approached Buster's engineering group at Peterson in late 1964, to put the project on the fast track. A concept model of the dozer, made out of two toy Cat tractors, was approved to go on to the next step . . . a full-size operating prototype. By late 1966, the prototype was ready for testing. Unique to this unit was its use of a single hydraulic cylinder, mounted on the front nose of each tractor, to control the movement of its massive blade. Caterpillar liked what it saw, even though further design work would be needed to bring the big dozer up to production standards. In 1967, Cat Research took over the project.

By late 1969, Caterpillar introduced a finalized version of the SxS D9G (29N left side/30N right). High-volume production dozing was what this brute was all about. With its 24-foot-wide blade, it was an ideal coal stripping dozer. The side-by-side machine also excelled at land reclamation and stockpiling. To push this big blade around, you needed horsepower, and with two D9G tractors combined, you had two Cat D353 diesels pumping out 770 flywheel-horsepower at your command. The SxS D9G was connected together by means of a rear tie-bar, a diagonal brace between the two inside track assemblies and at the front by the bulldozing blade. Operating controls used an air-over hydraulic system with quick disconnect lines. The operator controlled the operation of both tractors from the left unit.

When the regular production D9G became the D9H in mid-1974, the same transition occurred with the side-by-side dozer. The SxS D9H (99V left/12U right) produced more power than its predecessor, with 820 flywheel-horsepower now on hand. Most major specifications remained unchanged. The owner also had the option of converting both tractors to single dozer operation if a particular job contract required it. When the SxS D9H dozer's time finally came in 1977, only 13 sets had been sold. The SxS D9G saw 11 factory sets built. Add one more if you count the first Peterson prototype.

Buster Peterson was awarded a patent on the Side-by-Side Tractor concept in May 1972. Caterpillar purchased these patents from him, as it had done with the Quad-Trac designs.

TANDEM AND TRIPLE 657 SCRAPERS

During the mid-1960s, big earthmoving jobs were a fact of life in California, and one of the largest at the time was the San Luis Canal aqueduct project. Some of the

largest earthmoving contractors in the country were working on different parts of the mammoth operation project. At the "Reach One" site of the canal job, Guy F. Atkinson Co. was using tandem and triple LeTourneau Electric Diggers on its work site. At a different location near Modesto, California, Western Contracting Corporation had its five big Euclid Tandem TSS-40 scrapers in full swing. The writing on the wall was clear to Caterpillar and Buster Peterson. If they did not do something quickly, a lot of business was going to pass them by. Buster initiated a crash engineering program in 1964 to design a dual scraper of his own—the Tandem 657. The Tandem 657 consisted of two Cat 657 scrapers hooked together, utilizing multiple engine and steering control systems, all controlled by a single operator on the lead scraper. Operating tests were conducted at a nearby site in Castro Valley in October 1964. After the bugs were worked out of the new operating systems, Buster started to work on an even larger scraperﬂthe massive Triple 657.

The Peterson Triple 657 was essentially a tandem unit with another scraper added. But because of the length of the unit, a high-mounted operator's cab was fabricated for the front 657. This enabled the single operator to keep an eye on all three scrapers during operation. And with 186 feet of machine length, there was a lot of yellow Cat iron to keep your eyes on. With this giant's combined power rating of 2,580 flywheel-horsepower and a load capacity of 150 cubic yards, only the most skilled operators were allowed to take the controls.

In February 1965, Peterson shipped the Triple 657 and two sets of Tandem 657 scrapers to Peter Kiewit's contract at "Reach Three" of the canal project, for working a 23-mile stretch between Coalinga and Mendora. For the

Measuring some 186 feet in length, the Triple 657 resembled some sort of a monster land snake, as it twisted and turned over the uneven terrain. With six Cat diesels producing 2,580 flywheel-horsepower, the unit was the most powerful Caterpillar-based scraper ever produced. *Peterson*

next 21 months, the triple and tandem scrapers moved over 22 million cubic yards of earth on Kiewit's portion of the project. Once the contract was completed, Kiewit was so pleased with the performance of the 657 scraper teams, he decided to purchase the triple unit and one more 657, so he could convert the experimental machine into two more tandem sets.

The engineering knowledge Buster gained from the development of the tandem and triple scrapers would come in handy when Caterpillar research approached him about developing a push-pull system for tandem scraper use. The initial concept of the push-pull hitching system was conceived by Caterpillar's sales engineering group out of Joliet, Illinois. But to get it into iron quickly, the company needed the talents of Buster's engineering group. The final design was simple and efficient. A scraper would approach from the rear and "hook" the front unit when the two scrapers' push blocks met. The push blocks were spring cushioned to absorb the jolt on impact. Then a bail loop lowered from the front end and looped around the rear scraper hook. The rear scraper helped push the front unit while loading, and when the front unit was full, it then helped pull the rear unit for its loading cycle. To disengage the two scrapers, all that was required was the raising of the bail loop. It was that simple. Caterpillar adopted this system in 1968 for use with the 657, and later with the 627 and 637 scraper series.

HOEING APRON SCRAPER

One of Buster's most ambitious and complicated engineering concepts was the Hoeing Apron Scraper. This self-loading scraper utilized a tandem engine 657, with a large three-jointed backhoe fitted inside the stretched bowl of the unit. A third engine was mounted on top of the scraper, just to power all of the hydraulic functions. During field trials in 1967, the Hoeing Apron Scraper could literally swallow up five-foot diameter rocks, something that was unheard of for a normal scraper. With its giant hoeing backhoe, the scraper would reach out for its load on the move and pull it into the rear of the bowl. With a 60-cubic-yard capacity, it could carry over 16 cubic yards more than the standard 657.

But the Hoeing Apron had one very big drawback to its design—its complexity. The unit was so complicated to

The Triple 657's high-mounted operator's cab of the lead scraper sits stoically atop the machine. Only the most experienced and seasoned operators were allowed to sit at the controls of the Triple 657. With five articulation points, six engines, and a simply massive turning radius, there were a lot of things the operator had to keep his eyes on at all times. *Peterson*

One of Buster's most complicated and ambitious engineering designs was the Peterson Hoeing Apron Caterpillar 657. Testing on this unique scraper started in 1967, and would become part of Caterpillar's large self-loading evaluation testing program. The scraper was powered by three diesel engines—an eight-cylinder D346 up front and six-cylinder D343 units at the rear and on top of the scraper unit. Combined power output was a heady 1,300 flywheel-horsepower. But in the end, Caterpillar passed on the scraper concept, judging it too costly to produce. *ECO Collection*

operate that only the most skilled operator could keep up with all of the functions that had to be monitored constantly. The main control was a joystick with 10 microswitches on it. Even though the scraper proved to be a real digging machine, when Caterpillar was finalizing its choice for the best self-loading concept, it chose the push-pull design. The Hoeing Apron's complex design meant that mass production was out of the question. And the thought of supporting the scraper in the field would have given any parts manager nightmares. Buster received a patent in December 1972 for the "Hoe Scraper with Manipulating Apron." Like many of Buster's other patents, this one was purchased by Caterpillar.

TWIN-631B TAMPER

The Twin-631B Tamper was another example of Buster building a specialized machine suited to a customer's particular job requirements. The unit was designed for crews at Atkinson's Briones Dam contract in California to compact the extremely rocky material they were encountering. Buster's design called for two single-axle 631B scraper tractors, minus their scraper bowls. They were placed in line and connected by a large overhead box-section beam. The tires were removed and replaced with Hyster C400B compacting wheels, with 102 tamping feet per drum. Total power output for the rig was 720 flywheel-horsepower. The front of the unit, which was actually the rear of the 631B tractor, was equipped with a cushioned push-block for scraper loading duties. The operator's controls were also relocated to the rear of the 631B tractor, now making it the front. When it started operation in 1963, it looked like the unit was going in reverse, when in fact it was going forward. Caterpillar Research took an interest in Buster's unconventional design and considered it briefly as a possible "superpusher" for scraper operations. Researchers restored rubber tires to the design and ran it through tests, but the concept was put on hold as soon as Buster's Quad-Trac D9G tractors became available.

By March 1966, a more refined design of the Twin-631B Tamper was built by Peterson for use on the Oroville Dam project. The unit was much like the previous design, but now the operator's controls were in the front of the lead 631B tractor. The front ends of the 631B units faced the forward travel of the machine. But the cushioned push-block was history. This design was intended as a compactor only. In fact, it out performed every other compaction device used on the dam project.

CUSHIONED AIR-TRACK

During the late 1960s, Buster's engineering group started to give serious attention to a new tire concept called the Cushioned Air-Track. The Cushioned Air-Track was designed to protect the tires in rocky working conditions. The design consisted of a belt of special track rails with extra-wide track shoes bolted to them. This was then wrapped around the tire and secured. Although this idea had been tried several years earlier by wrapping a track around the rear tandem drive tires of a No. 12 grader, it was never meant for hard rock working situations.

Peterson experimented with a Cat 950 wheel loader, equipped with the steel belts wrapped around each tire. Early tests were encouraging. Again, Caterpillar Research

took a liking to the concept and started to put some serious resources into the project. Cat would eventually buy the patent from Buster, which was granted to him in August 1971.

Caterpillar's version of Buster's design was the Dystred Cushion Track. Instead of wrapping a normal tire in steel, Cat designed an entire wheel system, which included four sets of track assemblies fitted on inflated rubber drivers, mounted on special wheels and rims. The tire, or rubber driver, was smooth with no tread, with massive shaped upper shoulders that snugly held the track assembly in place. Caterpillar introduced the system in 1971 on one of its larger wheel loaders, calling it the Dystred 988 Cushion Track Loader.

By 1975, Caterpillar introduced an even more advanced design than the short-lived Dystred, calling it the Beadless Tire. The Beadless Tire differed in design from the Dystred in that it used a two-piece rim to support a rubber carcass. This rubber oval air chamber, reinforced with steel cable, had no bead or lip to seal against the rim. A mounting belt made of rubber, circumferentially wound with layers of steel cable, was wrapped around the inflatable carcass. Steel shoes then bolted directly to anchor plates molded into the mounting belt. The main purpose of this design was to protect the front tires from abrasive rock cuts. The Dystred design was required on all four wheels, while only the front wheels of the wheel loader were equipped with the beadless design. The rear tires were left stock. Caterpillar offered the Beadless Tire on the 988B and 992C wheel loaders, its largest models at the time. But by the early 1980s, technical glitches and a lack of industry interest brought the Beadless Tire program to an end. The engineering design work concerning the principle of a rubber belt, reinforced with steel cable, however, soon found a new home with the research group responsible for the Challenger agricultural tractor.

During the 1960s, Peterson built two different designs of compacting machines based on the single-axle tractor fronts of the 631B scraper. The model shown in March 1966 was the second and last design offered, the Peterson Twin-631B Tamper. This 720-flywheel-horsepower compactor was used at one major dam building project in 1966 and actually outperformed every other machine of its type. But the unit was never sold outright and was eventually dismantled. *ECO Collection*

7

THE BIG RISK

ELEVATED SPROCKET DRIVE TRIUMPHS

Successful companies are often tempted to modify or reinvent the very product or service that put their firms on the map, often with disastrous results. When such a move fails to please the market, it can be harmful, even fatal, to the company. But when it works, it can propel a firm to new heights, in profits, customer loyalty, and industry admiration. Caterpillar faced this decision in the late 1960s, when it considered modifying its industry-leading crawler tractor model line to an elevated drive-sprocket design.

The concept of an elevated sprocket for driving the track was not new to the industry. Other companies tried to utilize this design method in a production tractor as far back as 1917, when the Dayton-Dick Company of Quincy, Illinois, introduced its Leader Model 25-40 tractor with high-drive track design. This was followed in 1919 by its Model 18-36, also known as the Model C, which also utilized this track arrangement. But the Leader high-drive tractors never really caught on and were discontinued in late 1920. Another firm, Acme Harvester Company of Peoria, Illinois, also gave the high-drive concept a try with its Model 12-24, in 1918. But again, this was a short-lived model. Of the early firms experimenting with this drive concept, Cletrac of Cleveland, Ohio, was the most successful with its Model F 9-16 in 1920. Although its production run lasted only through 1922, quite a few of the small but extremely tough and durable tractors were built.

But even before these firms had experimented with the high-drive concept, both of Caterpillar's founding companies, Holt and Best, had looked into this type of track drive layout. In 1912, Holt built a special gas-powered trenching machine that utilized a high-drive sprocket design for the rear crawler tracks, with two steel wheels up front for steering. Holt had built a few of these units even before 1910, but these were steered by means of a single tiller-wheel. They also used a more conventional rear track design, and were steam-powered. Almost all of these special tractors

Unveiled at the 1996 MINExpo in Las Vegas, Nevada, the D11R CD Carrydozer (9XR) was the first of the series to be equipped with the 850-flywheel-horsepower Cat 3508B diesel. Full production on the big dozer officially got under way in April 1998. Weighing in at 239,550 pounds, it was the heaviest D11 model series ever produced, as of 2000. *Caterpillar*

Produced in 1914 and 1915, the Best C.L.B. "Humpback" 30 was the company's attempt at building an elevated-drive sprocket tractor for orchard and nursery work. Records indicate that only 45 of these unusual tractors were ever built. The "Humpback" 30 shown is part of the Fred C. Heidrick Ag History Center, and is the only known example of this rare tractor in existence today. *Randy Leffingwell*

were built to dig and clean out irrigation ditches in California, and were simply known as Holt Ditchers.

Best also produced a special tractor that utilized a high-mounted drive sprocket in the form of the C. L. Best Model 30 "Humpback." Produced from 1914 to 1915, it was mainly intended for orchard and vineyard work. Best applied this drive concept only to this one model. To some extent, its engineering was ahead of the times. But the high-drive sprocket design needed further work to become practical, which required funds Best could not afford to spend at the time.

The serious consideration of high-drive or triangle-track drive, as it was sometimes called, for use in a crawler tractor application went dormant in the minds of engineers

for decades. It was revived by a research engineer with Caterpillar named Bob Purcell, who was looking for a new drive system offering superior tractive capabilities. In 1965, Purcell designed a triangle-track drive system, with a single oscillating bogie wheel arrangement, to keep the bottom of the track firmly on the ground. He had the Caterpillar model shop build a prototype to his specifications. This was then incorporated into a highly modified garden tractor. The operator would sit on a rear-mounted seat that was attached to the front of the tractor by a swivel joint, and steer by means of two handlebars. Early tests at the Peoria

It's hard to believe, but Caterpillar's starting point in its elevated track drive program began with this little experimental test tractor, built primarily out of riding lawnmower bits and pieces. Conceived in 1965 by Caterpillar research engineer Bob Purcell, seated, it would provide the power for the triangle-track design. It surprised many at the Peoria Proving Grounds when it was able to provide enough traction to effortlessly pull a Jeep around the test center. *Bob Purcell Collection*

Even before the Best "Humpback" 30, Holt had built a specialized elevated track drive, gas-powered tractor, simply known as a Holt Ditcher. Produced around 1912, it was designed primarily to dig and clean out irrigation ditches in California. *Caterpillar*

The next big step in the development of Caterpillar's Hi-Drive system was this heavily modified prototype test D9G dozer. Originally built in 1970, it is pictured here undergoing tests at the Peoria Proving Grounds in September 1971. *ECO Collection*

Proving Grounds (PPG) confirmed that the design had incredible pulling power, and was in fact strong enough to pull a Jeep. Not bad for a cobbled-up lawn mower.

After these early tests, including extensive soil bin testing at the PPG to document and confirm the design's tractive capabilities, Cat engineers looked at how best to apply this concept to its machines. Interestingly, the crawler tractor was not the first beneficiary of the high-drive design. Instead, in 1967, another engineering group designed and built a set of triangle-drive tracks to be utilized on a 988 wheel loader. This group of research engineers was taking the drive concept down its own particular development path in accordance with their product group. But the use of this potent drive system soon found its way to the crawler tractor engineers, who were designing and building one of the largest such machines the company had yet conceived—the massive D10.

Back in 1954, and only a few months after the announcement of the D9, Caterpillar product developers were already thinking of an even larger tractor. This concept was basically a scaled-up version of the new D9, with a rigid suspension system and an enormous undercarriage. But the designs were all put on hold and eventually dismissed as being too large and expensive to produce and service with the existing manufacturing processes. During the following decade, the rise in large building and mining projects convinced Caterpillar that it would need a crawler tractor larger than the D9 series in the not too distant future. In 1969 management set up an engineering team to create a concept for the D10 project. A group from Cat Research was also invited into the D10 developmental team. Research had already produced many innovations that would eventually find their way onto the new dozer.

The team set up a list of objectives that were based on input from various Cat departments, such as Sales, Service, and Manufacturing, and of course, customers. These goals were high productivity, modular design, simplified maintenance, high operator efficiency, and transportability. By November 1969, the group had arrived at a two-track design, utilizing an elevated drive sprocket. To help in the approval process with upper management, a full-size mock-up of the D10 was built out of wood and cardboard to better illustrate the look of the new high-drive tractor.

The mock-up worked. Caterpillar management felt

there was great potential in the D10 and its drive concept. In early 1970, management authorized building a test bed machine to examine the elevated track drive system in action. In February engineers started converting a D9G tractor, and by June 1970, it was up and running. This D9G incorporated an elevated drive sprocket and a resilient mounted bogey undercarriage. A resilient undercarriage system allows the track rollers to float over obstacles for improved dozer and operator ride, reduced impact loading on rollers and roller frame, and better traction. In 1973, after two years of preliminary testing of the D9G test bed, work started on the building of the first D10 prototype from the ground up.

Cat executives did not take lightly the decision to proceed with the D10 project. Their crawler tractors were already considered the best in the world. Making a significant design change had as much potential to hurt them in the market as advance them, and they appeared to have more to lose than to gain. How would the company's loyal customer base react to this new design? And what consequences would follow if real work in the field were to prove the drive system just plain didn't work? The prospect of changing the basic drive design philosophy and debuting

The first prototype D10X1 was unveiled in July 1973 at a summer corporate meeting at Caterpillar's Tech Center. Of the early prototypes, this was the only one fitted with an open ROPS cab. It spent its entire testing life at the Caterpillar Peoria Proving Grounds. *Caterpillar*

Six weeks after the D10X1 was built, D10X2 was making its way down to Caterpillar's Arizona Proving Grounds. Looking much like the first prototype, it had a fully enclosed ROPS cab with air conditioning. Only D10X1 and X2 featured two upper track rollers in the design of the undercarriage. *John F. Cooper Collection*

This Caterpillar D10 tractor is one of the 10 preproduction pilot machines undergoing testing at the Arizona Proving Grounds in May 1977. The most discernible feature on the pilot D10 dozers was the ROPS bar designs covering the operator's cab. These would differ in the full production D10 units. *Caterpillar*

green light. Now the sleepless nights fell to the D10 management team. It was all in their hands.

On July 13, 1973, the first prototype D10, referred to as X-1, was finished. The following week at the Caterpillar Tech Center, the X-1 was shown for the first time to company officers and plant managers at their summer corporate meeting. All were impressed. After the meeting, the X-1 was secretly shipped over to the PPG for further evaluations. Six weeks later, X-2 was ready to roll and was on its way down to Cat's Arizona Proving Grounds.

The first two prototypes, X-1 and X-2, looked almost alike. The most notable difference was that X-1 had an open Rollover Protective Structures (ROPS) cage and X-2 had a fully enclosed ROPS cab. Most of the field performance evaluation testing was conducted with X-2.

In 1975, after two years of testing and redesign work of the original prototypes, two more units were built, X-3 and X-4. Many design alterations were performed on the dozers. The most obvious included a more refined ROPS cab and the elimination of the two upper track rollers on both sides. The engineers found that they just weren't needed.

During the testing of X-3 and X-4, Cat started raising a new assembly building in East Peoria in 1976. It would be known as Building SS, and would be the new home of the D10, along with future elevated sprocket tractor designs.

As testing continued with the prototypes, the D10 underwent further changes and refinements. All was ready

the change on the largest, most powerful single crawler tractor the company had ever built, made for a lot of hand-wringing in the big offices. There was quite a lot of debate as to the pros and cons of the issue at the uppermost levels of the corporation, and all understood the enormous risk the company was taking. But in the end, the benefits of the design were just too enticing. Top brass gave the project the

Pictured is the D10X3 prototype in 1975. At this point in the life of the big dozer, its overall layout was starting to enter its final design phase. Changes in the undercarriage, including an entirely new ROPS cab and the elimination of the two track rollers, are the most notable modifications. Not long after this unit started testing, D10X4 was built. It looked basically like D10X3, but with a slightly different ROPS cab design. *Caterpillar*

In the spring of 1978, full production D10 (84W and 76X) dozers started to roll off the assembly line at Caterpillar's Building SS Assembly Plant. The D10 pictured working here is an early unit with the single, large exhaust stack. Later models of the dozer would get a redesigned system with two exhaust stacks and repositioned air cleaner intakes. *Caterpillar*

The D10 was a great dozer, but it was also an equally superior ripping machine. The D10's 6-foot, single-shank ripping tooth could cut through solid rock like a hot knife through butter. This unit, pictured in August 1980 at the Arizona Proving Grounds, is one of the later models with the redesigned dual exhaust system. *Caterpillar*

An Impact Ripper was offered as an option on the better balanced and more powerful D11N (74Z) in 1987. Designed to fracture and rip rock, the Impact Ripper utilized a hydraulic impactor that transmitted powerful energy pulses through a specially designed ripper shank, which concentrated 450,000 pounds of impact at the ripper tip, 540 times a minute. Working weight of a D11N equipped with this massive ripper option was 225,950 pounds. *Caterpillar*

for the next phase in the program, the building of the pre-production machines. Starting in March 1977, 10 prepro-duction pilot D10s started to come off a temporary assem-bly line in the still-under-construction Building SS. These tractors were referred to as P-1 through P-10, and were shipped to various selected job sites across the United States. Although these field tests were to be conducted as clandestinely as possible, it's hard to hide the world's largest dozers when they're working out in the open. Whether working on a job site on an I-90 interstate pro-ject in Montana or in a coal mine in West Virginia, once the truckers got a look at them, that was it—the cat was out of the bag, so to speak. Word traveled fast by CB radio, and before long, companies like International Har-vester and Fiat-Allis had their men at the job sites to see for themselves what they were up against.

In mid-September 1977, Caterpillar officially announced the D10 project at a special press conference held at Caterpil-lar's Demonstration Area. A preproduction machine was on hand for a close-up inspection. What Cat had on its hands was not just the largest dozer it had ever built, but the largest, most powerful, and most productive dozer ever built, period. From this point forward, industry and customer perceptions of what a tracked dozer should be were forever changed.

In the spring of 1978, the first production D10 dozers started coming off the assembly line at the now-completed Building SS. There had never been a dozer quite like the massive D10. The first production units were powered by a turbocharged and aftercooled Cat D348 V-12 diesel engine, rated at 700 flywheel-horsepower. With its giant blade and rear ripper, the D10 was over 50 percent more productive than the D9H model. The dozer's 10U blade measured 19

feet, 10 inches across, with a 7-foot height. The large single shank ripper had a maximum ground penetrating depth of 70 inches. Equipped with this blade and ripper arrange-ment, the D10 weighed in at 191,100 pounds, or 95.5 tons.

Key to the design of the D10, of course, was its use of the elevated drive sprocket design, which removes the final drives from the work platform and from roller frame align-ment shock loads for extended powertrain life. Its modular design also allowed easy removal and installation of the final drives when servicing was required. Also, the resilient mounted undercarriage, with its four major track bogies per side, allowed the D10 to "ramp" over obstacles. This meant that the rollers and idlers were almost always in con-tact with the link rails, keeping more track on the ground for improved dozer ride and better traction. Dome-shaped rubber pads mounted both on the major bogies and the roller frames controlled their resiliency and travel.

Early D10 models were easily spotted by their use of a single, large exhaust stack. But some problems in the engine bay with the turbochargers and the routing of the exhausted system required a redesign incorporating a two-stack system, with relocated air cleaner intakes. This changeover took effect in 1980.

In January 1986, the last D10 came off of the assembly line in Building SS, and in February, the company started pro-duction of an upgraded version of the groundbreaking D10—the D11N. The D11N, upon first inspection, looked almost like the tractor it replaced. But there was a lot more to the D11N. A new powerplant, the Cat 3508 DITA V-8 diesel engine, rated at 817 gross horsepower and 770 fhp, now pow-ered the giant dozer. The track length had also increased, with an additional 21 inches on the ground. Overall working weight reached 205,948 pounds, or 103 tons. The 11U blade was now 20 feet, 10 inches wide, with a 7 feet, 7 inch height.

This D11R tractor, undergoing running engine tests at the East Peoria Building SS Assembly Plant, is nearing the end of its assembly procedure. In a few days, it will be ready for loading onto a reinforced flat railroad car, or be partially dismantled and shipped out by multiple semitruck loads. *ECO*

Operating capacity for the new blade was 45 cubic yards, compared with the D10's capacity of 38.2 cubic yards. Overall, the D11N was over 10 percent more productive than the D10. The D11N was a superior tractor in every way to its predecessor. Close to a thousand D10 dozers were built in its production run, and the D11N series would continue with this sales record for such a large machine. The D10 was a great dozer, but the D11N was an incredible one.

The D11N was the Number One choice for large mining operations around the world. But in early 1996, after a decade of dependable service, the D11N was upgraded to a new model version, the D11R. The D11R made significant changes to the overall efficiency of the tractor and its operator's controls, mostly through greater use of computer controls and monitoring systems. Most notable was the introduction of single-hand electronic steering and transmission controls. These were divided into two systems—Fingertip Controls (FTC) and Electronic Clutch and Brake (ECB), both mounted to the left of the operator. With enhanced operator comfort came increased productivity gains. Major specifications remained virtually unchanged, with the operating weight now up to 216,963 pounds, or 108 tons.

At the September 1996 MINExpo in Las Vegas, Nevada, Caterpillar unveiled a special version of its big dozer, the D11R CD Carrydozer. The D11R CD was intended for use in large-volume dozing applications, such as overburden stripping and land reclamation. The Carrydozer is basically a D11R with beefed up structural components, and a higher power rating from its improved 3508B EUI diesel, now rated at 915 gross horsepower and 850 fhp. The key feature of the Carrydozer is the design of its 22-foot-wide, 9-foot-high, 57-cubic-yard-capacity blade, which carries material inside the blade curvature for tremendous productivity gains. This increases the effective weight of the tractor, which enables it to push a larger pile of material in front of the blade. Operating weight was now rated at 239,550 pounds, or almost 120 tons. After

over a year of torturous field testing, the D11R CD was officially released for sale in April 1998.

During the testing program of the Carrydozer, engineering decided to upgrade the engine in the regular D11R with the more powerful unit found in the D11R CD. The improved D11R was officially introduced in August 1997. Most of the other improvements found in the Carrydozer also made their way into this more powerful version of the regular model.

The D10/D11 series of giant dozers are considered some of the finest track-type tractors ever produced for large earthmoving applications. Their contribution to the advancement of dozer technology is undeniable, especially the original D10. It is interesting to note that all of the early prototype and pilot test dozers built during the D10's developmental stage have been destroyed. That is, except for one—the first pilot D10 P-1. It was saved from the Arizona Proving Grounds and brought back to East Peoria in June 1989. There it was put on permanent display outside Building SS as a tribute to the hard work and dedication shown by the men and women at the plant who helped make the D10 a realityfland made earthmoving history at the same time.

The D11R (8ZR), which replaced the D11N in early 1996, was powered by a 770-fhp Cat 3508 diesel. In August 1997, power was increased once again with the 850-fhp 3508B diesel housed in the D11R (9TR). Working weight of the D11R was 225,500 pounds. The Impact Ripper option was not offered on the D11R. An 850-fhp version equipped with the optional single upper track roller is pictured in October 1998 at a coal mine in the Powder River Basin of Wyoming. *ECO*

The D11R CD Carrydozer gets its name from the specially designed bulldozing blade it utilizes. Large amounts of material are carried inside the curvature of the blade, enabling it to push larger loads in front of the blade, increasing productivity dramatically. Blade capacity for the Carrydozer is 57 cubic yards. The D11R CD pictured is working in a coal mine in central Ohio in July 1999. *ECO*

8

GROWING FORTUNES

RAPID PRODUCT LINE EXPANSION

During the 1970s, Caterpillar made many strategic moves in its earthmoving product lines, like the introduction of the elevated track drive system for track-type tractors already mentioned. But pressure from foreign competition was now becoming a serious threat to the company's health in the world market. As the major highway projects were reaching their peaks in the United States, Caterpillar sought out new market opportunities overseas. As time passed, the international marketplace would play a much larger role in Caterpillar's business activities and economic health. Overseas growth would really come into play during the energy crisis and mild recession of the mid-1970s. During this time period, domestic sales took a big hit, but international sales were steady, and in some areas, actually increased.

During the late 1960s, contractors started taking hydraulic excavators more seriously. As these machines increased in size and reliability, they began displacing cable-operated backhoe designs. American manufacturers, such as Bucyrus-Erie, Koehring, Insley, and Warner & Swasey, all offered hydraulic excavator designs in various sizes. Caterpillar, on the other hand, had nothing to offer in this market niche. To take advantage of what it perceived as a growing market opportunity, Caterpillar introduced its first fully hydraulic tracked excavator, the model 225, in 1972.

Caterpillar's first hydraulic excavator officially got its start in Research and Design in early 1969, when a full-size wooden mock-up, designated the X10, was shown to management to demonstrate the overall size and component planning of the project. By January 1970, the first full-size, 3/4-cubic-yard pilot unit, referred to as the 625X1, was put into iron. After this pilot model was approved, production of the hydraulic excavator program was transferred to the Aurora Assembly Plant in Illinois. Following further testing and design changes, such as relocating the operator's cab to the left side of

Caterpillar unveiled its very popular D400 series of 40-ton-capacity, articulated haulers in 1985, though the truck did carry the DJB name, but only briefly. The D400 was a permanent six-wheel-drive design, powered by a 385-flywheel-horsepower 3406 DITA diesel. The D400, when teamed with a Cat 245 excavator, was an unbeatable high-production match-up for its day. *Caterpillar*

The 625X1(shown in January 1970) was the pilot 3/4-cubic-yard Caterpillar hydraulic excavator. This model eventually formed the basis for the Model 225, after some design changes, such as the relocation of the operator's cab to the left side of the unit. *Larry Clancy Collection*

Released in 1973, the model 235 was the second hydraulic excavator to be offered by the company, after the introduction of the 225 in 1972. Like the 225, the 235 was completely designed and built by Caterpillar. *Caterpillar*

the machine, the new machine, named the model 225, was ready for full production in 1972.

The Caterpillar 225 excavator was 100 percent designed and built by the company. The 225 was powered by a Cat 3160 diesel, rated at 125 flywheel-horsepower. Machine travel was by hydrostatic drive. Average capacity range was from 1 to 1 3/8 cubic yards, depending on bucket size and material density. The 225 excavator was a good start for the company, which had more models nearing release.

The next hydraulic excavators to follow the model 225 were the 235 in 1973 and the big 245 in 1974. The 235 excavator was powered by a 195-flywheel-horsepower Cat 3306. Average capacity was right around 1 1/2 cubic yards. The larger 245 machine got its power from a Cat 3406 diesel, rated at 325 flywheel-horsepower. Bucket payload range was from 2 to 3 1/4 cubic yards.

On the opposite end of the product line from the 245 model series, Caterpillar introduced the smaller 215 excavator in 1976. Built in Belgium, the 215 was an 85-flywheel-horsepower machine with a 3/4-cubic-yard capacity.

To broaden the appeal of its larger hydraulic excavators, Caterpillar produced front shovel versions of the 235 and 245 model series. The 235 Front Shovel (FS) was introduced in 1978. Power was the same as in the standard version of the machine. Two bucket designs were offered. The front-dump design was rated at 3 cubic yards, while the bottom-dump version made do with 2.38 cubic yards. The larger model 245 FS shovel was first seen in 1976. Its capacity was 5 cubic yards for the front-dump bucket and 4 cubic yards for the bottom-dump version.

As imports of hydraulic excavators started to flood into Caterpillar's home market, especially from Japan, the company started to look for a way to bolster its offerings of this type of machine. The market was demanding smaller and more versatile hydraulic excavators. The worldwide recession in the early 1980s severely cut into Caterpillar's bottom line. To add smaller models quickly to its product line, Caterpillar formed a marketing agreement with Eder of Germany, a well-respected name in Europe in the production of highly productive and compact hydraulic excavators.

To further broaden its hydraulic excavator offerings in new market niches, Caterpillar built front shovel models from its largest machines, such as the 235 FS, which was introduced in 1978. This particular unit is equipped with a 3-cubic-yard front-dump bucket. A 2.38-cubic-yard bottom-dump bucket was the alternate choice. *Caterpillar*

Largest of the early Caterpillar hydraulic front shovels was the 245 FS, which was first seen in 1976. The 245 FS shown is loading a 35-ton capacity 769C hauler with a 4-cubic-yard bottom-dump bucket. Working weight of the excavator was 146,700 pounds. *Caterpillar*

The Mitsubishi-sourced Caterpillar E650, introduced in 1987, was the largest of all the E-series hydraulic excavators. The E650 was powered by a Mitsubishi S6B-TA diesel engine, rated at 375 flywheel-horsepower. Bucket capacity for the backhoe model was 3.9 cubic yards. A front shovel model was also offered with a 5-cubic-yard-capacity bucket. Working weight of the backhoe version was 140,238 pounds, while the front shovel weighed in at 142,200 pounds. *ECO Collection*

The DJB D550, the largest articulated hauler the company ever offered, was introduced in 1978, and like all DJB trucks, the drivetrain was completely Caterpillar sourced. The 3408 PCTA diesel engine produced 450 flywheel-horsepower. The powershift transmission came from the 988B program, while the two drive axles were from the 980B loader. Payload capacity was 55 tons. *ECO Collection*

The largest articulated hauler ever offered by Caterpillar, as of 1999, was the D550B, albeit briefly. Introduced in 1986 as an upgraded model of the D550, it was quietly removed from the product line in 1987 because of a lack of demand for an articulated 55-ton payload truck. The hauler was powered by a Cat 3408 diesel rated at 460 flywheel-horsepower, and was a six-wheel-drive layout, unlike the previous version, which had only four wheels driven. *ECO Collection*

Since its introduction in 1962, the dual-engined scrapers in Caterpillar's 657 series have been recognized as some of the finest large production scrapers ever built. The 657B model, which was introduced in 1969, features a power output of 950 flywheel-horsepower and a heaped payload capacity of 44 cubic yards. This machine, shown in July 1978, was a real money-making machine for contractors who used them. *Caterpillar*

In 1984, Caterpillar offered seven new models built by Eder to complement its larger machines. Tracked machines included the 205 LC, 211, and 213. Excavators mounted on wheeled chassis were the 206, 212, 214, and 224. These models basically filled the gaps in the product line in sizes smaller than the Cat 215 series.

Caterpillar further strengthened its position in the world excavator market in 1987, when it started to import hydraulic machines built by Mitsubishi of Japan. The close working relationship between the two companies actually dated back several years, when in 1962, to get around stringent Japanese import controls, Caterpillar announced that it was forming an equal-ownership manufacturing and marketing company with Mitsubishi Heavy Industries, Ltd., to be called Caterpillar Mitsubishi Ltd. Caterpillar products built in Japan included tracked dozers, and track and wheel loaders. The venture was fully implemented in 1963. In 1964 the company built its first factory in Sagamihara, which was not far from Tokyo. The first product built in the new plant, a D4 tractor, rolled off the assembly line in the spring of 1965. The partnership had been very successful for both companies, and in 1987, the joint venture was expanded to include hydraulic excavators, with the new name of the company to be called Shin Caterpillar Mitsubishi Ltd.

Caterpillar's global strategy for its excavator product line was now starting to fall into place. The company's venture in Japan made way for a flood of new models in 1987. The first of these imports, sometimes referred to as the E machines, were the E70, E110, E120, E140, E180, E240, E300, E450, and E650 series hydraulic excavators. In 1988 the E200B also joined the lineup.

In the earthmoving world, contractors were teaming up hydraulic excavators with a type of hauler known as an articulated truck. The combination of the two has replaced, in many instances, the need for self-propelled scrapers in certain working conditions. Articulated haul trucks go where other types of earthmoving equipment fear to tread. With their articulated steering chassis and all-wheel drive, they are practically unstoppable, even in muddy and wet conditions. Caterpillar did offer a type of articulated hauler in the 1950s and 1960s, utilizing one of its two- or four-wheel tractors attached to an Athey rocker rear-dump unit. But on steep grades, the performance of these haulers fell off dramatically because of the lack of all-wheel drive. Only the front wheels were powered.

The model 639D, released in 1979, was the most powerful of all the elevator-type loading scrapers offered by Caterpillar. The 700-flywheel-horsepower 639D was essentially a 633D with an extra engine in the rear, driving the scraper unit's wheels. Capacity for both models was 34 cubic yards heaped. Production on the 639D ended in 1984. *Caterpillar*

When the 50-ton-capacity model 773 hauler was introduced in 1970, it was only one of two trucks being offered by Caterpillar at the time. But the 773, with its D346 diesel pumping out 600 flywheel-horsepower, was an instant success. It would cement the company's position in the off-highway truck market once and for all as a true contender. *Caterpillar*

To increase the market share of its truck lines, Caterpillar offered tractor versions for pulling bottom-dump haulers. Shown is the 100-ton capacity 772 Coal Hauler, which was first released in 1974. The 772 tractor was based on the 773 hauler chassis, and it had the same engine and power ratings. The original 772 tractor was introduced in 1971. *Caterpillar*

Caterpillar entered the modern articulated haul truck market in a roundabout sort of way, when it agreed to provide complete drivetrains to an English company, DJB Engineering Ltd. Formed in August 1973, DJB Engineering Ltd. was founded by David John Bowes Brown in Peterlee, England, for the sole purpose of building articulated trucks. From the beginning, the DJB haulers incorporated Cat drivetrains, including engines, transmissions, and axles. In November 1974, the first DJB truck, the 27 1/2-ton-capacity D250, was unveiled. The DJB D250 was powered by a 235-flywheel-horsepower Cat 3306T diesel engine. Interest in the new truck was high and orders started to pour into the company. So big was demand that by September 1975, DJB Engineering had to move to larger facilities.

By June of 1976, a larger second model called the D300, rated with a 33-ton payload, was introduced. Even though these early trucks were designed by DJB, the souls of the trucks, their drivetrains, were Caterpillar iron through and through. Many Cat dealers carried the DJB line, since the drive components were fully warranted by Caterpillar. By the end of 1978, over 30 percent of all DJB trucks being built were coming to North America. In 1985, Caterpillar acquired the rights and designs for all of the articulated trucks built by DJB Engineering, though the haulers were still manufactured under contract in the United Kingdom. It was at this time that the DJB company name was dropped and changed to Artix Ltd. Finally, in early 1996, Caterpillar bought the manufacturing company, now referred to as Brown Group Holdings, which included all of the facilities and property in Peterlee. This acquisition made everything involved with the production and building of articulated trucks 100 percent Caterpillar.

Numerous models and variations of these articulated haulers have been built over the years. These include two-axle, two-wheel-drive; two-axle, four-wheel-drive; three-axle, four-wheel-drive; and three-axle, six-wheel-drive models. Some of the key model introductions included the two-axle D20D in 1992, the D22 and D25 in 1979, the D30C in 1985, the D35 in 1981, and the D40D in 1988. Three-axle versions included the D275, D330, and D350, all in 1978, and the D300B and D400, both in 1985. The largest models built were the two-axle DJB D44 in 1980 and the three-axle DJB D550 in 1978. The 44-ton-capacity D44 utilized a four-wheel-drive system. But the 55-ton payload D550 six-wheeled models were powered on the first two axles only, with the rear axle nonpowered. In 1986 both models were upgraded into the D44B and D550B. In the case of the D550B, the upgrade brought power to all six wheels. But the market for articulated trucks in this size range was not developing the way Caterpillar had hoped it would. By the end of 1987, both models were quietly removed from the product line.

Some of the other new product lines that first saw the light of day for Caterpillar in the 1970s and 1980s were backhoe tractor loaders in 1985; rubber-tired wheel skidders in 1971; logging and forest product machines in 1983; integrated tool carriers in 1984; and a host of paving products in 1985 that included cold planers, reclaimers and stabilizers, mixers, slipform pavers, asphalt pavers, and vibratory compactors.

The company hit a grand slam when it unveiled its first production 777 hauler in 1974. Rated at 85 tons, it quickly become the industry standard for this class size of haulers. Key features of the 777 were its powerful 870-flywheel-horsepower D348 diesel engine, oil-cooled disc brakes, and squared-off radiator and front decking design. The prototype 777 is shown undergoing final testing at the Cat Arizona Proving Grounds in January 1974. *Caterpillar*

For large coal mining operations, Caterpillar offered the 150-ton capacity 776 Coal Hauler in 1976. The 776 tractor was based on the chassis and the drivetrain of the 777. The bottom-dump was designed by Caterpillar, with the actual fabrication being handled by WOTCO, who also built the 100-ton-capacity trailer of the 772 Coal Hauler. *ECO Collection*

107

THE ESTABLISHED LINES

The company's core earthmoving product lines of the 1970s and 1980s also saw substantial increases in introductions of all-new model variations.

Caterpillar made significant changes in its scraper lines, eliminating all of its two-axle, four-wheel tractor scraper models by early 1979. The company also pulled the plug on its towed scraper units. The largest of all the track-type tractor-towed scrapers was the Model 491C, rated at 27 cubic yards struck and 35 heaped. It was phased out in 1970. The No. 60, which had been in the product line since 1952, finally was retired in 1972, making it the longest-running Cat towed scraper model type to remain in continuous production. The last model built, the 435G, built by Caterpillar in the United Kingdom, brought the entire towed scraper product line to a close in 1973.

On a happier note, new self-propelled scrapers, especially of the elevator type, were now being offered by Caterpillar in a wide variety of capacities and power outputs. For a standard type of loading scraper, the twin-powered model 637 from 1970 was a real standout performer. Powered by a Cat D343 diesel, rated at 415 flywheel-horsepower in the tractor, and a D333 in the rear scraper, with an output of 225 flywheel-horsepower, the 637 was capable of a combined 640 flywheel-horsepower. Capacity was 21 cubic yards struck and 30 heaped. The 637 was the perfect machine for midsized to large earthmoving jobs. In 1975 the model would become the 637D, with an increase in power to 705 flywheel-horsepower combined from a new Cat 3408 diesel in the tractor and a 3306 in the scraper. By 1985 it had become the 637E, with slightly revised lower power figures of 700 flywheel-horsepower.

Caterpillar launched three new model types of elevating scrapers during this period. The smallest was the 16-cubic-yard-capacity model 615 in 1982. In the middle was the model 623 in 1972. The 22-cubic-yard 623 was powered by a 300-flywheel-horsepower rated Cat D336 diesel. But in 1973, the scraper was quickly upgraded into the Model 623B, which was now powered by the Cat 3406, rated at 330 flywheel-horsepower. The largest of the elevating machines was the model 639D, which made the lineup in 1979. The 639D carried the same payload capacity, 34 cubic yards heaped, as did the 633D. But the 639D was a twin-powered scraper, with a Cat 3408 diesel in the nose, rated at 450 flywheel-horsepower, and a 250 flywheel-horsepower 3306 engine in the tail. With 700 flywheel-horsepower on tap, the 639D was the most powerful self-loading elevating type scraper the company would ever make as a full-production unit. But the 639D never quite found its niche in the marketplace. The scraper ended production in 1984, at the height of the worldwide recession, due to lack of demand.

Hauling units also made a good showing for the company, and many important introductions significantly opened up new markets for Caterpillar trucks. After the misstep of the electric-drive hauler program, the company got back on track in early 1970, with the release of the 50-ton-capacity 773.

The very popular 992 wheel loader was upgraded into the 992B model series in 1973. The powertrain and power output were the same as the previous model, though capacity increased to 10 cubic yards. The most notable exterior difference between the two models was the 992B's pin-on ROPS cab, which had a very distinctive rear slope to it. *Caterpillar*

The Caterpillar 992C is probably the greatest large-capacity wheel loader ever built. The much larger and more powerful 992C replaced the B model in late 1977. The 690-flywheel-horsepower 992C weighed in at 199,260 pounds, while the old B model tipped the scales at only 135,300 pounds. *Caterpillar*

The introduction of the 773 was delayed somewhat because of the large amount of resources that were being poured into the 779 project. Once that program was terminated, the full attention of the company's hauling group engineers could be brought to bear on the 50-ton-capacity truck program. The 773 was powered by the field-proven D346, with a solid 600 flywheel-horsepower output. The 773 looked much like its little brother, the 769B, only larger. In 1978 the truck became the 773B. This model version was now powered by the Cat 3412 diesel, rated at 650 flywheel-horsepower. In the new design, the rounded sheet-metal nose of the previous truck was gone. Now a squared off radiator housing design was introduced, along with an entirely new cab.

Caterpillar finally released a truck in 1974 that filled the void in its product line left by the cancellation of the 779 hauler. That truck, the 777, was a real success for Caterpillar. With a rated payload capacity of 85 tons, it was just what the marketplace was looking for. With a Cat D348 diesel pumping out 870 flywheel-horsepower, the truck was as bulletproof as you could get. The 777 was also the first Cat hauler to be released with the squared-off front-end treatment. This design approach has proven so well thought out that it still serves as the basic look for all Cat haulers today. In 1985 the model finally became a "B" series with the introduction of the 777B. New to this model was the use of the Cat 3508 diesel. Power output remained unchanged, but maximum capacity was now raised to 95 tons.

During the 1970s, Caterpillar complemented its off-highway hauler offerings by introducing a series of tractors for coal and earth hauling. These models were based on current rear-dump units, minus their dump bodies and associated hardware. In their place would be a full set of rear fenders and a fifth wheel for the attachment of a trailer. These models included the 768B and the 772 in 1971. In 1974 the 772 Coal Hauler tractor/trailer model was introduced with a 100-ton capacity. This was followed by the 776 Coal Hauler in 1976, which was capable of hauling 150 tons in its bottom-dump trailer.

The wheel loader models offered by Caterpillar during this time were numerous. Just about any size or power output machine required for a customer's particular job was available. From the small to the large, Cat had the wheel loader for you. Caterpillar's two largest mining offerings, the 988 and 992, were due for some serious makeovers. The classic 988, the company's first articulated steering loader, became the 988B in 1976. This new model now was powered by a Cat 3408 diesel, rated at 375 flywheel-horsepower. The 988B was also equipped with an entirely redesigned front end, including lift arms and new Z-bar loader linkage, which allowed for faster and fuller bucket loads. This was a good thing, since capacity was now up to 7 cubic yards.

Caterpillar breathed some new life into the 992 loader program in 1973, when it became a "B" model series. The 992B contained numerous mechanical changes aimed at increasing the reliability and productivity of the machine.

The powerplant and the horsepower output were unchanged from the previous 992 model, but capacity was now up to 10 cubic yards. New for this loader was a pin-on ROPS cab, which protected the operator in the event of a rollover accident. For the really big mining jobs, you wouldn't have to go looking any further than the 992C, which replaced the 992B in late 1977. The 992C was a very muscular mining loader. From any angle, the 992C looked like it meant business. Power and productivity were what this giant was all about. In the rear beat the heart of a V-12 Cat 3412 diesel, rated at 690 flywheel-horsepower. This extra power came in handy, since the loader's capacity had also risen, to 12.5 cubic yards. This was due in part to the redesigned lift arms, which included the use of Z-bar loader linkage design. By 1982 an updated series of the

Caterpillar replaced its popular 983B track loader in 1982 with the newly designed 973 hydrostatic drive model series. The 973 loader's 210-flywheel-horsepower Cat 3306 diesel is mounted in the rear of the unit for better weight distribution. Standard bucket capacity is 3.75 cubic yards. A 973 equipped with the optional "steel mill" extreme service package for working with hot slag is fitted to the machine. *Caterpillar*

The D7G series, first released in 1975, was the last of the D7 model dozers designed with conventional track drive. The D7G's Cat 3306 diesel produced 200 flywheel-horsepower. Other variations of the dozer included the D7G LGP in 1976 and the D7G SA in 1981. Even though Cat introduced an elevated track drive D7H in 1985, an imported version of the D7G model was still offered as of 1999. *Urs Peyer*

992C was released with an increase in capacity to 13.5 cubic yards. How good was the 992C? By the time the model was finally replaced by the redesigned 992D in 1992, over 2,500 units of the C model had been put into service worldwide, making it the best-selling large mining loader of all time.

The track-loader product line would go through some radical changes in the 1970s. Caterpillar started to introduce all-new, redesigned models in 1980, when it introduced the hydrostatic drive model 943. The 943 was the first of a new

The Caterpillar D9L, with its the elevated track drive, was the replacement for the legendary D9H dozer. However, the company left the conventional track drive model in the product line for one more year, just in case. The 1980 D9L was powered by a 460-flywheel-horsepower Cat 3412 diesel that evolved into the D10N model series by 1987. *Caterpillar*

Introduced in 1977, the Caterpillar D6D SA "Special Application" agricultural tractor proved to be a very popular model, especially in the western United States. Power for the tractor was supplied by the Cat 3306 diesel that generated at 125 drawbar-horsepower. The D6D SA tractor also formed the basis for two special units built to field test the future Mobil-trac System for the Challenger program. *Caterpillar*

generation of Z-bar bucket linkage track-loaders that featured hydrostatic drive and had their engines mounted in the rear for better operator vision and an overall greater machine balance. The concept of a rear-engined track-loader was nothing new for the company. Back in the mid-1960s, the original concept designs of the large 983 track-loader called for a rear-mounted engine. But management at the time thought the unit would stand out too much from the rest of the product line. It decided to keep all of the loader designs uniform, so the rear-engined concept was shelved temporarily. When it came time to revamp the entire line, the company revisited the rear-engine layout. Other models to follow the 943 were the 953 and 963 loaders in 1981, followed by the largest hydrostatic drive model, the 973, in 1982. The 973 was the replacement for the largest conventional front-engined track-loader built by Caterpillar, the 983B, which had been available since 1978.

The company had put a lot of thought and resources into improving and expanding all of its offerings during the late 1970s and 1980s, but nowhere were these efforts more noticeable than with the core business product line, the track-type tractors. As discussed in the previous chapter, the introduction of the elevated sprocket design on the gigantic D10 in 1977 turned the industry upside down. But Caterpillar was not going to stop there. More new models were to follow that would incorporate this revolutionary drive system, not just for the largest machines, but also for some of the smallest too.

After the introduction of the D10, the next new model to receive the elevated drive sprocket was the D9L in 1980. The D9L, with its 460 flywheel-horsepower, for the most part took the place of the very popular D9H series, even though that model was left in the product line

until 1981. This was done as a precautionary tactic just in case customers were not willing to give the elevated drive design a chance. In that event, Cat could still fall back on the conventional drive D9H. But these fears never materialized and the D9L was an instant hit. Next to follow the D9L was the D8L in late 1981. Rated at 335 flywheel-horsepower, it was the replacement for the D8K in North America. Other elevated-drive models to follow in the footsteps of the larger machines were the D4H, D5H, D6H, and D7H, all in 1985.

Caterpillar made a little more of its own personal history in 1972 when it introduced the D3. A conventional drive design, the model is significant in the fact that was the first time the company had issued the D3 designation to a tractor.

In 1987, not long after the launch of the D11N, Caterpillar released the rest of its larger N series dozers. The D8L was upgraded into the D9N, and the D9L was transformed into the D10N. This followed the same pattern as when the D10 was turned into the D11N in 1986. To fill the void in the dozer lineup left by the replacement of the D8L, a new D8N model was introduced.

During this time, there were dozens and dozens of various track-type tractor models built by Caterpillar in its factories around the world. This included plants in the United States, the United Kingdom, Japan, Australia, France, Brazil, Mexico, and Indonesia. Some of these units were imported into the United States, while others were used in each country's own domestic market or related territories. As for the larger mining machines, such as all of the D9, D10, and D11 series tractors, these have always been built exclusively at Caterpillar's East Peoria Assembly Plant in Illinois.

In 1986, Caterpillar introduced a special agricultural tractor called the AG6. With a longer main frame, 20-inch longer track roller frames, a fuel tank and an operator's cab repositioned 38 inches farther forward, this specialized tillage tractor was better balanced than the D6D SA. Other features included a VHP Variable Horsepower Cat 3306 diesel, rated at 200 flywheel-horsepower in gears 1 and 2, and 240 flywheel-horsepower in gears 3 through 5. An AG4 model was also briefly offered in 1986, but was soon dropped, with only seven listed as being built. The AG6 was withdrawn from the product line in 1993. *Caterpillar*

9

BACK TO THE FIELDS

MODERN AGRICULTURAL MTS TRACTORS

It would seem to many that from the late 1940s to the 1970s, Caterpillar downplayed the significance of the agricultural market to the company's overall bottom line. And to some extent, this was true. After World War II, the shift to earthmoving equipment for construction and mining was quite dramatic. Yes, the company did field the Special Application crawler tractors marketed especially for farming use in the 1960s and 1970s. The Cat SA tractors were well received in the western United States but made little impact elsewhere. But in the overall scheme of things, the builders of rubber-tired tractors were the clear and dominate choice down on the farm.

During the 1970s, Caterpillar started to take on a whole new attitude concerning the agricultural side of its business. Starting in early 1974, a group of engineers at Caterpillar's Vehicle Engineering, located at its Tech Center in Mossville, Illinois, was given the go-ahead to do initial concept research on a Cat-designed rubber-tired agricultural tractor. But in 1975, just as the new program was getting started, the entire project was put on hold.

In 1977 the rubber-tired ag tractor project was revived again by Vehicle Engineering. It gave management a series of concept designs and received approval in July 1977 to proceed to a full-size prototype. It was also felt that the design and buildup of the tractor should be moved to the Aurora, Illinois, plant, because of the expertise there in articulated wheel loader design production. By late 1979, the first prototype rubber-tired Cat 4x4 Ag Tractor, X-1, was ready for field testing.

The Cat 4x4 Ag Tractor utilized dual rubber-tired wheels at all four corners, all driven. The tractor steered by means of an articulated chassis. Painted in Cat yellow, it was a very modern-looking design. But early testing soon showed the areas in which design improvements would have to be

In 1997, Caterpillar introduced its wide-track Row-Crop Challenger tractors into the marketplace. Offered in Challenger 35, 45, and 55 model versions, these tractors come with a standard track base width of 80 inches, which is expandable to 120 inches. This setup provides superior turning ability under load and allows custom setting of the tracks to specific row crop widths. Standard Row-Crop Challengers base setting is 60 inches, which is expandable to 80 inches. *Caterpillar*

The Caterpillar Challenger 65 was a very innovative tractor in the farming industry when it was officially launched in late 1986. The Mobil-trac System, or "MTS" as it is more commonly known, produced far less ground compaction than comparable rubber-tired machines. The tractor shown is one of the early preproduction field-follow units, undergoing testing in December 1985. It was the design that would go into full production. *Caterpillar*

Caterpillar first considered producing an articulated, rubber-tired agricultural tractor in the late 1970s and early 1980s. This program eventually merged with the rubber-belted track concept that was being worked on by a separate engineering team. Pictured is the first Experimental 4x4 Ag Tractor X-1 in late 1979. *Larry Clancy Collection*

made. The 4x4 X-1 was just too heavy. It was also designed with front-axle oscillation, which proved to be too unstable in turns on uneven ground. To top it off, the X-1 was too expensive to build.

Cat engineers rolled up their sleeves, and by late 1980, unveiled the next step in the life of the project, the X-2 4x4 Ag Tractor. Sharing the same wheel, tire, and steering design layout, the X-2 looked much like the X-1, only painted silver this time. The second prototype utilized rear-axle oscillation, which greatly improved its handling characteristics. Also, the main articulated frame was of a much lighter and simplified design. Ground clearance was also increased for row crop purposes. Testing commenced on the X-2 ag prototype in March 1981 in California.

At this same time within the company, another parallel design program was under way investigating the merits of building a tractor with rubber tracks instead of tires. This program had started in late 1979, with the modification of a Cat D4E SA tractor, which had been equipped with a 240-flywheel-horsepower Cat 3306 diesel, mated to a Fuller 12-speed truck transmission. The purpose of the exercise was to test different powertrain combinations for agricultural tractor development use. While this testing was under way, another program was testing the feasibility of a rubber-tracked undercarriage for tractor use. These tests were performed in 1980 on a specially designed test unit simply referred to as the BTTB (Belt Track Test Bed). This test unit was built out of the rear end of a Cat 130G motor grader and was eventually tested with various rubber belt-drive layouts. In 1981 both of these programs came together to form a test unit referred to as the BAT mobile. The BAT (Belted Ag Tractor) was built out of the special test D4E SA unit, now equipped with a rubber-belted undercarriage and special bodywork painted red, yellow, and black. From a distance, it somewhat resembled a "Versatile" tractor, which was the whole point. Caterpillar wanted to draw as little attention to the BAT test mule as possible when testing it in actual field conditions. The BAT's main purpose was to test various engine, transmission, and undercarriage designs for possible use in an agricultural tractor.

After reviewing the BAT rubber-tracked program, Caterpillar management decided to merge the 4X4 Ag Tractor program with the BAT project to form one cohesive design team, whose sole purpose was to build a rubber-tracked ag tractor.

Following in the footsteps of the initial BAT prototype were two specially converted D6D SA tractors equipped with rubber-belted track undercarriages. Conversions started on these tractors in July 1983. These two test units (Cat Proving Ground Numbers 1A8070 and 1A8071) performed the bulk of the field and proving ground testing needed to bring the tractor concept up to preproduction status. Thousands of hours of testing were put on both units, both in controlled proving ground testing and in actual field use, especially in the western part of the United States. Various wheel bogie and track designs were tried in the quest for the most durable and functional combination, one that could stand up to the demands of heavy farming. Even after the Challenger design had been finalized, both of these units continued in service until 1987, at which time they were retired from testing duties.

In February 1984, the first rubber-belted tractor built

In late 1980, the second rubber-tired unit, identified as Experimental 4x4 Ag Tractor X-2, addressed many of the design shortcomings found in the original prototype. The silver 4x4 Ag X-2 is pictured here conducting tests pulling twin scrapers involved in laser-guided leveling of farm land near Bakersfield, California, in March 1981. *Caterpillar*

The first true test prototype to utilize rubber-belt friction drive in real-life field working conditions was the Belted Ag Tractor. More commonly referred to as the "BAT" mobile, it was built in 1981, after starting life in 1979 as a Caterpillar D4E SA tractor. It was painted in camouflaged colors of red, black, and yellow to give the impression of a "Versatile" brand tractor from a distance. *Caterpillar*

The first test tractor prototypes built after the engineering teams of the 4x4 Ag Tractor group were combined with the Rubber-Belted Drive project were the two heavily modified Cat D6D SA tractors from 1983. Equipped with MTS undercarriages, they performed most of the program's field testing, at both the Peoria and Arizona Proving Grounds, as well as farm locations throughout the United States. *John F. Cooper Collection*

115

The Belt Track Test Bed, or "BTTB" for short, was originally built out of a Model 130G motor grader at the Cat Decatur Assembly Plant in 1980. Its main purpose was to test different configurations of wheel arrangements for the rubber-belted test program. The design's wheel configurations consisted of two four-wheel layout designs, one three-wheel, one six-wheel, and one seven-wheel hi-drive setup pictured. All were built on the same 130G rear motor grader chassis. *Caterpillar*

The first pilot Challenger 855X1 tractor, test unit 1A8106, is pictured in February 1984. At this point in the design phase, the new ag tractor with MTS is starting to reach its final form. Note the front headlights in the lower frame area. These were a carryover from the 4x4 ag tractor concepts and also showed up on pilot 855X2, test unit 1A8116. They were eliminated in the pilot X3 and X4 prototypes, which looked pretty much like a production Challenger 65. *Altorfer, Inc. Collection*

from the ground up, to be referred to as the Challenger, was the 855 X-1. This was followed by the 855 X-2 a few weeks later. At this stage in the design process, the overall look was now taking on final shape. The rubber-belted undercarriage was also approaching its final design form. It is interesting to note that while these early Challenger prototypes were being built and tested, the rubber-tracked system was being considered by another Caterpillar engineering group for use on the Hard Mobile Launcher, better known as the HML (see last chapter, military machines).

While the field testing of the preproduction Challengers was under way, Caterpillar engineers built another rubber-belted tractor in 1986 called the Super BAT. The Super BAT was a highly modified D3B LGP-S crawler tractor, fitted with super low ground compaction rubber belts. The Super BAT, which was originally tested in 1985 with steel tracks, was built strictly for information gathering testing purposes, with only one ever produced.

By late 1985, preproduction Challenger tractors were being field tested all over the United States, with a heavy concentration of machines on the West Coast. Now referred to as the Challenger 65, the model officially was introduced by Caterpillar in late 1986, with full production commencing in 1987. The Challenger 65 was the industry's first full-production, large farming tractor to be totally designed around a rubber-belted track undercarriage, referred to by Cat as the Mobil-trac System (MTS). The MTS consisted of continuous rubber belts, reinforced with four layers of flexible steel cable, driven by the friction between the rear wheels with two-inch rubber rims bonded to them, and the belt itself. The benefits of this system included a high ground contact area, which reduced ground compaction immensely. The bogie-mounted midrollers, cushioned by an air suspension, allowed the Challenger to literally float over uneven field conditions, while increasing traction at the same time with far less slippage as compared to a rubber-tired machine.

Supplying power to the Challenger drive system was a Cat 3306 turbocharged and aftercooled, six-cylinder diesel engine, rated at 270 gross horsepower and 256 flywheel-horsepower. This was connected to a full power-shift, direct-drive transmission, with the choice of 10 tillage and transport gear speeds. Between the ideal tillage speed range of 4 to 7 miles per hour, the transmission offered six closely spaced gears to match to any field working conditions. The Challenger was equipped with a steering wheel, which, when turned, would engage a hydrostatic pump and motor that would deliver power to a steering differential that changed the speed of each belt. The more the wheel was turned, the greater the speed difference produced between the two drive belts. This enabled the Challenger to turn in its own length if desired, without pulling an implement, of course. For its day, the Challenger 65 was the state-of-the-art for a rubber-belted ag tractor.

The Challenger 65 was not without some growing pains out in the field. Reliability of the drive system was in question on some of the earlier machines placed in the marketplace. But

Caterpillar stood behind each machine sold and corrected all of the early design problemsflfrom increasing the tension of the friction belt drive, beefing up the bearings, changing belts—you name it. Cat was going to make each and every customer happy about the purchase of a Challenger. They had to be. The entire program depended on it. The competition would seize upon any weakness in the Cat product, and spread the word overnight as to the tractor's shortcomings. The company had to act quickly at all times to maintain customer loyalty, something that Caterpillar cherished most dearly.

In late 1990, Caterpillar introduced an upgraded model of the original Challenger in the form of the 65B, as well as an entirely new one, identified as the 75. The Challenger 65B was basically the same as its predecessor, except with many system improvements to increase reliability, and a Cat 3306 DITA diesel with increased power output of 285 gross horsepower. The Challenger 75 was essentially the 65B model with a more powerful Cat 3176 ATAAC diesel engine, rated at 325 gross horsepower.

Both of these models were once again upgraded in late 1992. The Challenger 65C and the 75C were almost identical to their predecessors, except for the design of the front wheels on the MTS. Gone were the tires mounted on steel rims. In their place were steel wheels, wrapped with grooved rubber belts.

Caterpillar added two more model lines to the Challenger lineup in 1993, with the 70C and the 85C. The 70C

Pictured in 1999 is the only surviving Challenger prototype D6D SA test tractor, unit 1A8070. It was purchased by a Caterpillar dealer, Ziegler, Inc., of Minneapolis, Minnesota, from the Peoria Proving Grounds inventory in 1993. The wheel bogies were missing from this unit because they were used in other research areas concerning the MTS testing program. This tractor's companion, 1A8071, which spent a large amount of its life at the Arizona Proving Grounds, was scrapped. *ECO*

THE MILITARY CHALLENGER

It's not surprising that a highly mobile tractor like the Challenger would somehow find a way to serve its country. The military had taken a keen interest in the Caterpillar's MTS, but it would take some years before a tractor unit would become fully operational in the armed services.

Caterpillar's first efforts to interest the military in a Challenger-type tractor began in 1986. The company surveyed Army engineers as to what they would like to see in future crawler tractor designs. The majority of the suggestions revolved around increased mobility, without losing any dozing ability. The tractor would also have to be within the transport capabilities of the C-130 aircraft. Based on these and other comments, Caterpillar initiated an internally funded design program in early 1987 to make such a tractor a reality. In 1988 the experimental unit was introduced as the Caterpillar 30/30 Engineer Support Tractor.

The 30/30 Engineer Support Tractor was designed strictly for military use. The 30/30 nomenclature stood for the original performance and design criteria targeted by the engineers— top speed of 30 miles per hour and weight at about 30,000 pounds. Even though it employed the MTS, it was reconfigured for the types of terrain a vehicle of this sort would encounter. The rear-drive wheels for the MTS were mounted high off the ground to keep them from being buried in mud and debris. This would also increase the drive system's longevity. The 30/30 was powered by a single Cat 3208, eight-cylinder diesel

engine, with two operating power modes. In the "travel" setting, the engine output was rated at 240 flywheel-horsepower, which would give the unit a top speed of 33 miles per hour forward, and 14 miles per hour in reverse. In the "work" mode, 170 flywheel-horsepower was available for dozing work with the unit's standard power angle tilt blade. The environmentally controlled operator's cab, with bullet-resistant laminated glass, was mounted in the front of the tractor, with the engine in the rear.

To keep costs in line during the developmental stages of the program, components systems from many current product machine lines were utilized. The rear differential steer unit was from the D8N track-type tractor; the fan and radiator, transmission, and torque converter were sourced from the 615 scraper; while the cab was a modified version from the 936 wheel loader program.

The 30/30 made the rounds of various military bases around the United States, and was also tested by the French and British armies. Because of budget cutbacks, however, Caterpillar never received a firm order for any production units. Only one 30/30 was ever built.

In April 1996, working directly with the military's Tank-Automotive and Armaments Command (TACOM), Caterpillar once again introduced two revised preproduction examples of an MTS tractor. The company called the tractor the Deployable Universal Combat Earthmover, more commonly referred to as the "DEUCE." The DEUCE program officially got its start in 1993 as an Army program

The Caterpillar 30/30 Engineer Support Tractor was the company's first effort at producing a mobile MTS dozer. Built in 1988, it was capable of being air-transported in a C-130, and it made the rounds to various military units for testing over the next several years. The nomenclature of the tractor represented the target design criteria of the program, 30 miles per hour and 30,000 pounds. But in the end, the 30/30 would never go into production. Only one 30/30 was ever built. *Caterpillar*

Caterpillar received another chance at building a highly mobile MTS military tractor in April 1996, when it unveiled its Deployable Universal Combat Earthmover, better known as the "DEUCE." Based heavily on the previous 30/30 design, the DEUCE was an extremely tough machine. From the start of testing, the DEUCE was a real powerhouse—so much so, in fact, that the company was awarded a production contract from the U.S. government in August 1996, for deliveries starting in 1997. *Caterpillar*

with the U.S. Army Engineer School (USAES). USAES started working with TACOM on ways to field the DEUCE tractor quickly. Several manufacturers expressed interest in the program, but in 1995, Caterpillar got the go ahead for its design, which was based heavily on the 30/30 experimental unit.

The Caterpillar DEUCE looked much like the original 30/30, only a bit meaner looking. The DEUCE was powered by a Cat 3126 diesel engine. As with the 30/30, two power modes are available—a 265-flywheel-horsepower "self-deployable" setting, and a 185-flywheel-horsepower setting for "earthmoving." The tractor could also be air transported and dropped from a C-130.

After successful testing of the two preproduction units, Caterpillar was awarded a production contract for the DEUCE in August 1996, for deliveries to commence in 1997. The first production DEUCEs began rolling off the line at Cat's Paving Products, Inc., plant, in Minneapolis, Minnesota, on September 9, 1997. (Regular Challenger tractors are built in DeKalb, Illinois.) The first four production units were tested by the Army and Caterpillar in early 1998. These tractors were the first 4 of a 36-unit DEUCE order placed by the U.S. Army. One additional unit was also shipped off for evaluations by the Canadian Army in early 1998.

The design of the MTS drive layout on the DEUCE was similar to the previous 30/30, in that the rear drive sprocket was elevated to keep it out of harm's way. This gave the unit tremendous maneuverability in deep mud, whether going forward or in reverse. Two power modes could be selected by the operator— 265 flywheel-horsepower for "self-deployable" and 185 flywheel-horsepower for "earthmoving." Digging capacity of the tractor is equal to that of a D5B. Top speed is 33 miles per hour. *Caterpillar*

carried the same operating specifications as the 65C, except that the 70C had special engine and transmission modifications that let first gear become a working gear for scraper and land leveling work. The 70C also had wider track widths, again for extra traction when pulling a scraper. The 85C was basically a 75C with a bigger 355-gross horsepower punch in gears 3 through 10.

In 1994 the company introduced the first of the new D-series Challengers in the form of the 65D. This was followed in 1996 by the 75D and 85D. The 70C model did not make it to a D-series, with its production run ending in 1995. The D-series Challengers were much like their predecessors, except with more power all around. The 65D was now rated at 300 gross horsepower, the 75D carried 330 gross horsepower, and the 85D boasted 370 gross horsepower.

Just when the market was getting used to the D Challengers, Caterpillar surprised everyone again with the release of all-new models in the fall of 1997. The new E series marked the first time in the life of the model line in which major changes were made to the appearance of the Challengers. The old body styles were nice, but these new designs, with their rounded edges and curves, were extremely modern and up-to-date in terms of styling. The new series included the 65E, the 75E, the 85E, and an all-new 95E model line. All models shared the same basic chassis design. Where they differed was in the drivetrains. The 65E utilized the Cat 3176C diesel, rated at 310 gross horsepower, while the 75E used an enhanced version of the same engine, producing 340 gross horsepower. Both the 85E and the 95E were powered by the Cat 3196C diesel engine, but once again with higher power in the latter model. The 85E was rated at 375 gross horsepower, while the 95E had a very

impressive output of 410 gross horsepower to work with. The 95E is the first Challenger to break the 400 horsepower barrier in the model line. With this much muscle, the 95E can take on the largest agricultural work without reaching its limits. In the marketplace, the 95E is definitely the top dog down on the farm.

THE ROW-CROP CHALLENGERS

In 1994, Caterpillar broadened its Challenger lineup with the introduction of a series of smaller Mobil-trac ag tractors referred to as "Row-Crop" Challengers. These tractors featured a MTS quite different in design from that of their larger brothers. The smaller tractors featured very large-diameter rear-drive wheels, which provided the tractor with 18.9 inches of crop clearance when working in 30-inch rows. Also of great importance was the tractor's use of a full range, powershift transmission, with 16 evenly spaced forward speeds and 9 reverse. The look of the tractors was also very impressive and would be the first hint as to what styling changes would show up on the bigger E series in 1997.

Between 1991 and 1992, Caterpillar designed and built three test tractor chassis utilizing the large-diameter drive wheel concept. Early tests were very encouraging—so much so, the tractor was given the go-ahead to proceed to preproduction status. By June 1993, the company unveiled the first preproduction model design as the Challenger 55. Even though the 55 was the first to reach preproduction build, it was not officially released for sale until 1995. The first two models officially introduced in 1994 were the Challenger 35 and 45 tractor lines. The Row-Crop Challenger 35 and 45 were both powered by the same Cat 3116 diesel engine. The 35 was rated with 150 drawbar-horsepower, while the 45 had just a bit more power on hand, with 170 drawbar-horse-power available. When the model 55 was finally introduced, it carried a much more powerful Cat 3126 diesel under the hood, which kicked out a healthy 191 drawbar-horsepower. Like the larger Challengers, the smaller Row-Crop tractors utilized the same basic chassis and body styles, but differed in their drivetrain setups.

In 1997 the company introduced a new wide-track feature to the Row-Crop Challenger product line. This enabled the wide-track tractor's base width of 80 inches to be increased to a maximum of 120 inches. For comparison, the standard chassis on the 35, 45, and 55 models is a 60-inch base width, which is expandable to 90 inches. With the two chassis available for the Row-Crop tractors, customers could custom match the tracks to Row-Crop width for cultivation, planting, or tillage. Spacing could also be set to follow the same path as grain carts, sprayers, or combines.

The smaller Challengers, along with their larger brethren, are some of the most sophisticated ag tractors available to the farmer and contractor alike. The Cat MTS has proven itself every bit as tough as its rubber-tired competition, whose manufacturers have been perfecting that technology literally for decades. For Caterpillar engineers to take a revolutionary drive concept from the 1980s and have it basically perfected by the 1990s is a tribute to the company's engineering might. Its efficiency in bringing this new design to market has inspired imitators. John Deere, the largest of the rubber-tired tractor manufacturers, has realized the design merits of low ground compaction, rubber-belted, friction-drive systems for ag use. In late 1997, that company unveiled the first of its new line of rubber-belted ag tractors into the marketplace. And as we all know, imitation is the sincerest form of flattery.

Caterpillar introduced its new line of Challenger Row-Crop tractors in 1994 with the models 35 and 45, followed by the Model 55 in 1995. Its MTS features 58-inch-diameter drive wheels that provide 18.9 inches of clearance over 30-inch rows. The first preproduction Row-Crop Challenger is shown in June 1993, and it happens to be a model 55. Even though the 55 was the first one built, it would be the last one officially introduced. *Caterpillar*

As of year 2000, the Model 95E was the most powerful Challenger ever offered by Caterpillar. Introduced in the fall of 1997, it has 410 gross horsepower on hand from its six-cylinder Cat 3196C diesel. The 95E has some pretty serious muscle to overcome the most demanding agricultural jobs. All of the E-series Challengers look virtually identical, except for their nomenclature. The difference is their powertrain setups, which are unique to each individual model line. *ECO*

121

10

WHEN SIZE MATTERS

**MAMMOTH MINING
EQUIPMENT**

For decades, Caterpillar equipment has played an important part in the success and overall productivity of large mining and quarry operations the world over. Caterpillar wrote the book on large crawler dozer utilization, with such standout performers as the D9 and D10 series bulldozers. But in the realm of the really, really big machines, such as the haulers and wheel loaders, other companies produced much larger equipment offerings.

Established manufacturers such as Euclid, Unit Rig, WABCO, and Terex all made larger rear-dump trucks than Caterpillar in the 1970s. The Cat offerings in the under 100-ton class were some of the best in the world. But in the over 100-ton market, Cat had nothing. The advantage that these competitive haulers had over Cat at the time was their diesel-electric drivetrains. All of Caterpillar's hauler designs were of a mechanical-drive design, that is, they utilized a diesel engine, a transmission, a driveshaft, and a rear-axle differential. The diesel-electric drives did away with everything but the engine. In their place were generators and electric wheel motors, mounted in the axle, or in the wheel hub assemblies themselves. Cat had gone down that road once before in the 1960s, and was not about to make the same mistakes twice. If the company was going to make a larger mining truck, it was going to have a mechanical drivetrain layout.

In the early 1980s, Caterpillar started to design larger haulers in some of the most popular tonnage categories, with proven market demand. The company was not about to make any rash moves, such as building a truck that was too large for the industry, as Terex had with its 350-ton-capacity 33-19 Titan in 1974, of which only one was built. No, Caterpillar would take a meticulous and methodical approach with its larger trucks, releasing them only after thousands of hours of proving ground testing, and then releasing them one by one, slowly chipping away at a competitor's market share. The company needed to be careful in the early 1980s. Money was tight and

As of 2000, the Caterpillar 24H is the world's largest motor grader available to the mining industry. Officially released for sale in the spring of 1996, the 24H was marketed to large mining operations as the ultimate "blade" for maintaining haul roads. With its 24-foot-wide moldboard blade, it can do the work of two 16H motor graders. *Caterpillar*

The 24H is powered by a 12-cylinder Cat 3412E diesel, rated at 540 gross horsepower and 500 flywheel-horsepower. With a working weight of 136,611 pounds, the 24H has the bulk and brawn to take on the toughest mining grading assignments. Although the 24H's height of 14 feet, 3 inches to the top of its cab isn't all that impressive, its overall length of almost 52 feet most certainly is. *ECO*

the worldwide financial recession was in full bloom. Its first target would be the 130- to 150-ton class of mining haulers, the most popular range at the time.

THE 785 AND 789

In May 1983, Caterpillar had the first of its new generation of mining haulers, the 785, ready for testing at the Arizona Proving Grounds. The 785 did not stray too far from the overall look of the highly successful 777 series. But the 785 was much larger, with a rated load capacity of 130 tons, with the ability to carry a maximum 150 tons when optioned accordingly. The 785 was powered by a Cat 3512 turbocharged and aftercooled V-12 diesel engine, with a power output of 1,380 gross horsepower and 1,290 flywheel-horsepower. This was mated to a Cat six-speed, electronically controlled, automatic transmission. Keeping all of this in top running order would be the world-class Cat dealer network. With such a large and dedicated number of dealers, service and parts would be close at hand when needed. The competition knew that if the truck was

The pilot 785 hauler, pictured in May 1983, started the ball rolling for Caterpillar's new line of large mechanical-drive mining trucks. Having the design look of the earlier 777 truck, it was capable of hauling a maximum load of 150 tons. Full production commenced on the 785 hauler in September 1984. *Caterpillar*

a real performer, it was going to be a struggle for them to retain market share. There was no way they could hold ground against the large dealer and parts network Caterpillar had established over the decades.

In September 1984, the 785 hauler was officially released for sale. Even with the economic recession, the 785 quickly found its niche. It wouldn't be long before the 785 series was the best-selling hauler in its tonnage class. Everything Caterpillar had hoped the 785 would be came to pass. It was a standout performer.

Not long after the introduction of the 785, Cat was preparing for its next mining truck introduction in the tonnage class just above the 785. The 170- to 195-ton class of haulers was well established in the marketplace, with many of the largest mining operations basing their current truck fleets on them. By the fall of 1986, the mining industry would have another hauler to watch out for its consideration—the Cat 789.

In many ways, the new 789 looked just like its little brother, the 785. But the 789 was a bit larger in overall size. Motivation for the big hauler was supplied by a Cat 3516 turbocharged and aftercooled V-16 diesel engine, mated to a six-speed, electronically controlled, automatic transmission. Power ratings for the V-16 were 1,800 gross horsepower and 1,705 flywheel-horsepower. The 789 was officially launched in the fall of 1986, and to no one's surprise was a major hit in the mining sector.

The 785 and 789 were very well-designed trucks from the beginning. It was not until fall 1992 that upgraded models were finally introduced as "B" series haulers. The 785B and 789B featured numerous mechanical and detail changes, though no drastic design alterations were called for. Improved Cat 3512 and 3516 diesel engines with Electronic Unit Injection (EUI) were now standard in both trucks, with power ratings remaining the same as the previous models. These new engines greatly increased fuel economy and reliability and reduced emissions. The tonnage range for both models was unchanged. Even with the economic downturn

in the United States in the early 1990s, the demand overseas for the new haulers more than made up for any sales shortfalls. In fact, the haulers were selling at an even greater pace, much to the dismay of the competition.

In mid-1998, the haulers were again updated, this time to 785C and 789C status. The big news with the C models was their use of the improved Cat 3512B and 3516B EUI diesels, with substantial power increases for both hauler lines. The 785C was now rated at 1,450 gross horsepower and 1,348 flywheel-horsepower, while the 789C carried a higher 1,900-gross horsepower and 1,791-flywheel-horsepower output rating. Tonnage capacity remained as before for both haulers.

The 785 hauler realized immediate success in the mining industry when it was released in 1984. With its 12-cylinder Cat 3512 diesel, rated at 1,380 gross horsepower and 1,290 flywheel-horsepower, the truck could really hustle out from under a shovel with a full 150 tons on board. *Caterpillar*

Caterpillar entered the 240-ton class of mining haulers in 1991 with the introduction of the 793. It was the world's largest mechanical drive truck at the time of its release. Up until that point, all 240-ton payload rear-dump haulers were diesel-electric-drive designs. *Caterpillar*

Building on the success of the 785 hauler program, Caterpillar released an even larger model, identified as the 789, in 1986. In 1992, this hauler was upgraded into the 789B. Power for the truck was supplied by a 16-cylinder Cat 3516 diesel, rated at 1,800 gross horsepower and 1,705 flywheel-horsepower. Maximum capacity was 195 tons. *ECO*

One of three specially built Caterpillar 789B tractors with a MEGA CH290 bottom-dump coal trailer is shown in this photograph. First delivered in July 1995, the massive 94-foot-long haulers transport coal at a lignite mine near Bismarck, North Dakota. Rated at 290 tons, they often carry payloads well in excess of 300 tons. The 789B trucks were ordered new from the Cat Decatur Assembly Plant, minus their dump bodies and associated hardware. Final conversions of the tractors were handled by Butler, the local Cat dealer in Bismarck. *ECO*

Within the first two years of their launch, the original 785 and 789 trucks became the world market sales leaders in their respective tonnage classes. Today, this is a record the 785C and 789C models still hold and will take into the next century.

THE 793

The next class of mining haulers above Caterpillar's 789 series was the 240-ton-capacity trucks. The 240-ton class was dominated in the marketplace by giant diesel-electric-drive haulers. Companies such as Dresser (now Komatsu), Unit Rig, and Wiseda all had models in this class field by the late 1980s. It appeared from the competition as

though any hauler introduction in the 240-ton range would have to be of a diesel-electric-drive powertrain. This conception was about to be proven wrong by Caterpillar's newest hauler, the 793 series.

The new 240-ton Caterpillar 793 hauler was the world's largest mechanical drive truck when it started to roll out of the Decatur Assembly Plant in January 1991. No one thought a truck of this size could be reliably equipped with a mechanical automatic transmission and rear differentialñno one, that is, but Cat. The new six-speed transmission was mated to the tried-and-true Cat 3516 diesel engine. But as installed in the 793, a higher power output was dialed in, producing a healthy 2,160 gross horsepower and 2,057 flywheel-horsepower. Overall, the 793 was a smart-looking truck. It was also the company's first hauler to feature the front access ladder mounted in front of the radiator, making it less steep and safer for the operator and maintenance crews. The first few fleets of the 793 were followed very closely by Cat engineers. The company had its reputation on the line with these trucks in the mining industry, and any perceived fault would surely be brought to the attention of prospective customers by the competition.

The 793 performed well in the field, but not without the typical growing pains encountered in a totally new design. These were quickly addressed in the autumn of 1992, with the introduction of the 793B series. The big hauler received the updated 3516 EUI diesel, the same as that found in the 789B. The 793B also was fitted with a second-generation, electronically controlled, six-speed power-shift transmission, which addressed some of the weaknesses that had surfaced during the early months of the 793 program introduction. The new unit offered improved powertrain service life, smoother shifting, and electronic control of driveline torque during forward and reverse shifts. After these upgrades, the big hauler really started to hit its stride in the marketplace. By mid-1996, over 550 units of the 793 and 793B haulers had been placed into service at mining locations throughout the world. This total surpassed the former market leader in the 240-ton class, the diesel-electric-drive Komatsu Dresser 830E. The 830E was a tough competitor to be sure, but the industry was finding the design benefits of Caterpillar's all-mechanical drivetrain tough to resist.

The company kept the pressure up on its competition by releasing a more powerful model of the big hauler in mid-1996, in the form of the 793C. As with its smaller brother, the 793C received the improved Cat 3516B EUI diesel, with the appropriate increase in power, to 2,300 gross horsepower and 2,166 flywheel-horsepower. Capacity remained at 240 tons. Other improvements included redesigned hydraulic systems, more robust transmission clutch plates and discs, and enhanced diagnostic electronics.

Caterpillar's big 240-ton hauler again gained further improvements with the introduction of the 793C in mid-1996. The big diesel engine in the 793C was now the cleaner burning and more powerful 3516B EUI unit, rated at 2,300 gross horsepower and 2,166 flywheel-horsepower. Still classified as a 240-ton hauler, with a maximum operating weight of 830,000 pounds, it is the best-selling truck in this size category in the world. *ECO*

The 793 became the 793B in 1992. Other than component upgrades made to improve reliability, the biggest change was the installation of the Cat 3516 EUI diesel. The Electronic Unit Injection on the engine significantly reduced smoke, increased fuel economy, and improved reliability through the reduction of complex mechanical linkages. Power and capacity were unchanged from the previous model. *ECO*

On September 29, 1998, at Caterpillar's Decatur Assembly Plant, the massive 797 mining hauler was officially introduced to the world. After the ceremonies, the pilot 797 chassis was dismantled and shipped to the Arizona Proving Grounds. Once there, its wheels, tires, and dump body, which were already at the Proving Grounds, were installed. Testing was under way in November. *ECO*

THE 797

During the mid-1990s, a new design class of haulers began to appear in the marketplace, often referred to as ultrahaulers. Based on just a two-axle design, these trucks were typically capable of carrying 300-plus tons of material. Caterpillar had decided that it needed to be in the thick of things at the beginning of this new market push. Even though Komatsu had gotten a head start with its AC traction-drive, 320-ton-capacity 930E Haulpak, Caterpillar had even bigger plans in the works.

On September 29, 1998, at its Decatur, Illinois, assembly plant, Caterpillar unveiled a truly astounding piece of engineering work—the massive 797. The 797 represents Cat engineering and manufacturing muscle at its finest. The 797 is not just big . . . it is truly huge! A truck would have to be to handle a 360-ton load on its back, and that is just what this hauler is rated to carry.

From concept to finished prototype, it took Caterpillar only 18 months to make the 797 a reality. The entire truck was designed with 3D computer technology, utilizing the latest and most advanced finite element and solid modeling software technology. The truck alone uses eight on-board computers to control and monitor all of its vital functions. Caterpillar's other mining haulers, to some degree, shared many design and component aspects with each other. But the 797 is all new, and not just a beefed up 793 series truck.

The 797 is powered by a newly developed Cat 3524B EUI diesel engine, which is aftercooled, with four single-stage turbochargers. Power ratings for this beast are a whopping 3,400 gross horsepower and 3,224 flywheel-horsepower, at just 1,750 rpm. The design is based on two modified 3512 engines, connected together inline, by an innovative flexible coupling. This is mated to a highly automated, electronically controlled, seven-speed, automatic-shift transmission, driving a large rear-mounted modular differential. This is the most sophisticated mechanical drivetrain the company has ever produced. Many in the industry thought it couldn't be done. But the company that has stayed true to its belief in the mechanical-drivetrain layout saw no reason to change direction now.

The load-bearing frame design of the 797 differs from that of the 793C hauler in that it is made up entirely of mild steel castings. Nine major castings are machined for a precise fit before being joined by robotic welders. The 793C uses a mixture of box section steel structures, with steel castings in critical areas. The 797 frame design uses far fewer welds and creates a structure that is incredibly strong, suitable for supporting the kinds of loads the truck will face on a daily basis.

Another key factor in the design of the 797 is its use of 63-inch rims, one of the first trucks in the industry to use them. Previously, the largest rims available were 57 inches, the industry standard for haulers over 200 tons capacity. Caterpillar worked closely with Michelin on the development of the tires that would support the massive truck. The tires, new 55/80R63 radials, are simply state-of-the-art as far as haul trucks are concerned. They have to be if they are going on a truck that is capable of a 40 mile-per-hour top speed, with a full 360-ton load on board.

By November 1998, the first 797 arrived at Cat's Arizona Proving Grounds to start closely monitored field evaluation testing. In December, it was joined by the second preproduction unit. Starting in June 1999, additional 797 haulers started to be put into large mining operations throughout North America. About 20 or so preproduction 797s are planned to be built in 1999. Full North American release will be in 2000, with full worldwide availability in 2001.

THE 994

In the late 1980s, Caterpillar started development of a large wheel loader that was almost twice as large as the then-current 992C model. The new design, called the 994, was primarily targeted at the large mining sector. Even though two previous concept designs developed by Caterpillar were identified as 994, they had no bearing on this project. In 1989 production started on the first prototype 994 at Caterpillar's newly formed Mining Vehicle Center (MVC), located within the Decatur assembly plant. By September 1990, the completed prototype was dedicated at the plant before being shipped to its new home at the Cyprus Sierrita copper mine in Arizona, which happens to be the property adjoining the Cat Proving Grounds, just south of Tucson.

The 994 was the largest wheel loader the company had ever built. Equipped with a standard bucket rated at 23 cubic yards, it ranked with some of the largest wheel loaders ever produced. The loader also utilized a mechanical drive layout. Power for this monster was supplied by the Cat 3516 EUI diesel, the same engine found in the 789 and 793 series of mining haulers. Output in this application was set at 1,336 gross horsepower and 1,250 flywheel-horsepower. The transmission was a Cat planetary, three-speed, powershift unit.

The 994 could perform a variety of digging assignments, a sort of jack-of-all-trades at a mining site. It could load 150-ton haulers in four passes, 195-ton units in five to six passes, and 240-ton trucks with seven passes, when equipped with the high-lift loader arm arrangement. The 994 could also serve as a backup for a mine's large electric cable shovel fleet. If a shovel is down for repairs, the loader can be brought in right away to take up the production slack. Once the shovel goes back on line, the loader can quickly travel to another work site within the mine. The 994 loader's mobility is one of its strongest selling points. Of course, its large 23-cubic-yard, 70,000-pound-capacity bucket doesn't hurt either.

If anything hurt the big Cat during its early months of operation, it was the tires that were originally specified for the unit. The original 49.5-57 68 L-4 series were just barely adequate for a wheel loader of the 994's size and performance capabilities. But at the time, there just wasn't any other choice available from the tire manufacturers. The tires were basically reinforced hauler rubber designs. Clearly, something else was needed. Soon, the tire manufacturers released a larger design, the 53.5/85-57, built only for wheel loader use. The tire made an immediate difference in the performance and productivity of the loader. During the first few years, other upgrades were introduced to improve the 994's performance and reliability, such as even larger 55/80R57 radial tires, beefed up front axle mountings and lift arm assemblies, improved cooling capabilities, and greater bucket options. Through all of these improvements, the nomenclature of the 994 remained unchanged.

In December 1998, Caterpillar introduced an upgraded model of its massive loader in the form of the 994D. From the outside, little was changed on the loader, outside of the decals and the curved exhaust tips replacing the flat top design with rain caps. But internally, significant changes had taken place. The new model was now equipped with the improved 3516B EUI diesel, with power increased to 1,375 gross horsepower and 1,250 flywheel-horsepower. The 994D also had key stress areas for the lift arms and frame strengthened. New for the operator was the revamping of the steering controls for the loader. The steering wheel was now replaced by a joystick control, mounted to the left of the operator's seat, called the Cat Steering and Transmission Integrated Control system, or STIC for short. Caterpillar also offers the STIC control system, along with other technical upgrade packages, for retrofitting to existing pre-D-series units. You would think that with all of these upgrades, the 994D might weigh a few pounds more than its predecessor. It does. This version now tips the scales at 421,600 pounds, almost 211 tons.

The 994 series is by far the best-selling large wheel loader in the world, and by quite a margin, with over 200 of the original models sold before being replaced by the D series. Like Caterpillar's successful mining haulers, 994 loaders can be found working in all types of digging applications throughout the world. Even though the 994D faces stiff competition from offerings from LeTourneau and Komatsu, the big Cat loader is ready to take on all comers, no matter what their size.

The second pilot 797 is shown with its dump body raised some 49 feet in the air in December 1998, at the Arizona Proving Grounds. The tires on the 797 are 55/80R63 series radials on 63-inch rims. These are some of the most technologically advanced tire designs in the world. With an overall width of 30 feet, the 797 is also one of the widest trucks in the world. *Caterpillar*

THE 5130 AND 5230

At the October 1992 MINExpo held in Las Vegas, Nevada, Caterpillar introduced the mining industry to a new product line of large hydraulic excavatorsflthe 5000 series. The 5130 FS was the first in the new model line to be put on display at the show. The 5130 was almost twice as large as the 245 series, then the biggest Cat-designed and built hydraulic excavator. The original design of the 5130 was equipped with an 11-cubic-yard shovel bucket, and was powered by a single Cat 3508 EUI diesel engine, rated at 700 flywheel-horsepower. Weight of the prototype unit was 320,000 pounds. But after months of rigorous field testing of the early field trial units, changes were made to the excavator in early 1994 that greatly increased its performance and overall reliability. The 3508 diesel had its power increased to 815 gross horsepower and 755 flywheel-horsepower. Capacity of the bucket went up to 13.75 cubic yards, and castings and high stress areas were beefed up, bringing the weight up to 375,000 pounds. By the end of the year, it had increased to 385,000 pounds for the front shovel model.

In late 1993, the first 5130 ME backhoe unit was introduced into service. Equipped with either a 10.2-cubic-yard dirt bucket or a 17.8-cubic-yard coal loading bucket, the 5130 ME proved to be a very productive and well-liked machine in the field. The weight of the mass excavator was a bit more than the front shovel model, with the unit coming in at 390,000 pounds. Both models of the 5130 were performance matched to haul trucks with 65 to 100 tons in capacity. Even though both versions have sold well since their introduction, the versatile backhoe model has found the greatest acceptance from large quarries and mining operations the world over.

In July 1997, Caterpillar introduced the upgraded 5130B versions of its popular midsize hydraulic mining excavator. More power was now available from a revamped 3508B EUI diesel, with an increased output of 860 gross horsepower and 800 flywheel-horsepower. Capacity of the front shovel was now rated at 14.5 cubic yards, with the backhoe version available with multiple bucket choices, ranging from a 13.7-cubic-yard rock bucket to a big 24-cubic-yard coal model. As the superstructures of the excavators keep getting stronger, bulk went up accordingly, with the mass excavator version weighing in at 401,000 pounds and the front shovel model coming in at 399,000 pounds. The backhoe 5130B ME was the first version to be built by Caterpillar and put into service. The first front shovel started working in October 1997.

Following the successful launch of the 5130, Caterpillar introduced an even larger 5230 hydraulic excavator in 1994. Officially launched in August, the 5230 FS was one of the largest pieces of earthmoving equipment ever designed by Caterpillar, incorporating the largest steel castings produced by the company. By 1995 the 5230 ME backhoe versions started to find their way into the marketplace. The 5230 was powered by a single Cat 3516 EUI quad-turbocharged and aftercooled diesel engine, able to produce 1,575 gross horsepower and 1,470 flywheel-horsepower. Capacity for the front shovel model was 22.2 cubic yards, while the backhoe version utilized a 20.3-cubic-yard general-purpose bucket, with an optional 31.4-cubic-yard coal loading version. The 5230 was certainly a husky brute, with the weight of the front shovel coming in at 693,800 pounds, while the backhoe was a bit less at 692,320 pounds. By 1997

There are big trucks, and then there is the 797. The gargantuan hauler has the ability to carry 360 tons, and it ranks as the world's largest mechanical drive hauler. Power to carry such a load is supplied by a 24-cylinder Cat 3524B diesel engine, rated at a whopping 3,400 gross horsepower and 3,224 flywheel-horsepower. Operating weight fully loaded is a staggering 1,230,000 pounds, or 615 tons. *Caterpillar*

To load a massive truck like the 797, only the largest, most technically advanced electric mining shovels need apply. At Syncrude's North Mine in northern Alberta, Canada, a 797 is being loaded by a 1,489-ton Harnischfeger P&H 4100TS mining shovel, equipped with a 100-ton plus, 58-cubic-yard-capacity bucket, which is capable of loading the giant truck in four quick passes. *Harnischfeger*

Caterpillar upgraded its big loader into the 994D in December 1998. The new D series was powered by a slightly more powerful 3516B engine, rated at 1,375 gross horsepower and 1,250 flywheel-horsepower, and its operating weight increased to a meaty 421,600 pounds. Bucket capacity remained unchanged. New "STIC" joystick steering controls replaced the steering wheel and also controlled the transmission gear selections. *Caterpillar*

the front shovel model was listed at 702,000 pounds and the mass excavator at 697,980 pounds. At 351 tons, the 5230 was a true mining heavyweight, with an appetite for digging tons of rock.

The big Cat mining shovel was a natural fit with the company's top-selling haulers. The 5230 FS is capable of loading the 785C in five passes, the 789C in six passes, and in a pinch, it can load the 793C in eight passes. The 360-ton 797 hauler amazingly exceeds the limits of the 5230. As big as the 5230 is, the 797 is just too large for the shovel to accommodate. The 5230 is most productive when teamed up with haul trucks in the 150- to 200-ton class size.

By mid-2000, the upgraded 5230B model is to be introduced, enhanced by the improved Cat 3516B EUI diesel engine, plus a host of other performance features. Bucket capacity remained consistent with the previous model.

With the introduction of the 797 hauler, it would seem plausible that Caterpillar would release a larger hydraulic shovel model to load this giant. In 1995 the

company was in the early design phase of the 54XX project. It looked as if the world market for a 30-plus-cubic-yard hydraulic shovel looked bright. But somewhere along the line, someone forgot to tell the prospective mining equipment buyers this, especially in the United States. With sales of this class of machine barely holding their own at best, Cat decided to put any further development work on the 54XX project on the back burner. There was plenty to do just keeping all of the other 5000 series excavator designs, including the smaller 5080 and 5110 programs, on the right track. But when this market heats back up, rest assured that Caterpillar will have the design capabilities to put just the right production tool in its customers' hands when needed.

THE 24H

It seems perfectly natural for the company that introduced the Auto Patrol, the industry's first true, fully self-propelled motor grader in 1931, to enter the new

The 994 loader's standard bucket is rated at 23 cubic yards, with a 70,000, pound payload capacity. The widest bucket available is just over 20 feet wide. When the loader was introduced, it weighed in at 385,297 pounds. By 1998, this had risen to 390,300 pounds. *Caterpillar*

Following pages
Released in late 1990, the Caterpillar 994 was the largest wheel loader ever offered by the company at the time. The 994 is designed around a mechanical drivetrain layout, with a 16-cylinder Cat 3516 diesel at its heart, pumping out 1,336 gross horsepower and 1,250 flywheel-horsepower. The loader shown was the first unit equipped with a 45-cubic-yard coal loading bucket for working at a coal mine in the Powder River Basin of Wyoming. *ECO*

The 5130 became the 5130B in 1997. The 5130B FS was rated at 14.5 cubic yards, while the backhoe 5130B ME carried a 13.7-cubic-yard bucket. The Cat 3508B diesel in the 5130B pumps out at 860 gross horsepower and 800 flywheel-horsepower. Overall operating weight had increased to 399,000 pounds for the front shovel, and 401,000 pounds for the backhoe version. *ECO*

Even though Caterpillar had been manufacturing hydraulic excavators since 1972, it had never attempted to build anything larger than its 245 series until late 1992, when the 13.75-cubic-yard-capacity, 5130 FS was unveiled. This first of the "5000" series machines was powered by a single Cat 3508 diesel, rated at 815 gross horsepower and 775 flywheel-horsepower with an operating weight of 385,000 pounds. *Urs Peyer*

The 5130's big brother is the 5230 mining excavator, released in 1994. The big excavator was powered by the ultra-reliable 3516 EUI, the same diesel engine that powered the 789, 793, and 994 mining machines. Power output as rated in the 5230 was 1,575 gross horsepower and 1,470 flywheel-horsepower. The 5230 FS shown can load the 195-ton Cat 789B hauler in six passes with its 22.2-cubic-yard bucket. *Caterpillar*

century producing the largest motor grader offered by any manufacturer—the 24H. Like its cousins, the 994 loader and the 793 hauler, the 24H started its life at Cat's MVC. During the early design stages of the grader's life in the early 1990s, it was referred to internally as the 18H project. But research showed that an even larger unit would be needed to do the job that Cat had in mind for this mining grader.

The key role that the 24H serves in a mining operation is in the production and maintenance of haul roads. As larger hauler fleets become more commonplace in the industry, the haul roads that these trucks travel on have to be built and maintained economically. The roads are subject to traffic of the most punishing sort and require constant repair. The 24H, with its 24-foot-wide moldboard blade, is well suited to the task. It can move almost 2.5 times the amount of material that the second largest Cat grader, the 16H, can. And with the 24H's wider blade, the grader makes fewer passes to do the same job a 16H would do with its 16-foot blade. If a mine was using six 16H graders for haul road maintenance, they would only need three 24H units. The savings in total operating

expenses these large models provide more than make up for the initial higher cost of the graders.

The 24H is powered by a Cat 3412E HEUI diesel engine, rated at 540 gross horsepower and 500 flywheel-horsepower. With this type of power, and a working weight of 136,611 pounds, the 24H can apply greater cutting forces to its blade, enabling it to take on the most difficult road surfaces.

Testing of the prototype 24H took up most of 1995, with the first field unit delivered to the Eagle Butte coal mine, located north of Gillette, Wyoming, in late 1995. The 24H was officially released for worldwide sales in the spring of 1996. In the marketplace, the big grader really has no direct competition. Its closest rival is probably its smaller brother, the 16H. There have only been a few motor graders produced that were larger than the 24H, such as the Champion 100T and the Acco Giant Grader. But the limited production of the Champion and the experimental nature of the Acco doomed them in the marketplace. When a mining company is looking for the biggest blade in town today, it needs look no further than the mighty 24H, the world's largest, full-production motor grader.

Caterpillar introduced a backhoe 5230 ME version in 1995. The 5230 ME is rated with a 21-cubic-yard rock bucket or a 36-cubic-yard version for loading coal. Maximum reach of the excavator is 58 feet, with a 30-foot, 9-inch digging depth. *Caterpillar*

11

GLOBAL COMPETITION

CORPORATE REORGANIZATION PAYS DIVIDENDS

Heading toward the end of the twentieth century, Caterpillar had become a true global corporate entity. Not just a company that produced for the home market and sold products internationally as an afterthought, but a totally integrated business environment with dealerships, joint ventures, and factories in every major part of the globe and in several not so major. But this transaction did not happen overnight, and a few decisions made by the company were bitter pills to take, but necessary if Caterpillar was to compete effectively in a global marketplace.

The worldwide recession starting in 1982 was Caterpillar's wake-up call to start rethinking its international position in the manufacturing of heavy equipment. This was the time period in which Detroit's big three of Ford, General Motors, and Chrysler had their backs to the wall fending off foreign imports, especially from Japan. From 1981 through 1985, the undervalued Japanese yen gave that country a distinct pricing advantage over U.S. competitors. This fact was made painfully clear to Caterpillar early on in the recession. Caterpillar equipment had always commanded a slightly higher price in the marketplace. Even as far back as Holt, the tractors were more expensive than the competition's. The company's quality of engineering, the dealerships, parts availability, even warranties, were second to none in the industry. But all of this takes money. It was necessary to make Caterpillar a lean, mean fighting machine, if it was not to join the fate of other companies in the so-called rust-belt of American manufacturing.

During the troubled times of the recession, the company was guided by the capable hands of Chairman Lee L. Morgan. It would not be an easy task, though. The company lost money for the first time in 50 years. Labor strikes also complicated matters. But it takes a big man to make the big decisions in

Caterpillar made a major breakaway from its previous wheel loader designs with the introduction of the 992G at the September 1996 MINExpo. The 992G loader utilizes a large, one-piece, cast-steel, box-section lift arm instead of the more traditional twin lift arm design. Power for the big 16-cubic-yard loader is supplied by an 800-flywheel-horsepower Cat 3508B EUI diesel. Working weight of the standard 992G with the Hi-Lift boom is 209,343 pounds. *Urs Peyer*

The 854G is another Caterpillar world title holder. In 1999, it was the largest and most powerful wheel dozer available to the mining market. Formerly known as the Tiger 790G, it is based on the 992G wheel loader platform and drivetrain. Its power output of 800 flywheel-horsepower is also the same as the big loaders. *Caterpillar*

a company the size of Caterpillar. Not everyone would be happy with the downsizing of plants and personnel, but if the company were to prosper in the long term, sacrifices were going to have to be made now. One area in which the company resisted cutbacks was in funding research and design.

As the company's manufacturing costs were reeled in, key business relations were established with major heavy equipment builders in various overseas markets. This bolstered the product lines with more diverse machine offerings, covering a broader band in the marketplace, especially for smaller sized machines. To better reflect the monumental changes happening within the company, it was decided to change the corporate name of the Caterpillar Tractor Company to Caterpillar, Inc. The company had been more than just a tractor company for some years. Now the name would reinforce this fact, rather than suggesting otherwise. In 1989 two new trademarks, sometimes referred to as the yellow-triangle logos, were introduced to further separate the company from its former self.

In 1990, Donald V. Fites took the helm of Caterpillar, Inc., as chairman and chief executive officer. Fites further expanded the corporate changes started by his predecessor. During the 1990s, Fites led the way for a complete corporate reorganization of all business activities. This included restructuring the company into 13 business units, or profit centers, and four service centers, streamlining the decision-making process to focus on the customers' needs. Spending on plant modernization and improvements, started in the late 1980s, continued on at a record pace, with the investment of some $1.8 billion in the company's facilities. As it turned out, it was money very well spent. The mid- to late-1990s were the company's most profitable years ever. It took a lot of work and sacrifice by the company and workers, but now Caterpillar was starting to see the outcome of its long-term strategy initiated years earlier. The development boom of this period was helping the earthmoving industry generally, but Caterpillar was perfectly poised to take advantage of opportune times.

The largest 300 series hydraulic excavator offered by Caterpillar, as of 2000, is the 375 L. Pictured is a 375 LME Mass Excavator, which carries a rated bucket of approximately 6 cubic yards. Power output of the big excavator is 428 flywheel-horsepower and working weight is 178,800 pounds. *ECO*

The 1990s saw new products added at record pace. The building of diesel engines for over-the-road, mid-to-large trucks was becoming one of the company's most profitable divisions. Caterpillar Engine Division offered diesel engines, not just for trucks and heavy machinery, but also for generator sets, marine applications, industrial uses, and even locomotives. In 1981, Caterpillar purchased the Solar Turbines Industrial Division of International Harvester Co., which added a full range of massive and powerful gas turbine powerplants. The company's large diesel engine offerings were also further expanded in late 1996, when the German firm of MaK Motoren GmbH became part of the Caterpillar family. Then in December 1997, Caterpillar agreed to purchase the Perkins company, a very highly regarded builder of smaller diesel engines, from Lucas Varity Plc. of England. These acquisitions provided Caterpillar with complete control of all engines being utilized in its equipment designs.

The 1990s would also be an important time for the company's paving equipment lines. Caterpillar first entered this market back in 1984, when it entered a manufacturing and marketing agreement with the CMI Corporation of Oklahoma for the production of paving products. In 1987 the association between the two companies was discontinued.

Many of Caterpillar's hydraulic excavators can be equipped with an incredible array of optional tools, such as hydraulic impact hammers, and demolition and scrap attachments. The company offers a broad assortment of specialized equipment to custom fit an excavator to a customer's exact working conditions. In addition to factory attachments, numerous aftermarket tools are also available for Cat excavators worldwide. *Urs Peyer*

For a high-productivity articulated hauler and hydraulic excavator match-up, it's hard to beat Caterpillar's state-of-the-art D400E Series II and 365B LME. The D400E Series II is a 405 flywheel-horsepower rated, 40-ton capacity articulated hauler. The 365B LME is rated at 374 flywheel-horsepower and has a working weight of 142,420 pounds. *Urs Peyer*

But Caterpillar was able to purchase from CMI the technology to manufacture pavement profilers, asphalt pavers, soil stabilizers, and road reclaimers. It was also able to buy CMI's wholly owned subsidiary, RayGo, Inc., of Minnesota, which added a broad range of soil and asphalt compactors. Caterpillar's paving product offerings were further increased in April 1991, when the company purchased Barber-Greene, a world-renowned producer of paving machines. Barber-Greene, which was established in 1916, was known for its material handling machines. But in 1931, the company built and demonstrated the first true asphalt paver the industry had ever seen. In 1958 it also developed the first paving machine that paved on crawlers and traveled on rubber tires for fast travel between job locations. Today, the pavers are still sold under the label Barber-Greene and are all marketed, along with Caterpillar machines, by Caterpillar Paving Products, Inc., headquartered in Minneapolis, Minnesota.

While Caterpillar had numerous business successes in the 1990s, the materials handling equipment business was not one of them. Caterpillar entered this market in late 1965, when it acquired the Towmotor Corporation. Founded in 1919, Towmotor was a pioneering company in the design of lift trucks. Even though the Towmotor line sold well for the company, it was never able to achieve higher than a third-place ranking in sales, behind the industry's Number One and Two sales leaders, Hyster and Yale.

In July 1992, as a way to slowly divest itself from the fork-lift industry, the company formed three lift-truck joint ventures with Mitsubishi Heavy Industries, Ltd. The ventures, known as Mitsubishi Caterpillar Forklift (MCF) America Inc., MCF Asia Pte Ltd., and MCF Europe B.V., were 80 percent owned by Mitsubishi, with Caterpillar maintaining a 20 percent stake. In 1998, Mitsubishi Heavy Industries agreed to take over full responsibility for the design work of all forklift trucks for the joint ventures. The transition was to be completed by the end of 1999.

During the 1990s, Caterpillar made major strides in the production and marketing of large mining equipment. These offerings were further bolstered in July 1997, when Caterpillar purchased the rights to the large wheel dozers produced by Tiger Engineering Pty, Ltd., of Australia. Tiger, with the assistance of Caterpillar Industrial Products, Inc., created a design concept for its first large, rubber-tired wheel dozer in 1980, at the request of Mount Newman Mining of Western Australia. The first model, identified as the 690A, was based largely on components from the Cat 992C wheel loader. The first 690A would officially be delivered to the mining company in 1982.

Tigers have always been sold and serviced through the Cat dealer network, both domestically and abroad. Sales of Tiger dozers were slow at first, but picked up significantly when the model 690B was released in 1985. The key

The Caterpillar 5080 FS, which was introduced in late 1993, is essentially a front shovel version of the 375 model series. It is powered by a 428-flywheel-horsepower Cat 3406C diesel. Bucket capacity is listed at 6.8 cubic yards, with an operating weight of 184,800 pounds. *Caterpillar*

The Caterpillar 980G was the first of the "larger" wheel loaders to be introduced in a G series with the streamlined bodywork, in 1995. Power output of the 980G is rated at 300 flywheel-horsepower, and its bucket capacity range from 5 to 7.5 cubic yards. *Urs Peyer*

The Caterpillar C series tractor backhoe loaders, which were officially introduced in 1996, are some of the most sophisticated machines of their type on the market today. The 436C shown is loaded with big performance features, such as its turbocharged Cat 3054T diesel, rated at 93 flywheel-horsepower, and its all-wheel-drive and steer capabilities. *Caterpillar*

design improvement of this model over the previous one was the replacement of the standard 992C torque converter with a unit sourced from the 773B hauler drivetrain. This change greatly improved the Tiger 690B dozer's overall working abilities while increasing reliability measurably. In 1993 the 690B became the 690D, after the release of the Caterpillar 992D loader. The 690D also utilized a front frame that was based on the D10N dozer. Of greatest significance was the use of STIC, Caterpillar's joystick control system, which eliminated the need for a steering wheel. Operators simply loved the control system, which helped increase the Tiger's overall productivity dramatically. This was one of the many reasons why the 690D became the best selling Tiger wheel dozer ever made. In 1994, Tiger released a companion model to its larger model called the 590. The Tiger 590 was based heavily on the Cat 990 wheel loader. When that loader became a Series II machine in 1996, the Tiger model evolved into a new 590B series.

In September 1996, Tiger Engineering introduced an even larger wheel dozer than the 690D, known as the 790G. The new model was based on the newly released Cat 992G wheel loader, with other front-end components from the D11R dozer. But this Tiger never had a chance to earn its stripes. Caterpillar purchased the intellectual property rights to design and manufacture the 790G, along with the 590B, by mid-1997. In early 1998, the former Tigers were integrated into the Caterpillar wheel dozer product line and released as the Cat 854G and 844 respectively. These new Cat machines joined the population of other Tiger wheel dozers, which number over 150 units worldwide.

Caterpillar also has Australian manufacturing ties in the production of underground mining equipment. Caterpillar Elphinstone Pty, Ltd., is a joint venture company of Caterpillar, Inc. and Dale B. Elphinstone Pty, Ltd., located in Tasmania, Australia. Elphinstone manufactures underground mining equipment, which includes Load-Haul-Dump (LHD) loaders, and rigid frame and articulated haulers. All Elphies, as the machines are called in Australia, utilize Caterpillar drivetrains, with the rigid frame trucks

being based heavily on regular production Cat haulers, such as the 769D and 773D. The low-profile LHD loaders and the articulated haulers are Elphinstone designs, but contain various Cat components, including the engines and transmissions. The largest and most advanced design of LHD underground loaders built by the company is its R2900 Supa 20, which was introduced in 1999.

Even though Caterpillar was adding new machine releases from these various joint ventures and acquisitions

Introduced in 1993, the Caterpillar 990 wheel loader was targeted at large quarry operations requiring a machine with a 11-cubic-yard capacity. The 990 was based largely on the 992D model, and both utilized the Cat 3412 diesel. However, the 990's engine produced less power due to its smaller bucket capacity. Originally rated with a 610-flywheel-horsepower power output, this was raised to 625 flywheel-horsepower with the introduction of the 990 Series II in late 1995. *Caterpillar*

at a blistering pace, just as much time and resources were being spent on keeping the established product lines at the very top in the marketplace, both in sophistication and productivity. Nowhere was this more evident than with the hydraulic excavators. The sheer number of new models and variations on these machines built by Caterpillar in the 1990s was staggering. It seemed like every few weeks a new model was popping up. An all-new generation of excavators called the 300-series was officially launched in early 1992. Combining the know-how of its earlier designs, with the Japan sourced E-series machines, these new excavators were brisling with technological muscle. These excavators were not only powerfully productive, they were smart too, with the latest microcomputer technology managing the

engine and hydraulic system, balancing engine speed and pump output for maximum control and efficiency. These excavators had it all. The first models released were the 320, 325, and 330. The 320 replaced the older E200B and 215D machines, the 325 took the place of the 225D, and the 330 eliminated the E300B. In 1993 the much larger 350 and 375 model series were released. The 350 took the place of the 235D, while the 375 would take over the top spot in the lineup from the popular 245D. But this was just the beginning. As the months went by, more and more 300-series machines were added to the hydraulic excavator product line, making it one of the most complete and comprehensive in the industry today.

When Caterpillar introduced its larger 5000-series mining excavators with the 5130 in late 1992, it opened up an all-new product chapter for the company. Following on the heels of the 5130's release, Caterpillar introduced the 5080 FS in late 1993. The 5080 FS was basically the front shovel version of the 375 backhoe model. After the launch of the large 5230 FS, the company started development on a midsized machine that would fit into the product line between the 5080 and the 5130. Identified as the model 5110, the first of these units, a Mass Excavator or backhoe version, was the first model to see the light of day in early 1996. After a few more of this type were produced, a front shovel version was also built. All of the original 5110 models were considered preproduction units and were not intended for manufacture as is. After thorough tear-downs and examinations of most of the prototype machines, changes were made to the basic design to improve its overall performance characteristics. In the fall of 2000, the excavator, now identified as the 5110B, will officially be released to the mining industry.

To complement its hydraulic excavator offerings, Caterpillar offers an incredible array of optional buckets, hammers, and various other attachments for all sorts of specialized jobs. Along with components from Balderson, a company that Caterpillar purchased in the late 1950s for the production of bulldozing blades, products from various other firms have been added to further expand the

Introduced in 1974, the Caterpillar 777 has been the industry's leading haul truck in the 85- to 95-ton class. The 777D, which was introduced in 1996, raised the industry standard one more notch with the new truck, which was now rated as a true 100-ton payload hauler. Power for the 777D is provided by a Cat 3508B EUI diesel, rated at 938 flywheel-horsepower. *ECO*

Starting in 1999, Caterpillar began releasing an entirely new
model line of versatile skid-steer loaders. These were part of the
company's new lines of compact earthmoving equipment that also
included miniexcavators and wheel loaders. Models of skid-steer loaders
offered include the 216, 226, 228, 236, 246, and 248.
The model 236 shown is powered by a Cat 3034 diesel, rated at
59 flywheel-horsepower. *Caterpillar*

availability of world-class attachments. These acquisitions
include the German firm of Vibra-Ram, a manufacturer of
demolition and scrap attachments, in 1996; the Dutch
firm of Veratech Holdings B.V., a producer of hydraulic
hammers, in 1998; and the Marion, Ohio, company,
Material Handling Crane Systems, Inc., which builds
components for hydraulic excavators used in the scrap and
material handling business, also in 1998. That same year,
Caterpillar also formed a joint venture company with the
Finland-based Tamrock Corporation., called Caterpillar
Impact Products Limited, headquartered in Slough in the
United Kingdom. Their principal products are a wide
variety of hydraulic impact hammers.

Another established Caterpillar model line to see significant changes was the wheel loader. The G-series
machines are some of the finest wheel loaders the company
has ever built. Starting in 1995, the first of the new series to

Caterpillar offers the most complete line of motor graders in the world today. The entire H series lineup from the late 1990s is pictured with the exception of the giant 24H grader. All of these models
are assembled at the Caterpillar Decatur Plant. *Caterpillar*

Second only to the model 24H in size, the Caterpillar 16H is one of the most popular mining motor graders around. The 16H, which replaced the 16G in late 1994, is powered by a 275-flywheel-horsepower Cat 3406 diesel. The moldboard blade of the grader is 16 feet wide. *Caterpillar*

Although the scrapers in Caterpillar's 627 series have been around since 1968, they are still among the most popular models available. Shown is a 627F, which was introduced in 1994. Power is supplied by a 330-flywheel-horsepower Cat 3406C diesel in the tractor, and a 3306, rated at 225 flywheel-horsepower, in the rear scraper. Total output is 555 flywheel-horsepower. Payload capacity is 14 cubic yards struck and 20 heaped. *Caterpillar*

be introduced was the small 914G, followed a few months later by the larger 980G. Both models featured very streamlined designs with sloping rear-end bodywork, which gave the operators a better rearward view. Other G models were to follow, but the largest of them all in the 1990s was the innovative 992G. Unveiled in September 1996 at the MINExpo in Las Vegas, Nevada, the 992G was a technical marvel to behold. Designed as the replacement for the 992D, the 992G broke new design ground for Caterpillar. What makes the 992G loader unique is its utilization of a one-piece, cast-steel, box-section front lift arm design, instead of the former twin-boom configuration. The 992G was no lightweight, but a powerhouse with the muscle and capacity to take on the big jobs. With a Cat 3508B EUI diesel engine, pounding out 880 gross horsepower and 800 flywheel-horsepower and a large 16-cubic-yard bucket, it was a perfectly sized machine for loading 100-ton-capacity haulers, such as the Caterpillar 777D, which it can load in four quick passes.

Starting in 1998, the company introduced several new models of Cat Compact Machines that were smaller than anything it had built before. These new machines fell into three new categories: Mini Hydraulic Excavators, Compact Wheel Loaders, and Skid Steer Loaders. The mini excavators consisted of the models 301.5 and the 302.5. Compact loaders included the models 902 and 906. In 1999 the full line of skid steer loaders was finally released, consisting of six models, the 216, 226, 228, 236, 246, and the 248. These compact designs offer amazing flexibility for contractors needing very rugged and versatile machines in a smaller package.

Caterpillar's hauler offerings were also upgraded and improved throughout the 1990s. For the rear-dump truck line, newly revised D-series quarry and mining haulers started to be introduced in late 1995 with the releases of the 769D and 775D. In 1996 the 771D, 773D, and 777D models were also put to work. For articulated haulers, the highly refined Series II trucks were first offered in 1998 with the D250E Series II and the D300E Series II. Then in early 1999, the D350E Series II and D400E Series II articulated haulers rounded out the company's three-axle designs. As an alternative choice for contractors, the D400E II is also offered with a newly designed rear-ejector dump box, which allows the hauler to dump on-the-run, spreading the load as it goes. This saves time and increases the productivity of the D400E II considerably.

Caterpillar kept the scraper line fairly consistent through the 1990s, upgrading models to improve emissions and productivity. The company still offers the most complete line of big scrapers in the world. But sales have continued to decline as the decade has progressed. This has less to do with the quality of the machines, which is very high, and more to do with a change in the industry to a combination of hydraulic excavators and articulated haulers. They have taken over many of the jobs that were considered ideal for a self-powered scraper, especially short-haul earthmoving operations. For longer travel distances, the scraper is still the superior choice. The company released only one completely new scraper line during this time, the model 611. The 611, introduced in 1999, is a conventional, single-engined unit, rated at 10 cubic yards struck and 15 heaped. The mighty 657E model series remains at the top of Cat's scraper line, with the

The Caterpillar 657E is currently the largest scraper offered for sale. Introduced in 1962, it is the only real choice for the big jobs that require big scrapers. This 657E is equipped with the optional coal scraper body, rated at 58.7 cubic yards struck and a whopping 72.6 heaped. Engine in the tractor is a Cat 3412E, while the scraper unit makes do with the 3408E. Rated variable power output in gears 1 and 2 is 950 flywheel-horsepower, but in gears 3 through 8, power jumps to 1,045 flywheel-horsepower. *Caterpillar*

Released in 1995, the D9R is a worthy successor to the very popular D9N. The D9R gets its power from a Cat 3408C diesel, rated at 443 gross horsepower and 405 flywheel-horsepower. It's available with two steering systems: the standard clutch and brake arrangement, or the optional differential steering, which delivers uninterrupted power to both tracks while turning. Operating weight of the dozer equipped with a single shank ripper is 104,538 pounds. *Caterpillar*

Caterpillar has offered rubber-tired logging skidders as well as two-track units for years. As of 2000, two tracked models are offered: the 517 and the 527. These models replaced the previous D4H TSK and D5H TSK. This is a 150-flywheel-horsepower Model 527 skidder, first released in 1996. *Caterpillar*

same payload capacities as years past. The 657E is currently the largest production scraper in the world.

As in decades past, the track-type tractor models built by the company are without a doubt some of the world's finest, most technologically advanced dozers. Their only real competition comes from Komatsu in Japan, which has worked hard to compete with Cat's engineering excellence. The competition is good, giving Caterpillar strong incentive to keep introducing more refined dozers, with cutting-edge computer controls and diagnostic systems. At the top of Cat's tractor product line are the R-series dozers, including the D8R and D9R released in 1995, followed by the D6R, D7R, D10R, and the mighty D11R. As with the D11R, the D10R is equipped with Fingertip Controls (FTC), allowing the operator to control steering, machine direction, and gear selection with a single hand from the left side of the seat.

RETURN OF THE COMBINE

Caterpillar machines were born in the fields. It was the founding firms of Best and Holt, and their combine harvesters, that made Caterpillar possible. Without the Best and Holt combines, the history of track-type tractors would have been very different indeed. Yet, as the years passed,

Caterpillar strayed from its roots to pursue the great growth of the construction and mining industries. And how fitting, as we enter a new millennium, that the company comes full circle. In 1997, Caterpillar reentered the combine harvester business after an absence of some 62 years.

After the consolidation of Holt and Best in 1925, Caterpillar Tractor Co. set up a new wholly owned subsidiary company in Stockton, California, in 1926 called the Western Harvester Co., which would take over the operations of the Holt Harvester Works. Western's sole purpose was to build and market combine harvesters and attachments, principally for the western United States. In March 1929, Caterpillar announced that it was going to build a new plant in East Peoria, Illinois, to take over harvester production from the old Stockton plant due to the impending sale of the property. Full production was to commence in the new Building HH in 1930. Now the combines would be built and marketed as Caterpillar machines. Three models were offered—the Model Thirty-Four, Thirty-Six, and Thirty-Eight. But after five years of marketing the machines, Caterpillar's business interests had shifted away from agriculture toward construction. The U.S. Stock Market crash of 1929, and the Great Depression that followed, didn't help matters either. So in 1935 the company sold the licensing rights to build and market the three combine models to Deere & Company. Caterpillar was now out of the harvesting business.

Not until the early 1990s would Caterpillar engineers again take an interest in the combine market. In 1993, Caterpillar, along with an independent outside firm, built and tested an experimental harvester called the Bi-Rotor Combine. The Bi-Rotor concept machine was even showcased at a few farming exhibitions to gauge customer reactions. But the time still was not right. After careful analysis of the project, management decided that producing all of the machine's other component systems, other than the bi-rotor mechanism itself, would be just too expensive. Another way would have to be found.

As of 2000, the D10R is Caterpillar's second-largest mining dozer offering, right behind the legendary D11R. Introduced in 1996 as a replacement for the D10N, the D10R is powered by a Cat 3412E diesel, rated at 613 gross horsepower and 570 flywheel-horsepower. Operating weight with ripper is 146,106 pounds. The D10R is offered with Fingertip Controls (FTC), just as in the D11R. *ECO*

A diesel Thirty-Five tractor pulling a Caterpillar Thirty-Six combine is pictured working in Humboldt, Minnesota, in October 1933. The Thirty-Six was by far the most popular Caterpillar-built combine, with some 4,001 units produced between 1927 and 1935, before its sale to Deere & Company. *Caterpillar*

The joint agreement made in 1997 between Caterpillar and Claas allowed the Claas-designed combines to be marketed in North America and Caterpillar Challenger tractors to be sold in Europe under the Claas name. A Challenger 85E wears the signature green-and-white Claas. All models of Challengers are marketed in Europe, including the Row-Crop tractors. *Urs Peyer*

Across the Midwest, the sight of a Caterpillar LEXION combine matched to Challenger tractors is becoming more and more of a common sight during harvesting season. Pictured is the top-of-the-line LEXION 485 equipped with the Mobil-trac System, loading a grain hopper attached to a Cat VSP70 "Versatile Flotation System" undercarriage, which is being pulled by a Challenger 55 Row-Crop tractor. *Caterpillar*

Instead of building an entirely new unit, the company decided to seek out a possible partnership or joint venture with an established combine manufacturer. They considered New Holland as a possible partner in this venture. But once Caterpillar engineers made a trip to Germany to look at the combines being built by Claas KGaA, located in Harsewinkel, they knew they had found the right machines to carry the CAT name. Caterpillar had previously worked with Claas through its Industrial Products division, starting in 1987, when it supplied Cat engines and specially-designed MTS (Mobil-trac Systems) for use with the German-built Commandor 116 CS and 228 CS tracked combine model lines.

In February 1997, Caterpillar and Claas officially announced the forming of a joint venture company to be called Caterpillar Claas America. This venture would allow Claas combines to be sold and serviced in North America as Caterpillar machines. In return, the complete line of Caterpillar Challenger Ag tractors would be marketed as Claas units throughout all of the company's dealerships in Europe. Even though these Challengers would bear the Claas name and colors of green and white, their heart and soul would be Caterpillar.

The first models of Caterpillar LEXION combines to be introduced were the Models 460, 465, 480, and 485 in the fall of 1997. This was followed by the LEXION 450 in 1998 and the 470 in fall 1999. The LEXION combines are marketed by the type of separation systems they employ. The 450, 460, and 465 utilize a straw walker separation system. The 470, 480, and 485 use a rotary separation method. The LEXION 450, 460, 470, and 480 ride on rubber tires, while the 465 and 485 are equipped with the rubber-belted Mobil-trac System in the front. This gives these machines unprecedented traveling performance in the field, and reduces ground compaction dramatically. All LEXION machines feature Cat Diesel power.

The long-term cooperation between the two companies seems full of promise. In September 1999, Caterpillar Claas America officially broke ground for an entirely new assembly plant in Omaha, Nebraska. Full LEXION production is anticipated to begin by the end of 2001. This

plant will supply combines for the North American and Australia markets. All others will be covered by Claas, with machines built in Germany. Caterpillar combines will now be seen bringing in the harvest, just as in times past with Best and Holt machines. Although the horse and mule teams and the steamers of old are gone, Caterpillar has returned to harvest the fields of the new millennium.

A Caterpillar LEXION 485, harvesting in the fall of 1999 in central Illinois, tries to get as much work done as possible before the sun sets. The 485 is equipped with the Mobil-trac System, which allows the combine to "float" over ruts in the field and reduces soil compaction dramatically. *ECO*

12

THE GOOD, THE BAD AND THE UGLY

MILITARY, EXPERIMENTAL, AND PROTOTYPE MACHINES

Some of the most interesting Caterpillar equipment designs are those that you don't see. These machines live in the world of military applications, early prototype developments, and experimental designs . . . very hush-hush for most of us on the outside. But many of these creations pushed the boundaries of what could be done in equipment design in their day. The prototypes are the most interesting because they give an insight to the engineering process of taking a machine concept from paper to iron. In many cases, they are almost exactly like the production model. In others, a few different designs might have to be tried to get the right performance and reliability requirements to survive in a very competitive marketplace. As for the experimentals, these machine designs often test a new design theory or concept. Sometimes they evolve into a production machine. In other cases they raise costs or deficiencies that suspend or terminate the project.

In today's world of manufacturing earthmoving equipment, you can build and test a machine with powerful computer-aided design programs. These enable a design engineer to visualize each part of the machine in 3D computer imagery, and to test it with finite computer stress analysis. Computer testing can shave years off the development of any machine design. In the past, before the age of computer design, engineers had no good way to test their designs short of putting them into "iron." Design work was therefore a very expensive endeavor, even more so if the design didn't work out because the development costs were lost.

Of course, before production can begin, even a computer-aided design must be built in iron and tested. At this point, engineers want a controlled atmosphere, for observation, and a bit of secrecy, too, to keep competitors guessing. That's why Caterpillar has operated its own proving ground facilities over the years. Here a design can be tested in part or in whole, out of sight from prying eyes. The company has numerous testing locations, but the major ones are the Peoria Proving Grounds, better known as the PPG, and Tucson Proving Grounds.

The Caterpillar 657 Dual-Bowl was part of the company's high-production, self-loading scraper test program in 1967. The unit consisted of two independently operated 24-cubic-yard heaped scraper bowls, hooked together in the middle. Engines in this prototype were the same as a standard 657 scraper, and were rated at 900 flywheel-horsepower. Operating weight of the Dual-Bowl was 159,100 pounds. *ECO Collection*

The Holt 120 Long-Track, Model T-24, was built in 1918 as a possible heavy artillery prime mover for use with the U.S. Army in Europe. With its big six-cylinder Holt M-8 gas motor, the tractor tested well during preliminary Army demonstrations. But after the armistice was signed, the tractor was no longer needed. Only one unit is listed as ever being built. *Caterpillar*

For large machines and hot weather testing, Caterpillar established the Phoenix Proving Grounds in 1945, just west of Phoenix, on land leased from the state of Arizona. In 1990 it established the Tucson Proving Grounds, just south of its namesake. Located about 170 miles south of the former Phoenix site, this complex, which is adjacent to a large copper mining installation, is ideal for testing mining equipment. The Tucson Proving Grounds is divided into two separate operations, Test and Development, established in April 1990, and Tinaja (pronounced Tin-ah-ah) Hills

Training Center, Marketing Support's new training and conference facility. Its doors opened in October 1990. The PPG and the Tucson Proving Grounds give Caterpillar a decisive advantage since many of its competitors do not have their own private testing grounds. And no competitor has a testing and development facility of the scope and scale of the PPG and Tucson Proving Grounds. Extensive testing and development makes a difference in terms of durability and quality.

MILITARY MACHINES

Caterpillar has designed many pieces of equipment over the years, specifically destined for military use. In fact, the invention of the tracked-type tank during World War I was influenced by Holt's designs at the time. Benjamin Holt did not invent the tank, but his demonstrations of his tracked tractors to interested countries, especially Great Britain, definitely influenced their thinking concerning crawler tracks in the battlefield.

Along with the modified commercial tractors Holt built for military applications already discussed in Chapters 1 and 2, a few were designed from the outset for military purposes. In 1916 the company tried to get the attention of the Ordnance Department with its Holt 12 (Model Series F-KEB) tractor. The little tractor was powered by a four-cylinder, 3 3/4x5 1/2-inch bore and stroke, enclosed-head Beaver motor. Unique to this design was its roller-bearing mounted cast frame. But the government wasn't biting on this one. Records indicate only one was built, and it was shipped to the Army for testing, never to be heard from again.

In late 1915, the Holt 18 (Model Series E-JEB) muley was introduced as another possible government model. This model was equipped with a four-cylinder, 4 1/2x6-inch bore and stroke, enclosed-head Beaver engine. Only five of these tractors were eventually produced, but they seem to have been tested by various government agencies until about 1918, when Holt gave up on the design. Of the five built, two were special builds. One was classified as a Model T-11A with special track links, and the other, a Model T-11B, was equipped with an eight-cylinder, Hershel-Spillman motor. All of the Beaver-engined Holt 18 units, including the specials, and the Holt 12, were designed and built in Peoria.

Holt, working with the U.S. Army Ordnance Department, introduced a small artillery tractor in 1918, identified as the 2 1/2-Ton (T-13). The 2 1/2-Ton Artillery Tractor Model 1918, as it was referred to by the military, was powered by a 70-horsepower Cadillac V-8 gas engine. In field service, the 2 1/2-Ton was expected to replace a six-horse team. Unlike a horse, however, the tractor couldn't cross deep water, one of its many faults to come to the surface during deployment. These tractors were built under license by the Federal Motor Truck Company, which accounted for 87 units, and the Interstate Motor Co., which made only 7, all intended for military use.

Other Holt artillery tractor designs were the long-track models from 1917 to 1918. These machines were designed to traverse rough, uneven ground and be able to climb steep banks. In 1917 the first of these special tractors started testing at the Peoria plant. Identified by the factory as the Holt 45 Long-Track, the military had their own

During World War II, Caterpillar built two models of heavy artillery tractors referred to as "High Speed D6 and D7 Heavy Tractor M1." Produced between 1942 and 1943, both tractors featured transmission gears and engine governors with increased rpm settings, different from regular production models, which enabled the units to travel at 11 miles per hour. Pictured is a High Speed D7 with front-mounted Hyster winch, reinforced frame, and crew area for four. *ECO Collection*

name for it . . . the 10-ton Artillery Tractor M1917. Based on the 45 muley, its longer track assemblies allowed it, in theory, to climb a bank of earth without damaging the front end of the tractor. In 1918 an improved version of the concept was tested, with improved track designs that were just a bit shorter in length than the original test unit. This tractor was also based on the 45 muley. The largest of the extended-track experiments was the big Holt 120 Long-Track. Tested by the U.S. Army in 1918, the Long-Track 120 (T-24) was a real beast. Weighing in at about 30,000 pounds, it was a formidable artillery tractor, capable of towing 20 tons. This special tractor design was essentially a regular 120, with the front tiller-wheel removed. In its place were long crawler track assemblies that ran the length of the unit. In testing, the tractor performed quite well. Its biggest problem was its timing. Once the armistice was signed, the need for the 120 Long-Track evaporated. Only one Long-Track 120 Model T-24 was ever built.

Another area in which Holt designs influenced military decision-making was in the production of the experimental, self-propelled, tracked gun mounts. The first of these was the Holt 55-I (T-15) in 1917. Weighing in at 56,000 pounds, the unit was originally tested with a 3-inch antiaircraft gun. This was later removed and replaced with a big 8-inch howitzer. This tracked gun mount is the earliest known self-propelled chassis used by the U.S. Army with an artillery weapon. Early tests confirmed that the design had merit.

After the completion of the 55-I, Pliny E. Holt, the man most credited with the design work on the Caterpillar gun mount, was persuaded by the U.S. Army Ordnance Department to leave Holt Manufacturing. He was focused solely on assisting the Army with further development of the tracked gun mounts. These first gun mounts were built by the Ordinance Department, under the supervision of Pliny Holt. They include the Mark I, the Mark II, the Mark III, and the Mark IV. All of these creations were produced in 1918.

Other models to follow, which were assembled at the Stockton plant, were the Mark VI in 1920; the Mark VII in 1919; the Mark VII Cargo Carrier in 1918, better known as the Tractor, Caisson Mk VII; the Mark VIII in 1918; the Mark IX in 1921; and, also in 1921, the Mark X, better known as the "4.7-inch Gun Motor Carriage Mk X," later classified as the M1922E. Although all of these Caterpillar gun mounts were classified as experimental prototypes, they would lay the foundation for all U.S. military self-propelled, heavy artillery gun mounts to come.

Holt didn't build any mobile tanks outright for the U.S. Army, but he did help in the development of a few designs worth mentioning. One of these was the Holt 6-ton Special Tractor in 1917. This unit was the chassis for the U.S. Renault two-man tank, of which 225 were built, all by Maxwell and other subcontracting companies in Dayton, Ohio.

Even more unique were two very odd tank designs developed in conjunction with the U.S. Ordnance Department. The first of these was the Holt T-18 Gas and Electric Tank, Vehicle B-Model E, codeveloped with General Electric in 1917, of which only one was built. The other was the Holt T-20 Doble Steam Tank, Vehicle A-Model E, in 1918. Again, only one of these steam-powered tanks was

Caterpillar also manufactured two fully factory-armored dozers, the D6A and D7A, for Allied service in World War II. This is a D6A, serial number 1T03001, with rear-mounted Hyster winch and hydraulic cylinder-controlled, extreme service angle-dozer blade. The full armor plating worn by these tractors made servicing of them in the field extremely difficult. *ECO Collection*

ever built, and it was said to have been shipped to France, never to be heard of again.

The majority of the crawler tractors used by the different branches of the U.S. armed services were, for the most part, standard production machines, with special requested options to make them suitable for military use. Many of these tractors have already been mentioned in earlier chapters, but there were a few that were much more than just off-the-shelf machines. In the 1940s, Caterpillar produced special models of its D6 and D7 tractors that were designed strictly for wartime use. For the rapid deployment of artillery pieces and cargo carriers, Caterpillar built high-speed units, identified by the military as the

In 1962, Caterpillar officially released its versatile 830M articulated wheel tractor-dozer into military service. The 830M was designed for use with three government-purchased pull-scrapers provided by other manufacturers. Initially rated at 420 gross horsepower and 335 flywheel-horsepower, an improved model, the 830MB, was released in the mid-1960s, with an increased power output of 448 gross horsepower and 357 flywheel-horsepower. *Caterpillar*

Caterpillar's involvement with the military GOER program actually got its start in 1959, with an experimental truck called the XM437E1. Through the experience of this trial machine, the company secured a government contract for production units in 1960 and released them in 1961. Shown is an eight-ton GOER M877, which is essentially the M520 model equipped with a materials handling crane. *Caterpillar*

High-Speed D6 and D7 Heavy Tractor M1. Both of these units were powered by engines found in their regular production counterparts. The biggest drivetrain changes were different transmission gears and engine governors with increased rpm settings. Other changes included front frame extensions for mounting heavy-duty Hyster winches. Both units also sported larger seating and deck areas that were surrounded by 18-inch metal sidewalls. In all, some

453 of the High-Speed D6 tractors were built between 1942 and 1943. Although the High-Speed D7 was introduced into service at the same time as the D6, records do not indicate how many were produced.

Two more special heavy tractors produced for World War II military needs were the Armored D6A and D7A models from late 1942. The D6A (S.N. 1T03001) and the D7A (S.N. 1T01001) used the same drivetrain as their conventional counterparts and were both direct-drive machines. These tractors were equipped with factory-designed armor plating that covered the entire machine, with rear mounted Hyster D7N winches. Both machines also utilized a specially designed angle-dozer blade, controlled by two hydraulic cylinders mounted on either side of the front end, also fully armored. This was an unusual feature not found on Caterpillar tractors of the time, since all of the rest used cable-controlled blades. These tractors were some of the most bullet-proof designs Caterpillar ever created, literally. Only about 45 units of the Armored D6A tractor were built, while some 138 were produced of the D7A.

Not all of the special equipment built over the years for military use was of a tracked-type machines. In the 1960s, Caterpillar introduced an articulated wheel tractor-dozer identified as the 830M. Introduced into service in October 1962, the 830M was a front-engined, four-wheel-drive, articulated rubber-tired tractor, equipped with a dozing blade. It was capable of numerous earthmoving tasks, including pulling scrapers, of which three different types were available—a hydraulic controlled Euclid unit and two cable-controlled designs, one from LeTourneau-Westinghouse, and another from Curtiss-Wright. Caterpillar was not awarded a contract for a scraper design of its own. The original 830M was powered by a six-cylinder, Cat D343 diesel engine, rated at 420 gross horsepower and 335 flywheel-horsepower. By the

Caterpillar's prototype of the Armored Universal Engineer Tractor, or AUET, pictured in 1961. Even though the government chose a competing design, the final production machine, the M9 Armored Combat Earthmover (ACE), didn't begin production until 1989. After some 28 years of testing of a combat earthmover tractor concept, the final product wound up looking very much like the original Caterpillar design. *Caterpillar*

mid-1960s, an improved 830MB model was introduced with more power. It was rated at 448 gross horsepower and 357 flywheel-horsepower. Capable of speeds of up to 30 miles per hour, with an average cruising speed of 25 miles per hour, the 830MB could maintain a brisk pace in a convoy with other equipment.

Another rubber-tired vehicle that Caterpillar was heavily involved in was the GOER project. The GOER was an all-wheel-drive, articulated, completely amphibious truck design, built in various configurations to meet specified job requirements. The Caterpillar-built GOERs were all powered by a six-cylinder, Cat D333 engine, rated at 213 flywheel-horsepower. The early engines were set up to burn a variety of fuels, but later versions with the D333C powerplant ran strictly on diesel. In low gear ranges, the GOER had four-wheel-drive capabilities. On the road, the unit was driven by only its front wheels. Top speed was listed at 30 miles per hour, but because the axles were solid mounted, with no suspension system to speak of, a speed of 20 to 25 miles per hour was more suitable for operator comfort and control.

The Caterpillar GOER project actually got its start in 1959, as the Truck, Cargo, Logistical, High Mobility, 16-ton, 4X4, XM437, better known as the XM437E1. The experience

of building this larger prototype helped Caterpillar acquire the design and development contract in 1960 for a family of 8-ton GOER vehicles, under the direction of the Army Tank Automotive Command. In 1961, Caterpillar introduced three versions of the GOER—the 8-ton M520 Cargo Vehicle, the 10-ton M553 Recovery Vehicle, and the 2,500-gallon M559 Tanker. When the M520 was equipped with a material handling crane, its designation changed to the M877.

Caterpillar also built larger 15- and 20-ton versions of the GOER. In 1961 the company built the 15-ton XM438E2, which was a continuation of the early truck design from 1959. But this contract would eventually be awarded to LeTourneau-Westinghouse for production. Caterpillar also built the 20-ton XM554 Recovery Vehicle, which was a much larger version of the M553. Only Caterpillar built the 20-ton wrecker GOER.

During the 1960s, Caterpillar participated in the design and production of a specialized vehicle called the Armored Universal Engineer Tractor, or simply the AUET. Conceived in 1958 by the U.S. Army Engineer Research and Development Laboratories, the vehicle was to be able to function as a dozer, a scraper, a troop and cargo carrier, and a prime mover. Initially, both Caterpillar and International Harvester

Somewhat of a controversial design in its day, the Caterpillar/Martin-Marietta Hard Mobile Launcher, or HML, was designed for land-based deployment of the small nuclear ICBM, code-named Midgetman. Caterpillar designed the tractor, while Martin-Marietta was responsible for the trailer. Both utilized Caterpillar's Mobil-trac System. Even though the HML was unveiled in 1985, its rubber-track system was actually borrowed from the Challenger program. *Caterpillar*

The prototype Caterpillar DW16 was the forerunner of the production 619B. The DW16, shown here in May 1958, is equipped with a No. 442 scraper unit. Although the units looked similar, there were some minor differences, such as the grille. Vital statistics for the DW16 were 212 gross horsepower, and 13 cubic yards struck and 16 heaped. The 619B was rated at 225 gross horsepower, with 14 cubic yards struck and 18 heaped. *Caterpillar*

built prototypes of the versatile machine. The Caterpillar AUET was powered by a six-cylinder, Cat D333 diesel engine, rated at 300 gross horsepower. The hydro-pneumatic suspension system was quite advanced for its time. The operator had the choice of a resilient operation or a rigid setting. The AUET was also an amphibious design. Throughout 1961, Caterpillar tested every function of its design. With testing completed in Peoria, Caterpillar shipped its prototype off to Fort Belvoir in July 1962.

Although further prototypes were tested, the Army gravitated toward the design put forth by International Harvester. Or so it seemed. The UET, as it was now

referred to, would go through numerous design changes as well as several suppliers. Finally in 1989, the Army approved the production of an engineering tractor, now identified as the M9 Armored Combat Earthmover, or ACE for short. Built by the BMY Company of York, Pennsylvania, it looked much like the original Caterpillar design produced some 28 years earlier. Government bureaucracy and budget cuts are to blame for the overly long gestation period of the UET/ACE tractor program. The entire program could be a case study on how not to build and test a proposed military vehicle. With almost three decades of effort by several manufacturers, the approved machine had not evolved substantially from the original offering.

Another truly remarkable military vehicle, coproduced by Caterpillar and Martin-Marietta's Denver Aerospace division, was the Hard Mobile Launcher, more commonly referred to as the HML. Unveiled in September 1985, the HML was a test vehicle designed for use with a small, single-warhead nuclear ICBM, code named Midgetman. The purpose of the mobile launch vehicle was to keep the location of the missile flexible, and therefore more resistant to a targeted attack. The moving carrier was part of our nuclear deterrence system against the Soviet Union. The HML consisted of a Caterpillar-designed crew module, or prime mover, utilizing the company's latest MTS technology. The towed missile module trailer was the design of Martin-Marietta and it also incorporated the Cat rubber Mobil-trac System. The front tractor was powered by a single Cat 3412 V-12 diesel engine, rated at 750 horsepower. This engine also supplied all the power requirements of the missile module trailer, including its track system. Designed with a maximum attainable top speed of 50 miles per hour, it would be able to relocate its missile package quickly. The rubber-tracked undercarriage would also allow the unit to cross rugged desert areas, something that was of prime importance in the initial

The starting point for Caterpillar's big 600 series high-speed, three-axle scraper units from the 1960s was the DW25, shown here in March 1959. Design elements from the DW25, showed up in all of the two-axle tractors in the 600 series. The closest production models to this prototype were probably the 630A for its looks and the 650 because of its drivetrain. This DW25 is equipped with an experimental hydraulic-controlled RM189 scraper. *Jim Gee Collection*

The first of two concept High-Speed Tractor-Scraper prototypes to be tested by Caterpillar is shown in November 1964. This unit is based on a highly modified D8 tractor and the 28-cubic-yard No. 632 scraper. This model was followed up with the High-Speed Tracked 657 Tractor-Scraper from 1967. *ECO Collection*

The 659 Cross Belt Loader, built in 1967, was another scraper design being considered by Caterpillar for its self-loading scraper program. It was designed for the high-speed loading of bottom-dump wagons. The 659 was powered by a Cat D346 in the front, a D343 in the rear, and a D333 on top powering the belt loader, totaling 1,140 flywheel-horsepower. Total machine weight was 143,000 pounds. *ECO Collection*

design. Overall weight of the HML, including its 30,000-pound ICBM payload package, was 175,000 pounds. But in the end, the government chose a rival design produced by Boeing Aerospace and Goodyear Aerospace. Only one HML was ever built.

EARTHMOVING MACHINERY

The great amount of earthmoving equipment designed and built over the decades by Caterpillar includes numerous experimental prototypes. Just about every machine manufactured by the company had to start out somewhere. These engineering exercises are among the reasons the company's products enjoy their enviable reputation in the marketplace.

The late 1950s, 1960s, and 1970s was a time of prolific experimental machinery. One model line that received an immense amount of attention during this period was the self-propelled scrapers. Caterpillar started to make the change to all hydraulic-controlled scraper bowls by the late 1950s. In fact, one of the first prototypes was based on a design by Buster Peterson, produced by Research and Design. The design was competing with two other creations produced by the Joliet scraper factory design team. Initially both of the latter designs were a mixture of cable

and hydraulic controls. But the Peterson-inspired design made the Joliet team take another look. The result, in 1959, was the elimination of all cable controls. By mid-1960, management gave the nod to the designs from the Joliet team, while the Peterson-influenced scraper concept was terminated.

The 1960s saw Caterpillar build and test many scraper designs in the quest for the most productive self-loading machine. One of the first of these creations was the High-Speed Tractor-Scraper in 1964. This early design utilized a heavily modified D8 crawler tractor, with its operator seat and controls relocated to the left side of the engine compartment. The scraper was a 28-cubic-yard-capacity No. 632 unit, with a modified gooseneck that could attach to the upper area of the D8 tractor. Putting out 305 horsepower, the entire unit was capable of a top speed of 12 miles per hour.

In 1966 this concept was taken to the next level with the High-Speed Tracked 657 Tractor-Scraper. This machine utilized the 44-cubic-yard-capacity scraper unit of a regular 657 model. The rear tires were removed and replaced with a set of high-speed track assemblies, powered by the rear 400 flywheel-horsepower, six-cylinder diesel engine. The tractor pulling this monster was again a highly modified D8, much like the unit from 1964, but with even more alterations

This Light Weight Scraper, better known as the LWS, was an ultrafuturistic Caterpillar scraper design from June 1966. Power for the front two drive axles was supplied by a single Cat 1673 diesel, rated at 207 flywheel-horsepower, and total operating weight was a very trim 28,000 pounds empty. Caterpillar engineers had envisioned an even larger model, powered by two diesel engines, front and rear, rated at 600 flywheel-horsepower total. Capacity of the larger unit was to have been 32 cubic yards struck and 44 heaped, but in the end, only one of the smaller 10-cubic-yard struck and 13 heaped units was ever built. *Jim Gee Collection*

This truck, pictured in August 1965, was the first diesel-electric-drive, 100-ton capacity, Caterpillar 783 side-dump hauler to be built. Its drivetrain consisted of a Cat D348 diesel, rated at 1,000 gross horsepower and 960 flywheel-horsepower, powering two Cat-designed electric traction motors in the middle drive axle. The side-dump box could dump left or right. *ECO Collection*

to accommodate the larger 657 scraper. Power output for the tractor was listed at 360 flywheel-horsepower from its six-cylinder engine. Total weight of the unit was 169,950 pounds. For comparison, the regular 657 model weighed in at 125,500 pounds.

Three more large rubber-tired, self-loading experimental machines would make it into testing at Caterpillar's Peoria Proving Grounds in 1967. One of these was Buster Peterson's 657 Hoeing Apron Scraper. The other two machines were created by Caterpillar Research Design engineers. These were the 657 Dual-Bowl Scraper and the 659 Cross Belt Loader. The 657 Dual-Bowl design consisted of a standard production 657 tractor front and rear power module. The scraper consisted of two 24-cubic-yard heaped capacity bowls, hooked together in the middle for independent operation. First the front bowl was loaded, then the rear unit. Engines both front and rear were the standard units found in the regular 657 model. The 657 Dual-Bowl was rated at 900 flywheel-horsepower.

The 659 Cross Belt Loader was an elevating loader design, with a right-side belt loading conveyor. Its main function was to be a high-capacity loader for bottom-dump haulers. The 659 was built mainly out of existing 657 components, with the addition of the elevator and belt loaders. A surge bin was placed over the cross belt and held the material that was being loaded by the 659, while a bottom-dump wagon pulled alongside. At that point, the operator would engage the belt loader and fill the hauler instantly. This way, the 659 never needed to stop loading itself, even if a bottom-dump was not in position yet. Like the Dual-Bowl design, the 659 utilized the engines of the 657, but with an additional six-cylinder, 240 flywheel-horsepower unit, mounted on top to drive the belt loader. Total power output was a whopping 1,140 flywheel-horsepower. The loading ability of the 659 was equally impressive, rated at

3,000 cubic yards an hour. It produced some of the lowest cost-per-ton production figures ever seen for this type of application. But in the end, the 659 proved too costly to manufacture. After all of the prototypes were tested, Caterpillar finally decided that the most cost efficient design was the push-pull system with the cushioned hitch.

Another scraper design briefly embraced by Caterpillar engineers was a dual-tired, tandem-axle, lightweight scraper concept. This unit, identified as the Caterpillar 3D01 Light Weight Scraper, or LWS, was very futuristic in

continued on page 163

After management decided against the side-dump concept, Caterpillar engineers tried to keep the 783 program alive by redesigning the original prototype with a rear-dump body in 1967. The operator's cab and front end were also brought up to current model 779 standards, but it was too late. Because of other problems with the diesel-electric-drive hauler program, the 783 was simply left to fade away. Only one unit is listed as ever being built. *ECO Collection*

In the 1960s, the world's largest mining vehicle was the experimental 240-ton-capacity Caterpillar 786 Coal Hauler. Unveiled in October 1965, the 786 had dual tractors at both ends, complete with separate operator's cabs. The 786 was always facing forward, no matter how it was situated in the mining pit. *Caterpillar*

The 786 utilized a diesel-electric-drive system that was powered by two V-12 Cat D348 diesels, rated at 2,000 gross horsepower and 1,920 flywheel-horsepower combined, one per tractor unit. Only the front axle of each tractor was powered. Thundering down a haul road, the 96-foot-long 786 was capable of speeds in excess of 30 miles per hour with a full 240 tons of coal on board. *Caterpillar*

Featuring relocated engines and radiators, the first of two preproduction 786 tractors is pictured at the Decatur Assembly Plant in July 1968. In all, four sets were eventually built like this. Only the pilot machine had the engines on top of the upper decking. All of the 786's coal hoppers were fabricated at the Joliet Plant. The spreader bar on the two tractors shown acts as a stand-in for the hopper, so all of the dual controls can be thoroughly tested. *Caterpillar*

Caterpillar also produced a couple of heavy-duty hauler concepts that were capable of being driven on paved roadways. The first of these to make it into iron was the 23-Ton Truck in 1967. This 23-ton-capacity hauler was of a four-axle design, and steered with the first, second, and fourth units. Power was supplied by a six-cylinder Cat 1673 diesel, rated at 324 flywheel-horsepower. The truck provided a high load-to-weight ratio, low ground pressure, and compensated strut suspension for a soft ride. Empty weight of the truck was 23,000 pounds. *ECO Collection*

The second on/off highway concept was the 25-Ton Truck, unveiled in 1967. It was also a four-axle design, but not like the system found on the 23-Ton. The 25-Ton was an 8x8, all-wheel-drive layout, with dual wheels used on all axles. The steering was by means of an articulated front end. Power was supplied by an eight-cylinder, Cat 1676 diesel, rated at 340 flywheel-horsepower, with the drive wheels fully suspended on rubber torsion springs. But in the end, management felt that these concepts would ultimately be too costly to mass produce. Only one of each of these mechanical-drive trucks was ever built. *ECO Collection*

Before the "hi-drive" track layout concept ever saw the light of day on a dozer, it was first used on the experimental 988 Track Loader, pictured here in April 1967. Because tire cuts were very costly on large wheel loaders working in rock, it was thought that a tracked articulated loader might make a better choice for hard rock digging situations. *Bob Purcell Collection*

Continued from page 159

design, as well in looks, when it was unveiled at the Proving Grounds in June 1966. The concept of the LWS was first visualized in 1964, with design specifications finalized in 1965. The scraper concept was powered by a single six-cylinder, 207-flywheel-horsepower diesel engine. This supplied power, via the same transmission found in the GOER, to the front two axles of the tractor. Tandem wheels and tires were mounted on the front axles, while the rear scraper unit used a more conventional design of single tires on one axle. There was no rear powerplant on this design. Capacity of the scraper was 10 cubic yards struck and 13 heaped.

As mentioned in Chapter 5, Caterpillar veered off course slightly in 1965, when the hauler division took a keen interest in diesel-electric-drive systems. Along with the limited production 779, the company built two other models that utilized diesel-electric drive—the 100-ton-capacity 783 and the massive 240-ton-capacity 786 Coal Hauler. As with the 779, these electric-drive haulers were spearheaded by Ralph H. Kress, who was the manager of truck development at the time.

The prototype Caterpillar 783 was rated as a 100-ton-capacity hauler. Unique design features of the 783 included a three-axle design, with only the middle axle being driven. The truck was also fitted with a side-dumping body, capable of unloading from the right or left side, at the discretion of the operator. The engine in the 783 was the same as that found in the 779, a single Cat D348 V-12 diesel, rated

Other variations on the 988 Track Loader were tried by Caterpillar engineers as the testing program proceeded, such as this unit in October 1968, with the triangle-track assemblies only mounted on the front as a cost-cutting move. Another version, also built out of a used 988 loader in June 1968, utilized a more conventional "low-sprocket" track design to compare the two layouts in side by side working situations. *ECO Collection*

Caterpillar built its first pilot 988 Carry Loader in 1967. Designed as a load-and-carry wheel loader for large quarry operations, it could load both of its buckets and travel to different areas of the work site for the custom blending of materials quickly. Combined load capacity was 13 cubic yards. The first pre-production unit was built in October 1969, with the model introduction in January 1970. But just as fast, the loader was withdrawn from sale, due to severe frame fatigue problems showing up in the prototype units. None survive today. *ECO Collection*

at 1,000 gross horsepower and 960 flywheel-horsepower. The electric-drive system was of Caterpillar origin, with two traction motors mounted inside the main drive axle. Both the front and rear axle steered the truck. The 783 started testing in August 1965. It was even shown at the American Mining Congress show in October 1965. But field trials in 1966 showed a few of the design concepts of the 783 were in doubt. To help save the 783 program, engineers redesigned the prototype hauler in 1967. This time it was equipped with a more conventional rear-dump box. But the new design was too little, too late. Although the truck continued testing, no real consideration was given to putting the unit into production. Only one 783 was ever built.

Largest of all of the Caterpillar diesel-electric-drive creations was the giant 786 Coal Hauler. Introduced in October 1965, it shared many of the same drivetrain components found in the 779 and 783 haulers. The 786 utilized two drive systems, one in each tractor, powering the front axle on each unit. With two Cat D348 diesels, the giant bottom-dump was capable of generating 2,000 gross horsepower and 1,920 flywheel-horsepower. The giant hopper was rated at 240 tons, making it the world's largest hauler in its day. The 786 was produced in conjunction with Southwestern Illinois Coal Corporation of southern Illinois. The design of the 786 was actually based on a concept hauler sketched out in September 1952 by Kress, when he was working with Dart Trucks. Testing of the first prototype 786 (1A) took place throughout 1966 and 1967 at Southwestern Illinois Coal's Captain Mine. This would lead to four preproduction 786 (81A/80A) haulers being built, with the first ready by July 1968. These four units differed from the original prototype in that they had modified tractor designs. The Decatur assembly plant was responsible for building the tractors, while the Joliet plant fabricated the massive hoppers. The 786 was 96 feet in length, and weighed in fully loaded at 670,000 pounds. All five units worked at the Captain Mine until just after 1969, when all work on the electric-drive hauler programs by Caterpillar ended. For liability reasons, all of the giant 786 haulers were parked. Soon they were simply relegated to the Captain Mine's bone-yard, were they were scavenged for parts throughout most of the 1970s. By the mid-1980s, the last remaining remnants of the five 786 haulers were cut up for scrap, eliminating any trace of Caterpillar's involvement with these early diesel-electric-drive trucks.

It is interesting to note that Caterpillar Research Engineers had put forth a design proposal in March 1965 for an ultralarge, 100-cubic-yard, dual-bowl scraper, utilizing the diesel-electric tractor designs of the 786. With 2,000 flywheel-horsepower combined and a 300,000-pound payload, the unit would have been something to see. This Cat proposal was an alternative design to that of the Peterson Triple 657. But a unit of this size would have had too limited a market impact to justify its development costs.

Large wheel loader experimental prototypes also had their place with the company's imaginative research engineers. During the early years of the development of the elevated-sprocket design, some of the first working prototypes were not designed for crawler tractors, but were instead tested on the 988 wheel loader. In April 1967, the company's Research Department started evaluation testing on a new 988 wheel loader, fitted with triangle-track drive assemblies at all four corners. Most importantly, this vehicle was to test the validity of the high-drive sprocket design, but it was also to assess the practicality of replacing the 988 loader's tires with tracks for working in harsh, rocky conditions. At one time, there was even talk of making the 988 tracked-loader a production model, to be identified as the 991. But it was not to be. Interest in Buster Peterson's Cushioned Air-Track, the forerunner of the Cat Beadless Tire program, caused management to kill the triangle-track loader concepts, in favor of the track-belted tires. They deemed this concept more practical and cost-effective than the more complicated triangle-track assemblies. But you can't keep a good idea down. The concept would reappear on the early test beds of the D10 tractor, and the rest is earthmoving history.

Another wheel loader design that almost made it into production was the 988 Carry Loader. First tested in 1967, the Carry Loader consisted of a 325-flywheel-horsepower 988 with a rear-mounted loader attachment to accompany the front unit. This would essentially double the operating capacity of the 988 to 13 cubic yards. The Carry Loader was mainly aimed at quarry operations where the mixing of different materials was a necessity. Carrying the load in two buckets would balance the machine better and promote better tire wear. By October

1969, the first preproduction Carry Loader was ready for testing. Caterpillar officially announced the loader in January 1970, but within weeks of its introduction, it was pulled from the product line. Severe stress cracks were starting to appear on the frames of the test machines, prompting the company to kill the project then and there. After this, all of the test Carry Loaders were scrapped.

During the development stages of the 992 wheel loader project, Cat engineers built an even larger diesel-electric experimental machine identified as the 994. This first 994 loader creation had nothing in common with the development of the more modern 994 offering of the 1990s. The experimental 994 was first tested by Caterpillar in early 1969 at its Peoria Proving Grounds. It was powered by the same engine found in the electric-drive trucks, the D348 V-12 diesel, rated at 1,000 gross horsepower and 960 flywheel-horsepower. All wheels were driven by electric traction motors. Bucket capacity was rated at 20 cubic yards and was of an ejector type. Bucket linkage was a unique four bar design. But when management pulled the plug on development of the electric-drive

In the late 1960s and early 1970s, some heavy equipment manufacturers had brief love affairs with turbine-powered mining equipment. Caterpillar examined the benefits of the high power-to-weight ratios of the turbine engine layout by building this experimental 992 Gas Turbine Loader in August 1973. But the oil embargo and escalating fuel prices doomed all of these creations, including the 992 design, by 1974. This was because turbine engines literally gulped fuel. Caterpillar also built an experimental 621 Turbine Scraper in 1968, but its survival skills were no better than the others. *ECO Collection*

trucks, the experimental 994 loader went with them. All work on the diesel-electric 994 stopped in January 1970.

During the design of the prototype 994, a Quad-Track version, identified as the 995, was also drawn up. In fact, engineers also were planning to put triangle-track assemblies on a 992 and call it a 993. But these designs only existed on paper. None were ever put into iron.

Today, Caterpillar continues to build experimental prototypes to test its machines of tomorrow. As always, prior to production, these designs are closely guarded company secrets. In time, truckers may see test models working and spread the word via cellular phones or the Internet, giving competitors and the public a glimpse of Caterpillar's newest innovations. Until that moment, we can only guess what the future of earthmoving holds. Yet given the company's successes in so many designs and applications, from the fields to the mines to the highways connecting our cities and towns, we know, in a way, what to expect. Only the most productive and dependable machine is worthy to wear the color of Caterpillar Yellow.

This odd-looking quad-track creation, pictured at the Peoria Proving Grounds in December 1967, was homemade by the Cat Research Department. It is a variable-weight towing vehicle, designed to test drawbar and tractive effort of large D8 and D9 tractors, especially the Quad-Trac and SxS D9G dozers, in rough conditions. Two men were required for its operation—one to drive the unit and the other to record test readouts. *ECO Collection*

BIBLIOGRAPHY

Crimson, Fred W. *U.S. Military Wheeled Vehicles.* Sarasota, Florida: Crestline Publishing Co., 1983

Crimson, Fred W. *U.S. Military Tracked Vehicles.* Osceola, Wisconsin: MBI Publishing Co., 1992

The Caterpillar Story. Peoria, Illinois: Caterpillar, Inc., 1990.

Gowenlock, Philip G. *The Letourneau Legend.* Brisbane, Australia: Paddington Publications, 1996.

LaVoie, Bob. *Caterpillar Gas Tractor-Restoration & Interchange Manual.* Osceola, Wisconsin: Motorbooks International, 1996.

Leffingwell, Randy. *Caterpillar.* Osceola, Wisconsin: Motorbooks International, 1994.

Letourneau, P. A. *Russell Graders Photo Archive.* Minneapolis, Minnesota: Iconografix, 1993.

Letourneau, P. A. *Holt Tractors Photo Archive.* Minneapolis, Minnesota: Iconografix, 1993.

Letourneau, P. A. *Caterpillar Military Tractors Vol. 1.* Minneapolis, Minnesota: Iconografix, 1994.

Letourneau, P. A. *Caterpillar Military Tractors Vol. 2.* Minneapolis, Minnesota: Iconografix, 1994.

Letourneau, P. A. *Caterpillar Photo Gallery.* Hudson, Wisconsin: Iconografix, 1997.

Nichols, Herbert L., Jr., Moving the Earth (Third Edition), New York, New York: McGraw-Hill Publishing Co., 1976.

Payne, Walter A. *Benjamin Holt—The Story of the Caterpillar Tractor.* Stockton, California: University of the Pacific, 1982.

GLOSSARY

Belt horsepower - Belt horsepower is an older reference for flywheel horsepower and is used mainly in the description of power ratings for agricultural equipment and tractors.

Drawbar horsepower - Drawbar horsepower is the machine's flywheel (or belt) horsepower, minus friction and slippage losses in the drive mechanism and the tracks or tires.

Flywheel horsepower - Flywheel horsepower, sometimes referred to as net horsepower, is the actual horsepower output, with all accessories connected, including the fan, air compressor, generator and hydraulic pump. This rating is the one most used when comparing one model to another.

Gross horsepower - Gross horsepower is the output of the engine or motor as installed in the machine, without the major accessories connected.

Heaped - The soil or material carried above the sides of a body, scraper bowl, or bucket.

ROPS - Rollover Protective Structures are reinforced canopies and/or cabs that comply with the U.S. Department of Labor's occupational health standards, effective April 5, 1972. This required all new tractors built on or after September 1, 1972 to be equipped with ROPS. Equipment built between July 1, 1969 and September 1, 1972 would have to be retrofitted with ROPS systems that were capable of bearing twice the weight of the vehicle "at the point of impact."

Struck - The soil or material made level with the top of the sides of a body, scraper bowl, or bucket.

INDEX